# MARY AND MARTHA

# MARY AND MARTHA

## Women in the World of Jesus

SATOKO YAMAGUCHI

ORBIS BOOKS

**Maryknoll, New York 10545**

Founded in 1970, Orbis Books endeavors to publish works that enlighten the mind, nourish the spirit, and challenge the conscience. The publishing arm of the Maryknoll Fathers & Brothers, Orbis seeks to explore the global dimensions of the Christian faith and mission, to invite dialogue with diverse cultures and religious traditions, and to serve the cause of reconciliation and peace. The books published reflect the views of their authors and do not represent the official position of the Maryknoll Society. To learn more about Maryknoll and Orbis Books, please visit our website at www.maryknoll.com.

Queries regarding rights and permissions should be addressed to: Orbis Books, P. O. Box 308, Maryknoll, New York 10545-0308.

Published by Orbis Books, Maryknoll, NY 10545-0308
Manuscript editing and typesetting by Joan Weber Laflamme
Manufactured in the United States of America

**Library of Congress Cataloging-in-Publication Data**

Yamaguchi, Satoko.
      Mary and Martha : women in the world of Jesus / Satoko Yamaguchi.
         p. cm.
      Includes bibliographical references and index.
      ISBN 1-57075-401-2 (pbk.)
         1. Women–Biblical teaching. 2. Women in Christianity–History–Early church, ca. 30-600. I. Title.

   BS2545.W65 Y35 2002
   225.9'5'0082–dc21

                                                                      2001036921

*To my partner Masa, my friends, and women and men of all colors*
*in feminist friendship*

# Contents

# Acknowledgments

This work was motivated, carried out, and completed in sisterhood. About fifteen years ago I was a mathematics teacher, actively involved in women's liberation movements in Japan. Some Christian women, including myself, had just started ecumenical gatherings in order to challenge patriarchal aspects of messages and practices in the church. It was not an easy task. We had different denominational backgrounds, faced different problems, and embraced different future visions. The major commonality we shared was that most of us were put under patriarchal interpretations of the Bible, the authority of which was a given in the Japanese church setting, and that we had few tools to carry on our challenge.

In the midst of such a struggle, I encountered Elisabeth Schüssler Fiorenza's book *In Memory of Her.* It inspired me and empowered me deeply. The book literally changed my life. With great encouragement and support from Sasagu Arai, my friend and an established theologian in Japan, I translated the book into Japanese. At that time my partner Masahiro (Masa) obtained scholarship information and encouraged me to study feminist theology in the United States. I quit my job and moved to Cambridge, Massachusetts, originally planning for one year of study at Women's Theological Center. This plan changed to an extended two-year study at Episcopal Divinity School (EDS) in its Master of Arts program. Then the whole family moved for my further study in its doctoral program, and Masa also became a student there after twenty years of work as a minister in the United Church of Christ in Japan (UCCJ).

Although such a decision required me to be strongly determined to make a commitment to feminist liberation theology at the expense of certain other things, I know that not every woman has this kind of privileged opportunity. Therefore, my study of feminist liberation theology in Cambridge started both as an appreciative response to pioneer feminist theologians and as a means of my compassionate solidarity with other women in Japan.

The greater Boston Theological Institute's cross registration system allowed me to enjoy a variety of feminist courses not only at EDS but also at Harvard Divinity School (HDS), Weston School of Theology (WST), Boston College, and elsewhere. At the outset, Elisabeth Schüssler Fiorenza encouraged me strongly to take courses at HDS rather than just audit them, and it became the basis for my further studies. Also at the very early stage, Carter Heyward's courses at EDS challenged me to question radically the orthodox christology, something which did not occur to me before but which became a central concern in my further studies. I was fortunate to have Katie Geneva Cannon as my student-life adviser at EDS; her encouragement sustained my energy when such help was most needed.

During my student life in Cambridge, I encountered and learned so much from women with diverse particularities in ethnicity, class, and gender (including different sexual orientations). My compassionate solidarity has expanded to women and men of all colors who are committed to transforming our world for a better future. Gradually I embraced the idea of writing a book that would introduce feminist scholarship to ordinary women and men in order to offer tools for their struggles in the patriarchal church.

In the actual writing process I was helped by countless women. I am most indebted to my thesis adviser, Joanna Dewey, for her guidance with extraordinary patience. She is an educator who lets her students choose what they want to study and write, while offering professional help and care. I am also profoundly indebted to my formal and informal readers, whose critical and supportive comments on my drafts helped me a great deal. They are Alison Cheek, Kwok Pui-lan, Lucretia Yaghjian, Elisabeth Schüssler Fiorenza, Lieve Troch, and Elaine Wainwright.

Elisabeth Schüssler Fiorenza spent much time as a "friend" and an informal reader, although I could never adequately respond to her criticism. For this I do not know how I could ever express my deep heartfelt gratitude. I can only say that all of my commitment to feminist theology, including my studying in Cambridge and my recent co-founding and co-directing, with Hisako Kinukawa, the Center for Feminist Theology and Ministry in Japan, started from my encounter with her book *In Memory of Her* and has always been supported by her feminist friendship. My special gratitude goes also to Lieve Troch, whose encouragement pushed me to enter the doctoral program in the first place, and whose visit from the Netherlands to Cambridge at the most difficult time of my writing rescued me from a crisis. I am also indebted beyond words to Elaine Wainwright, who has constantly offered criticism and support, both face to face while she was in Cambridge and from the opposite side of the globe after she returned to Australia.

Further academic support was given through personal communications with Luise Schottroff, Bernadette Brooten, Kathleen Corley, Richard Horsley, Louis Feldman, and Lawrence Wills. Precious insights, much support, and sustaining energy came to me from many friends in various ways. They include women of various religious affiliations in Japan, Korea, Taiwan, Australia, Germany, Switzerland, the Netherlands, Canada, and the United States.

On a more practical level I was helped very much by the supportive staff of the library of the WST/EDS, especially by Sarah Faith Spencer, Anne Reece, and Gregory J. Sakal. I was also greatly helped by my thesis editors: at the early stage by Frank Kampmann, who was my exchange tutor, and at the final stage by Pauline Allsop, with whom I shared the Bible and Archaeology Prize for our dissertations at EDS in 1996.

After graduation, Bernadette Brooten urged me to publish my dissertation, giving me warm encouragement accompanied by concrete advice. In the process of revising my dissertation to become a book for ordinary readers, my colleagues and students at New York Theological Seminary and Newark School of Theology read parts of my early drafts and gave me helpful comments and encouragement. Pauline Allsop in Canada, Kathleen Rushton in New Zealand, and Elaine Wainwright in Australia read through the entire manuscript and made numerous valuable comments. Lastly for editorial work, David Mckintosh, my translator friend in Tokyo, helped me with endnotes, and Bonnie Woods, my artist friend and editor in Boston, worked on the entire manuscript to transform my Japanese-English into a readable English, while keeping the flavor of my writing. I wish every feminist writer in the world for whom English is the second language had the good luck to have an editor like Bonnie. Finally, I feel lucky to have had Susan Perry at Orbis Books as my final editor. She is an excellent editor who worked for me and with me always in a supportive and encouraging way.

Without all of the sisterhood and various support, this work could not have been done. My heartfelt gratitude to each of them goes beyond words. My experience tells that something impossible otherwise will surely become possible when a woman lives in a circle of feminist friendship, not exclusive of men. My work proposes a new way to read the Bible, to look at our Christian history, and to re-vision our Christian identities. I sincerely hope that this book will inspire and empower women and men of all colors who are committed to transforming our spiritual and social world for a better future.

# Introduction

## Re-visioning the Past to Transform the Present

Feminist biblical scholarship has shown that there were many different versions of stories coexisting in the oral world. To hear different versions of biblical stories, especially those of women, is important because, first, the Bible contains primarily elite male text-versions of biblical stories, and, second, hearing possible women's versions affects our understanding of our Christian origins and traditions, and thus our Christian identities.

By presenting a feminist re-visioning of Martha and Mary in the Johannine gospel from a Japanese feminist perspective, I hope both to challenge and to contribute to Johannine scholarship in particular, and to biblical scholarship in general. However, since the majority of the women with whom I work are not part of academic theological institutions, I hope to write this book in a way that is accessible and helpful for them.

My hope is to encourage women of all colors in their diverse contexts to become familiar with the results of feminist scholarship and to participate in the global feminist endeavor of re-visioning our Christian past and Christian identities. Such a collaboration is especially important now at the beginning of the twenty-first century, when multicultural and interreligious dialogues have become increasingly important for global peace.[1]

In this book I am going to introduce feminist scholarly tools that can be used to construct a new historical imagination, the foundation for rereading the Bible. A new historical imagination more inclusive of the social world of Christian origins is very important because our understanding of such a historical context affects our interpretation of biblical messages.

Next, after expanding our historical imagination, I offer my reading of the story of Martha and Mary as an example of how to approach biblical texts. I hope to show that a feminist reading can make a difference in our reading of biblical texts, particularly when it is based on a different historical imagination by someone from a different context, in my case, that of a Japanese Christian woman.

*1*

## Rereading of the Johannine Gospel

I have chosen a text of the Johannine gospel for two major reasons. First, this gospel is used as a major basis for the christology formulated in 325 c.e. in the Nicene Creed. Today this "orthodox" christology is identified by the church as the "core" of the Christian faith. As such, feminist rereadings of this gospel are indispensable for examining the relevance of standard interpretations of the gospel and of the christology that is supposed to be based on it. However, thus far few critical feminist studies have been directed to this gospel.[2]

Second, I believe it is important to understand the cultural embeddedness of this gospel. It is called the "spiritual" gospel; that is, it is claimed to be more spiritual than the other canonical gospels. "Spiritual" in this context implies speaking of divine things that disregard or transcend worldly things. However, once I expanded my historical imagination to include the social, cultural, and political worlds in which the gospel was written, I have come to see more and more clearly the cultural embeddedness of this or any other gospel. This includes the cultural embeddedness of the "christological" titles, the use of the "father-son" language and of the "I am" revelations for understanding who Jesus was for the communities. It will help us better to understand the messages of the gospel and to hear with more sensitive ears the voices and stories suppressed but present in the gospel.[3]

I have chosen to expand our historical imagination broadly to include the Greco-Roman world rather than to focus on certain regions. I do this mainly because there is little consensus among scholars concerning exactly where this gospel was written. Except for general agreement that it was probably written in a city in the Greco-Roman world in the latter half of the first century, there is little consensus on the author/s and the editor/s, on the process of composition, or on the precise time and place it was written.

*Authorship.* Most scholars believe that the gospel was written by an anonymous male author, but that it was attributed to the apostle John to claim a certain authenticity and authority. However, some scholars still strongly argue for the authorship of the apostle John. Some scholars claim plural authors, and others claim female authorship may be probable.[4]

Most scholars assume that the author/s of the gospel did not write the gospel from scratch. The author/s had access to both old and new traditions, probably both oral and written, from which the author/s selected, combined, rearranged, and modified texts and sayings.[5]

Most scholars assume that there was a male editor or editors. They often assume as well that the editor/s added chapter 21 and made other minor revisions so that the gospel would be accepted by the mainstream Petrine church authority at the end of the first century. When it comes to more detailed analyses, however, scholars' opinions differ considerably.[6]

Keeping these differing possibilities in mind, I will use the term *author/s* rather than *John* or *the author*. In referring to the gospel, I will use the term *the Johannine gospel*, instead of *The Gospel According to John*, to avoid the strong connotation of a single male author. I use the word *Johannine communities* in referring to the communities in which the gospel was composed and to which it was primarily addressed. The plural form is preferred to the singular form for two reasons: first, the Johannine communities seem to have existed at more than one place, and second, different views, practices, and strands of traditions existed within them.[7]

*Time.* Most scholars now assume that the basic compilation of the gospel took place between 80 and 90 C.E., and that minor reediting was done later. Scholars once assigned later periods for the date of composition, because this gospel appears to have assumed the audience's knowledge of some stories told in the synoptic gospels (Markan, Matthean, and Lukan gospels). Generally, recent scholarly awareness of the long-term existence of oral traditions behind written gospels has shifted the date of the composition or writing of this gospel to the earlier period, between 80 and 90.[8]

*Place of Composition.* Ephesus in Asia Minor is high on the list of possible locations, but the possibility of other cities remains open, whether in Asia Minor, Syria, Palestine, Transjordan, or Egypt. Thus, it appears that many cities in the vast Roman province may be candidates for the place of composition as well as for the location of the Johannine communities.[9]

*Language.* The Johannine gospel was written in *koiné* (common) Greek, the daily language of the Greco-Roman world. This gospel, however, shows a limited vocabulary and some peculiar uses of language. Because of this, some scholars suspect that the language of the gospel is an "anti-language" that is typical of antisocial sects. There are also some scholars who claim that the language of the gospel is an immigrant language: Although Greek was not the primary language of the author/s, it was used for the sake of a mixed audience. It seems plausible that the author/s (and some of the community members) could have immigrated from a region where Hebrew or Aramaic was the daily language to a region where Greek was the common neighborhood language. Thus, while there is an enormous body of scholarly publications on the gospel, no clear consensus emerges. A broad historical imagination regarding the Greco-Roman world, rather than a narrowly focused one, will be helpful for reading the Johannine gospel.[10]

## Some Key Terms and Concepts

Sometimes it is more helpful not to define terms in order to leave our understanding of certain terms open and flexible. In this way we may gain new understandings as our study and dialogue with other people proceed. Here, for the sake of convenience, I would like to explain briefly how I understand and use some of the important terms and concepts in this book.

*Identity* or *self-identity* refers to our understanding of who we are with respect to various social markers of ethnicity, class, gender, and some others, such as age or physical features. Our identity formation is not fixed or permanent but is constantly changing depending on how we evaluate the various social markers in our history and traditions.[11]

By *history* I refer to historiography or historical narrative that refers to real events. This contrasts with *fiction*, which is created, although often with some taste of verisimilitude (an appearance of being real or historical). However, as long as historians narrate past events, this activity involves the collection, selection, and redaction (editing) of available data, as well as the choices of language, vocabulary, structure, ordering, rhetorical style (or means of persuasive argumentation), and narrative style. History writing is a complex, ideological, and creative form of composition. Thus, history—as well as fiction—is *story*. It is always culture- and ideology-laden and never objective or value-neutral. It is always important for us to have inclusive historical knowledge in order to better understand our ancestors' lives and struggles.[12]

*Tradition* refers to the beliefs and practices that are created and maintained in a communal setting for a certain duration of time. As such, tradition is a historical and communal construct that always involves complex power interplay in a community.[13]

*Patriarchy* is a male-centered hierarchical social system. This structure serves male interests at the expense of others or "the other," and involves multiple interlocking discriminations, including various forms of sexism, racism, classism, and colonialism.

The word *kyriarchy* is a combination of *kyrios* (master, lord) and *patriarchy*. It was coined by Elisabeth Schüssler Fiorenza to show clearly the structure of patriarchal domination by a few elite males over the majority of women and men.[14]

*Feminism* refers to political ideologies and movements that challenge various forms of patriarchy. By *feminist*, I refer to a political stance, and a person, that challenges patriarchal oppression and the marginalization of women and that strives to transform the world toward a realization of wholeness and well-being of all.[15]

I use the word *re-member*, following Mary Rose D'Angelo, who says "it conveys . . . the ideas of bringing what has been hidden out of the shadows of history, of putting together what has been dismembered and of making someone a member of oneself/of the community in a new way."[16]

In this book I strive for inclusive language, avoiding the sexism of English grammatical custom. Throughout I use the generic form of a word such as *god* or *prophet* regardless of gender. The English-language custom of using a standard form for males and a derived form for females strikes me as sexist. This custom identifies the male with the standard being while rendering the female deviant; it can have a devastating effect on women's self-identities (as well as on men's).[17]

In regard to the Christian Bible, I replace the terms *Old Testament* and *New Testament* with *Hebrew Bible* and *Christian Testament*. Use of the former reflects the Christian-centric view of the Hebrew Bible or the Jewish Bible.

Regarding the terms related to Christian origins, I use the term *reign-of-God movement*, referring to the one particular movement in which Jesus of Nazareth was a representative figure, among many *Jewish reign-of-God movements* at the time. I use the phrases *the earliest Christian movements* or *the earliest Christian communities* to refer to the movements or communities that continued after Jesus' death that were still part of the diverse Judaism in the first century and probably into the early second century. In other words, women and men, both in the reign-of-God movement and in the earliest Christian movements, were Jewish people, if not by birth, then by faith or way of life. During the second century Christian movements gradually became independent of Judaism. The phrases *the early Christian movements* or *the early Christian communities* refer to those times in the second and third centuries when participants no longer identified themselves as part of a diverse Judaism.[18]

It is important, however, to note that even at the time of the early Christian movements, the word *Christian* did not mean those people whose "orthodox" faith would be narrowly defined in the fourth century. Both the earliest and the early Christians had various biblical writings in Hebrew and in Greek. But they did not have *the* Hebrew Bible or *the* Christian Testament—or the concept of Christian canon. They had a much greater variety of biblical stories in oral forms. In other words, both their beliefs and practices were diverse. Similar things can be said about early *Judaism* as a whole. Before the formation of the Talmud in the sixth century, Jewish beliefs and practices were very diverse.

Finally, a remark is necessary regarding the use of the word *Jewish* and related terms. An adequate understanding of these terms is important. First, we have a tragic history of conflicts between "Jews" and "Christians," although they have the same biblical Jewish ancestors. Second, the Johannine gospel uses the word *Judeans* many times, the use of which became one basis for later anti-Judaism and anti-Semitism. In addition, the word *Judeans* was used in an ambiguous way in the first-century Greco-Roman world.

As we trace back the history of Israel, tribal ancestors of *Jewish* people seem to have been called *Hebrews*, probably deriving from *apiru/habiru* (outlaw), designating those who were social outcasts of Canaanite city states. After the Exodus experience, when they established the tribal confederacy of Israel in the twelfth century B.C.E., they identified themselves as *Israel* and *Israelites*. Israel then underwent transformation. It became a monarchy in the tenth century B.C.E., and at this time the first temple was built in Jerusalem. Israel was divided into the northern state of Israel and the southern state of Judah at the end of tenth century B.C.E. Israel was destroyed toward the end of the eighth century B.C.E., and Judah, including the temple in Jerusalem, was destroyed in the early sixth century B.C.E. All of the Jewish people now lost their national identity, regardless of whether they lived in *the land of Israel* (Palestine) or in *diaspora* (dispersed to various places outside of Palestine). They were able, however, to rebuild the second temple in Jerusalem at the end of the sixth century B.C.E. and maintained their religious and ethnic identity as the *people of God* or *Israel*, while outsiders referred to them generally as *Judeans (Jews)*.[19]

Among the "people of God" or "Israel," distinctions were made between *Judeans* (from Judea, the southern part of Palestine), *Galileans* (from Galilee, the northern part of Palestine), *Samaritans* (from Samaria, the middle of Palestine), and *Pereans* (from Perea, the land east of the Jordan). However, the Romans and other people called the entire land of Palestine *Judea* and all of its inhabitants *Judeans (Jews)*. In the same way, Israelites themselves often called all other ethnic groups *gentiles* (in Hebrew, *goyim*; in Greek, *ethnoi*; in English, *nations*), disregarding any differences among Romans, Greeks, Egyptians, and so on.[20]

At the same time, Greco-Roman inscriptions indicate that the word *Judean* and its variants were used in a very broad sense. These terms were applied to persons who were *Judeans* either by geographic origin (born and raised in Judea), by ethnicity (Israelites by birth), or by religious belief or practice (affiliation to Jewish traditions in one way or another). Therefore, when we read the word *Judean* and its variants in the Greco-Roman texts, such as the gospels of the Christian Testament, we need to be aware of these diverse uses that were not clearly defined.[21]

Based on these observations, I will use specific terms when preferable and possible, but on other occasions I will use the word *Jewish* as an umbrella term, referring to the people Israel (Jews) and the matters broadly related to them.

Now, we will proceed to expand our historical imagination of the first-century Greco-Roman world. Along the way we will see how this new historical imagination illuminates aspects of the earliest Christian communities. As we proceed to studying Johannine texts in Part Two, we will incorporate our new understanding of history and other insights to hear the story of the Johannine gospel with new ears.[22]

PART ONE

*Searching for a*
*New Historical Imagination*

# 1

## Looking at Christian History in a New Way

Everyone knows that the Christian Testament is ancient literature. Yes, it is written in the ancient language of vernacular Greek *(koiné)*. The authors of the Christian Testament writings and their earliest audience lived in a world that was very different from the world we know today. When we read stories in the Christian Testament, however, we tend to forget this. Unconsciously, we visualize women and men in the Bible as if they were our neighbors, living in houses and towns like ours, eating meals like ours, and speaking the exact words that are written in the Bible.

Furthermore, we tend to understand many words in the Bible in the way we have been taught in church. For example, when we read words such as "Christ," "Son of God," and "Savior" in printed texts, we think we already know their meanings. We do not wonder what kind of images the first-century audience had when they listened to these words in stories.

Since the social world in which they lived was so different from that of our day, it is quite likely that we miss some of the points made in stories, or that we misunderstand their messages. If we wish to understand better the messages of the stories as communicated to their original audiences, we must expand our "historical imagination" to include the world in which these stories were told.

### A New Historical Imagination

Historical imagination is different from the fantasies or illusions or groundless speculations we freely embrace while reading fairy tales or watching Disney movies. Historical imagination is an imagination we can expand within certain limitations as it has to be based on scholarly information. Only with the help of this type of historical imagination can we read ancient literature and begin to understand, never perfectly but better, the messages that were communicated to its earliest audience.[1]

At the same time, we should not forget that stories in the Christian Testament were written and edited by a small group of people, probably all of whom were men, who had privileged access to writing. The majority of women and men in the first century did not read or write. Certainly they did not have the luxury to buy expensive writing materials for stories as long as the gospels. One notebook-size sheet of papyrus probably would have cost the equivalent of today's $30-35 in Egypt, which was the least expensive place to buy these materials. Writing was laborious, inconvenient, and time consuming.[2]

One contemporary story helps us understand the actual writing task in the first century. At a monastery in present-day northern Iraq, ink is made in the traditional way for scribal activities, that is, for copying biblical texts by hand. The monks have discovered that plurals can suddenly become singulars and that many other changes can occur while the written materials are drying. This is because flies swarm on the papyrus and drink the wet ink! Later, the monks carefully examine the written texts to find spots where parts of words are missing. They make corrections here and there and then dry the pages again.[3]

The first century was an oral world. Even the written documents were read aloud as if in a storytelling gathering. People communicated with each other by telling stories: for education, for entertainment, and for religious activities. At each storytelling session, stories were changed and modified in a variety of ways to meet the needs of the audience. In other words, in the oral world a written story was only one version of many possible versions of the same story, told and retold with a variety of nuances. If we wish to restore the earliest Christian messages in a more balanced or inclusive way, we need to attempt to listen not only to the male authors' versions but also to the nuances of ordinary people's versions, especially those of women.

A more women-focused historical imagination is necessary, because even when we are informed of the ancient historical background, most of the information comes from privileged male perspectives and focuses on privileged men's lives. Too often we are left with an unanswered question: How much of this information is relevant for women, especially for ordinary women?

A historical imagination that includes the context of non-Christian cultures is also necessary, because Christianity was not a major religion at that time. Or, more precisely, Christianity was not yet an independent religion; it was part of the diverse traditions of Judaism, which was itself not a major religion in the first-century world. The earliest Christians lived as part of tiny Jewish minority groups in the midst of a society where there were many other religions, most of which were more popular and powerful than Judaism.

We will seek information from a variety of disciplines, such as historiography, archeology, sociology, anthropology, and linguistics. In doing this, we will attempt to obtain women-focused information as much as possible, especially from various critical feminist research. By drawing upon varied scholarly information, I hope to show a broad picture of the ancient world in which we can imagine ordinary women and men much more clearly than before.[4]

## Cautionary Remarks

One caution is necessary about the tentative nature of this new historical imagination. Even if we obtain information carefully from multi-disciplinary studies, this information is not necessarily a fair reflection of ancient people. For example, recently many biblical scholars have been using cultural anthropological studies to fill in the gap between the modern "Western" culture of individualism (in a high-tech capitalist society) and the ancient "Mediterranean" culture of kinship-orientation (such as would occur in a preindustrial agrarian society). This is an important endeavor, but we have to be very careful when we use anthropological information and theories. We should not forget that anthropological theories have been constructed mainly through combined studies of ancient literature and research on the so-called primitive villages today.

First of all, ancient literature was written almost exclusively by privileged males who reflected the perspectives of a tiny elite male group rather than the reality of the majority of ordinary people, particularly women. Second, anthropological theories are based on present-day research, ignoring the time difference of almost two thousand years. Furthermore, anthropological research and analyses have been made predominantly through Western middle-class male perspectives and tend to reinforce ethnic and gender stereotypes, overlooking and ignoring various different and even contradictory aspects among certain groups of people. Recently, these theories have been criticized by many anthropologists themselves, including anthropologists who are women. Unfortunately, however, most biblical scholars still rely, and rather uncritically, on cultural anthropological theories. So, we should be cautious and continually ask questions. For example, how relevant were the dualistic concepts of male/female, public/private, and honor/shame for ordinary women in that world? [5]

Similarly, information from archeological discoveries is helpful, but cautions should be taken in drawing conclusions based on this information. Since the mid-twentieth century, archeological excavations have advanced greatly. Among many things, archeological discoveries often shed light on the previously unknown circumstances of ordinary people's lives. But, again, we cannot uncritically rely on this information because the interpretations of archeological discoveries are constantly being challenged by more recent discoveries as well as by differing interpretations.[6]

## Reading of Spiral Movements

When we read biblical stories, we need to envision a spiral-like movement: First, using multi-disciplinary studies, we shall expand our historical imagination broadly to the ancient world. This will produce a rough sketch, as if done with a thick brush and ink. It will ignore many particularities and subtleties of the real world of ordinary people. We must also keep in mind the tentativeness of such information. After drawing this general background sketch, we must read biblical texts carefully and critically, as such a reading may yield clues that will lead to a better understanding of the particular situations in which the original authors and audiences lived. Then we should revisit our first sketch and explore the background information in more detail on certain specific aspects, in order to return to the texts as more informed and sensitized readers. With this spiral movement in mind, we will pay particular attention to ordinary women.

Since it is impossible to draw a comprehensive picture of the entire world of first-century women in this small book, we will focus on six areas that seem most helpful for a re-visioning of the first-century Jewish women in general, and for listening to the story of the Johannine gospel in particular. They are (1) daily lives of Jewish women and men in the first century, (2) deities and religious leadership, (3) prophecy and "I Am" revelations, (4) healing and sign-working, (5) storytelling and tradition-making, and (6) persecution and patriarchalization.

# 2

## Daily Lives of Jewish Women and Men in the First Century

In this chapter we will attempt to envision the conditions of daily life of Jewish women and men in their first-century context. We will ask questions such as: What did the first-century world look like? How were their society and economic system organized? Their family structure and functions? What kind of work did they do for living? What were their houses like? How many times a day did they eat, and what, and how? More and more questions will come to mind, but let us address these questions first.

### The Roman Colonial World

The primary world of the Christian Testament in the first century C.E. consisted of an advanced agrarian society. It was preindustrial, and people worked with tools, using the technology of the animal-drawn and iron-tipped plow.[1]

In this world the fundamental political landscape for everyone—male and female, free and enslaved, young and old—was the Pax Romana (Roman Peace). It was a "peaceful" Roman Empire, established through military and economic conquests during the previous three centuries, encompassing the parts of Asia, Europe, and Africa that surround the Mediterranean Sea.

Throughout these vast provinces, Rome kept order by its generous policy of allowing various ethnic groups to live according to their own respective laws and customs, as long as they did not conflict with Roman political and economic interests. At the same time, Roman military posts were placed throughout the empire. Jewish people lived not only in Palestine, but also in diaspora (various places outside of Palestine) in the Mediterranean areas. All of these places were Roman colonies during the first century.

In this society, under Roman colonial rule, a small group of elite males dominated the entire populace. The vast majority of the people suffered economic exploitation, which maintained the prosperity of the empire. The elite class of people—the top 2 or 3 percent of the whole population—controlled more than 50 percent of the wealth of the society and lived in luxury with enormous power. Their retainers, those who served the elite class directly, made up about 5 to 7 percent of the population. The retainers included lower-level aristocrats (mostly landowners and wealthy merchants), lower-level military officers, financial bureaucrats, clerks, tax farmers, rent collectors, personal estate managers, judges, jailers, doctors, scholars, scribes, and other religious functionaries. Religious functionaries included a few privileged priests, rabbis, and scribes, both male and female. Although the wealth of the retainers was much less than that of the elite, the retainers were still privileged people in their society. The elite and their retainers together made up less than 10 percent of the whole population and maintained the social status quo.

There was no middle-class majority as we understand the term today. The remaining 90 percent of the populace worked basically for their own survival and lived in poverty. The majority were peasant farmers. Others were fishers, merchants, artisans, day laborers, and service workers. The bottom 10 percent consisted of "the expendables," a term that also included beggars, bandits, and criminals.

### The Exploitative Economic System

The Roman economic system was structured in hierarchical layers of patron-client (or patron-mediator/agent-client) relationships that were maintained by various reciprocal exchanges of "goods and services." At the top was the Roman emperor as the chief patron of his client kings—including the Jewish kings, such as Herod the Great and his sons, who offered tribute and gifts to their patron emperor. Each of these client kings was served by chief administrators, and under those administrators were various lesser administrators, chief tax collectors, business agents, and so on. The emperor, kings, aristocrats, and the Roman government owned the best land and some major occupational trades. The rights to administer or control these lands and trades were contracted to their favored clients. These clients were often organized on kinship bases or chosen from those who would offer the best benefit to their patrons at the cost of exploiting those who worked under them.[2]

Such a political and kinship-embedded economic structure, with its highly centralized redistribution system, escalated the impoverishment of rural peasants, while it offered some benefits for urban citizens. This increased not only the economic but also the cultural gaps between urban and rural people and intensified the hatred between the two groups. However, ordinary urban people were not rich. They all suffered from heavy taxation. Jewish people suffered triple taxation: taxes to the Roman government, taxes to the Jewish client-government, and tithes (offering one-tenth of one's income) to the Jerusalem temple.

Accumulation of debts was a familiar reality for many people, but especially for the peasants. Drought, famine, disease, and heavy taxation—all contributed to peasants' downward shift from small-landowner farmer to tenant farmer. To pay debts, family members might be sold into slavery, beginning with the daughters. The whole family's collapse into slavery was a real possibility for many peasant families, but it was an especially threatening situation for most daughters.[3]

Widespread malnutrition and hunger, together with undesirable sanitary situations, made people susceptible to various diseases. Although there were doctors, poor people usually could not afford their services. Ordinary people often had to rely on magic or the miraculous. Widespread physical suffering was common and seems to have been perceived as the inevitable lot of humanity.

Women often died in childbirth, and infant mortality was also very high. Especially in the rural areas, where the majority of the poor people lived, about 30 percent died within the first year, 50 percent by age ten, and 75 percent by age twenty-six. Most of those who survived to the age of thirty suffered from problems of internal parasites, tooth loss, and/or weakened eyesight. In the urban areas the general life span may have been longer, but still only a small percentage lived to age fifty or more. So, if Jesus was about thirty when he started his public life, he was not a young man but was considered a mature person, having lived a longer life than most of his contemporaries.[4]

### Jewish Resistance Movements

For the exploited and colonized Jews, daily reality under the rule of the Roman emperor and his Jewish client kings was a catastrophe. Many Jewish people longed for their God's immediate intervention and for the realization of the *basileia* (reign of God). While there were various visions of *basileia* among different Jewish people, the prototype (historical root model) was the Davidic kingdom. It was remembered in Jewish communities as the kingdom in which the people designated the one who would be the *messiah* (anointed king in Hebrew; christ in Greek) who would rule the nation with justice.[5]

Several religious and political resistance movements in Palestine held various visions of *basileia* and *messiah*. Some were prophetic movements, and some were military-oriented messianic movements. When Herod the Great, the Jewish client king, died in 4 B.C.E., several disturbances broke out that stemmed from messianic resistance movements. The first Jewish revolt directed against Rome occurred in 66-70 C.E. This powerful movement led by Simon bar Giora was supported by the populace. It ended with the destruction of the Jerusalem temple, the central worship place for the Jews. A second wave of Jewish revolt occurred during the years 132-35. It was a large, well-planned revolt that also received wide-based popular support. Only after extended, costly battles did the Roman government finally annihilate the messianic movements in 135 C.E. Some leaders of these messianic movements appear to have been executed as Jewish kingly messiahs.[6]

Extant records do not tell us how women were involved in these messianic movements, but they do tell us that thousands of women and men, especially of the lower classes, were crucified by the Romans. Crucifixion was practiced to punish political criminals and dangerous robbers and to deter the lower classes from committing rebellious crimes. There seems to be no reason to exclude women from having participated in these messianic movements.[7]

## Family Life and Work Environments

The political philosophy of Aristotle (fourth century B.C.E.) still wielded a strong influence over Roman laws. According to Aristotle, the family was the smallest unit of the city state, and thus the formation and maintenance of the family by the "ideal natural order" is the basis for the prosperity of the state. The principal "natural order" was the control of the body by the soul, which is embodied in three basic human relationships: father over children (who are "in an undeveloped form"), male over females (who are "without full authority"), and master over slaves (who lack "the deliberate part" of the soul). First-century Roman law basically followed this principle. A household unit included the father as the head of the family; his wife, sons, and daughters; non-married relatives such as family widows or sisters; male and female slaves; freedmen and freedwomen (former slaves); other clients who sought protection from the "patriarch"; and residential properties.[8]

According to Roman law, which was applied basically to all residents of the Roman provinces, a married woman was not included in her husband's family even though she lived with him in his household unless she had a special contract. By law, she was still under her father's authority, although by tradition she was subject to her husband. A wife's primary duty was to give her husband a son, an heir for her husband's family line. While a husband, as a father, had decision-making power over his children, a wife as a mother had no legal rights whatsoever over the children.[9]

Maintenance of the patriarchal family line and its assets was the basic tenet of Roman family law. Monogamy was the rule, but a marriage between individuals of unequal social status or a marriage between slaves was not acknowledged as a formal marriage. A man in military service could not marry. If a soldier was already married, his marriage was automatically dissolved upon his entry into military service or upon his captivity in war.[10]

As an increase in the population—that is, the birth rate—was of great political concern to leaders of the Roman Empire, girls were married in their early to mid teens. Legislation of Augustus in 18 B.C.E. and 9 C.E. penalized celibacy. Unmarried women between the ages of twenty and fifty were penalized by a ban on receiving legacies under wills and a 1 percent tax on women who had certain assets. A woman who divorced or was divorced by her husband had to remarry within six months (later changed to eighteen months), and a widow had to remarry within a year (later changed to two years), unless she already had three children or, if she was a slave, four children. Although these laws were probably not strictly observed throughout the empire, many women were forced into consecutive marriages.[11]

In spite of the strictly patriarchal legal structure of families, in reality there were a variety of households, including households headed by women or those consisting of brothers only, sisters only, or brothers and sisters combined. Likewise, people's daily lives did not always proceed in accordance with the law. In addition, each ethnic group could follow its traditional laws and customs to a certain degree. Generally speaking, although work environments varied by sexual, geographic, and ethnic differences, the greatest differences were in social and economic status. Let us look at the lives of women and men more closely according to their social and economic status.

### Peasant Farmers

In Roman colonies in the first century, most people were peasants who formed semi-autonomous agrarian village communities that provided the economic base for urban citizens. A typical rural family had six members who lived in a house that consisted of one or two small rooms. The size of the room was about 3 x 4 meters (8 x 12 feet) to 5 x 5 meters (14 x 14 feet). This small house was connected to other similar houses, making a compound. The houses shared stairs to upper rooms or to a flat roof and faced a common yard that was located at the center of a house-compound. Houses were commonly made of stone with some wood, and poorer houses were made of clay bricks and mud. Floors were mostly earthen, often covered with a woolen carpet or straw mat. Typical furniture included beds, folding chairs, a table, and chests, although extremely poor families slept on the floor.[12]

In the central common yard several families shared ovens, water tanks, and other facilities used in daily life. People not only worked and cooked food in the central common yard but also often took meals there. A house, with its extension to the central common yard, was a dwelling space and a work space for women, men, and children. In a typical poor household, children started working at the age of six. Young and old, women and men—all had to work to ensure survival.[13]

Major crops were wheat, barley, millet, legumes, olives, and grapes. Sheep and goat raising were also trades in which both men and women worked. Peasant men worked in the fields almost year-round. After the spring harvest of wheat and barley, the dry summer season from mid-June to mid-September was the time when work in the field was not heavy. Nevertheless, they always had to supplement their farming with fishing, craft-making, or day-to-day temporary labor.[14]

This was also true of peasant women. Ordinary peasant women worked in the fields almost year-round and supplemented their farm income by making and selling their handcrafts or by working as various kinds of day laborers, including wet-nurses and domestic servants for wealthy families. Men were primarily responsible for the work in the fields. Although women also worked in the fields, their primary responsibility was for domestic work. It appears that women's double workload has a very long cultural history.[15]

The daily management of the house, hospitality, and the care of guests were assigned to women. This included grinding grain, baking, cooking, feeding babies and children, washing, cleaning, and making beds. Spinning and making clothes, drawing water from the village well, processing food for preservation, and making handcrafts and pottery for domestic use were also women's work. All these domestic tasks were done in the house or dwelling/work space and in the central common yard.[16]

Women who were living in the same building complex worked together on time-consuming tasks such as spinning and weaving. This offered peasant women social occasions for the exchange of village news and all kinds of storytelling. However, women's activities were not restricted to their houses or common yards. Besides working in the field, they went to the well to draw water and to the market to shop or work. In these circumstances a young woman and a young man could meet on their own.[17]

We may assume that the patriarchal social system offered some power and privilege to men over women, even among the very poor peasants. The basic division of work, especially the primary assignment of domestic work to women, may have also offered men better access to superior public positions. At the same time, however, we should recognize that in their first-century daily lives the distinction in our modern understanding between the public sphere (supposedly for men's activities) and the private sphere (supposedly for women's activities) seems irrelevant, at least in practice. First of all, the "private" sphere for ordinary people in the agrarian world was the basis for economic activities. A household was the unit of both production and consumption for a family, and from this "management of the household" (*oikonomia* in Greek) comes our word "economy." Many economic transactions were traditionally made by bartering things of mutual value with someone who was known by the family, although such family- and village-based exchanges were increasingly replaced by a centralized redistribution system in the first-century Roman Empire.[18]

In the lives of poor villagers, who were threatened not only by war and famine but also by robbers and disease, a supportive neighborhood would have been of great importance. This must have been especially true for women, because the women cooked daily meals together and borrowed utensils and materials from each other. This may be one reason that women highly valued hospitality. There must have been occasions when each woman was helped by others in times of crisis and hardship. A biblical text tells of a woman who lost a drachma coin (a day's wage) and searched the whole house for it. When she found the coin, "she called together her friends and neighbors, saying 'Rejoice with me, for I have found the coin that I had lost'" (Lk 15:8-10).[19]

Most people ate two daily meals. Breakfast typically consisted of bread dipped in olive oil, or bread with some type of vegetable. The very poor ate bread and garlic or bread with salt, if they could afford it. The evening meal, eaten at twilight, was the main meal of the day, and the standard diet included three basic components: bread, olive oil, and figs. Palestine was usually self-sufficient in the production of figs, and they were eaten on a regular basis. Figs were commonly processed by drying or pressing. A cooked food, such as fish, vegetables, eggs, legumes (beans, lentils), and on very rare occasions meat, might have been included in supper—again, only if the people could afford it.[20]

On the Sabbath, Jews were to eat three meals. The Sabbath meal was to be festive and might have included two cooked foods. On such occasions people drank much wine, usually diluted with a large quantity of water. Wine was considered a festive beverage, not only for Jews but also for other people at various celebrations.

The synoptic gospels remind us that Jesus' disciples plucked "heads of grain" to rub them and eat them in the grain field as a Sabbath meal (Mk 2:23-28; Mt 12:1-8; Lk 6:1-5). They were undoubtedly among the many, many poor people, especially women and children, who could not afford the customs of the "standard" meal.

### Peasant Fishers

For many of the peasant people in Palestine, fishing was the major family business. Certain place names indicate the importance of fishing in Palestine. The central city Jerusalem had a "fish gate." The disciples Andrew, Peter, and Philip were from Bethsaida (temple of the fish-god) on the northern shore of the Sea of Galilee (Jn 1:44). Mary Magdalene came from Magdala on the western shore of the Sea of Galilee (Jn 20:1). The name Magdala derives from the Hebrew *migdal* (tower), which probably referred to the towers on which fish were hung to dry in the sun and wind. The Greek name of Magdala was Tarichaeae (fish factory), where fish was salted.[21]

In the first-century Roman Empire, kinship ties were the basis for workshop or trade relationships, and relatives usually worked together. However, all of the workers were embedded in a large, complex political economy with layers of patrons, agents, and clients. Even the village fishers who had their own boats were involved in the system in one way or another. Fishing encompassed a range of tasks such as boat building and repairs; net making, mending, washing, drying, and folding; and fish sorting. All members of the family worked on these time-consuming tasks, and sometimes they had to hire seasonal or day laborers.[22]

The fishing trade also included the processing of fish. Processed fish, either cured and pickled, or dried and salted, was a staple food throughout the Mediterranean region. Some fishers worked individually on all aspects of fishing, processing, and selling; others worked cooperatively on these tasks. The distribution of the catch was controlled by government-approved whole-salers. In a highly regulated and taxed hierarchical political economy, regard-less of whether the fisher owned or rented a boat, or had hired workers, the "surplus" went to the agents and ruling elite. The families of peasant fishers worked essentially for survival, as was also the case for peasant farmers.[23]

And, as was true for peasant farmers, women worked outside of their houses all the time. It is true that the patriarchal social system gave privilege to men. However, the elite male ideology of public/male versus private/female seems to have been irrelevant for the daily life practices of the majority of women. This also held for merchants, artisans, and other urban workers.

### Merchants, Artisans, and Other Urban Workers

In addition to peasants, other groups of people who worked in various trades and services were embedded in the complex political economy of layers of patrons, agents, and clients. These people lived mainly in urban areas and, except for a small group of aristocratic merchants, the majority of these urban citizens resided in apartment houses *(insulae)* crowded near the centers of towns and cities. Such apartment houses were usually four to five stories high, made mostly of stone, wood, and mud. The *insulae* were the most common residences in all major towns throughout the Roman Empire.[24]

The shop/work space of merchants and artisans was located on the ground floor of these apartment buildings, with an arched opening facing the street. The width of the work space was often about 3 to 5 meters (8 to 14 feet), with a depth of about 4 to 8 meters (12 to 24 feet) and a height of about 4 meters (12 feet). In a back corner a ladder often led to a mezzanine that had an opening for a window (with no glass) above the shop entrance. This was the living space of the typical urban family of four persons, who worked be-low.

Sometimes the ground level of these buildings had more floor space. On the other hand, the higher the story, the more numerous were the units per story; these smaller, higher spaces were for the poorer tenants. These apart-ment buildings were notorious for their shabby construction, crowded condi-tions, poor ventilation, and vulnerability to fire. Only people with spacious houses could afford to have kitchens. Most people cooked food on portable grills in crowded, dark, and poorly ventilated rooms or ate regularly at "fast food" shops in the neighborhood. It was a society in which the rich ate "in" (food prepared by slaves and servants), and the poor ate "out."

There was neither running water nor a toilet facility in these housing units. The Roman government seems to have provided basic public toilets in every neighborhood, but we do not have much information about them. On the other hand, we have plenty of information about public baths. Both archeo-logical and literary evidence tells us that there were numerous government-owned public baths accessible to ordinary people for an inexpensive fee. A variety of public-bath-related words occur regularly in popular magical spells used for wishes and curses by ordinary women as well as men, which suggests that ordinary people could use public baths in their daily lives.[25]

In the first-century Roman world, as we have seen, rural women worked variously in farming, shepherding/goat-herding, and fishing. At the same time many poor urban women worked as shopkeepers and vendors of commodities such as salt, fish, grains, vegetables, sesame seeds, spices, honey, ointments, perfumes, handcrafts, and clothing. Textile trades such as spinning, dyeing, weaving, and the making and selling of clothes of wool, cotton, linen, and silk were typical trades for women. Other women worked as fish-processors, bakers, confectioners, hair stylists, lime-burners, makers of ointments, hosts of taverns, tax collectors, tentmakers, stenographers, and midwives and doctors.[26]

There were many *collegia* (clubs, societies) that artisans formed to help each other. In Greco-Roman times, as more women worked as artisans, women's involvement in various *collegia* increased. *Collegia* members often enjoyed meals together and used familial terms among themselves, such as father, mother, brother, and sister.[27]

In almost all of these trades, women were discriminated against in their wages and earned generally less than half of what men earned. While a man's wage covered his daily expenses, a woman's income hardly supported her economic needs. Since the above-mentioned apartment buildings or tenement houses (cheap rental houses) in towns made no provision for home baking, poor townspeople had to buy everything they needed, including their daily bread, fuel, and other provisions. The economy of a woman's household, without a man, often forced her to work as a prostitute.[28]

Artisans and merchants often worked in pairs or groups; usually a pair was male and female, but sometimes it was all male or all female. Many pairs or groups traveled widely throughout the provinces of the Roman Empire, led by the demand for their trade. It goes without saying that the first century's traveling conditions were difficult.[29]

A large selection of wheeled vehicles was available to travelers, but the cost of renting or buying a vehicle was beyond the reach of ordinary artisans. People usually traveled on foot, risking the flying stones that were thrown by passing vehicles. A donkey could be rented to carry baggage, but this increased expenses. Furthermore, a donkey could be "borrowed" or requisitioned on the spot by any Roman soldier or official. These officials could also require not only the donkey but also various services of any traveler, often unexpectedly delaying travel. A soldier could compel a person to carry his pack for a mile, and he could also compel an artisan to mend his pack or sandals. And such services were likely to be unpaid.

The average inn was like a courtyard surrounded by rooms. Poor travelers wrapped themselves in their cloaks and slept on the ground where the baggage was piled and animals were tethered. Even for those who could afford to rent beds in the rooms, a sound sleep was difficult because of bedbugs and thieves. Governmental officials or police were often out of reach or barely helpful, especially for travelers or strangers. Travelers had to protect themselves. In the countryside throughout the vast empire, roads were often hilly and mountain passes might be blocked by unexpected snowfalls, spring floods, or hailstorms. Travelers had to bear extreme changes of temperature and terrain. Furthermore, the dangers associated with mountain pirates as well as wild animals, such as bears, wolves, and wild boars, could happen anytime.

Sea travel was no less dangerous. There were no passenger ships available, and cargo ships took passengers on a stand-by basis. The ship provided only drinking water, and the passengers had to take turns cooking at the hearth in the galley of an oar-driven ship. As there were no cabins, passengers lived on deck, using their own tents if they had any. People had to struggle to protect themselves, their belongings, and their merchandise from harsh weather and thieves. Furthermore, shipwrecks were not unusual, and it was highly improbable that the survivors of an accident would be rescued by another ship.

Travel companions were indispensable for both women and men, not only for conversation but also for all kinds of practical collaboration. Little wonder that the itinerant preachers in the reign-of-God movement as well as Christian missionaries traveled in pairs. It must have been a great relief for many traveling Jews that synagogues offered them places to stay. While business travel was fraught with danger and hardships, it offered excellent occasions for missionary work.

### Slaves

In the Greco-Roman world slavery was taken for granted. Many different kinds of people were forced into the complex system of Roman slavery. The lowest group of slaves consisted of condemned criminals. Most of them were sent to work in mines or galleys (oar-driven ships). Some were killed in amphitheaters as gladiators, fighting each other or wild beasts for Roman entertainment.[30]

The majority, regardless of their ethnic background, had become slaves by being born to enslaved mothers, by being captured in war, or through kidnapping by pirates or brigands. These slaves, considered the property of their owners, included both women and men working on the lands of aristocratic absentee-landowners, at various factories, or at all kinds of menial work. There also were many abandoned female babies and daughters sold into slavery by their poverty-stricken parents. Many of these girls, if rescued, were raised by slave owners for the sex trade; they worked as prostitutes, actors, and entertainers at brothels, inns, and public baths.

There were, on the other hand, more "privileged" slaves who worked in wealthy homes. These slaves not only undertook domestic menial tasks but were often given special education and training; many became private tutors for the minor children of the household as well as trusted agents and administrators in business affairs. While most women, slave or free, did not have any training beyond traditional household skills, some women slaves received special education and training and worked as administrators, doctors, midwives, nurses, infirmary attendants, caretakers for children, tutors, readers, clerks, secretaries, stenographers, ladies' maids, masseuses, hair stylists, mirror holders, clothes folders, dancers, harpists, flutists, and other entertainers. They were also wool workers, weavers, seamstresses, and laundry women.

Slave "marriages" were not formal but were generally respected by custom. Oftentimes, urban slaves were freed in adulthood by their owner's will, by mutual agreement (mostly that they would continue to serve at their owner's households), or in recognition and reward for faithful service. Slave women were also frequently freed so they could marry their previous owner. The freed-slave wife, however, could not divorce without her husband's consent.

Urban freed slaves were likely to be more highly educated and to enjoy greater economic security than the freeborn poor. Since slaves were an integral part of the estate of their owners, slaves of prestigious families or persons often enjoyed more prestigious positions than poor free persons. In such complex forms of slavery, a poor free woman might gain more prestige by marrying a slave of a prestigious household than by marrying a poor free man.

It was taken for granted, however, that all slaves, both women and men, were available sexually for their master and the master's guests. A Roman novel, *The Golden Ass*, written by Apuleius in the second century, describes a slave girl who welcomes her master's guest into the house, washes his feet, prepares and offers the meal, makes up a bed, guides the guest to the bedroom, and sleeps with him. All of these tasks were seen as an ordinary part of her duties.[31]

Some of the earliest Christian communities seem to have practiced ransoming slaves. Drawing on community funds, they "purchased" and freed some slaves, especially those who were enslaved for debt and those who escaped from abusive owners. Some of Paul's words reflect this practice: "You were bought with a price: do not become slaves of human masters" (1 Cor 7:23). Such practices might well have offered the last hope for many desperate women and men.[32]

### *The Privileged Few*

Royal and aristocratic men were at the top of the social ladder in the first-century Roman Empire, and they exercised tremendous power over their subordinates. Women in this circle also exercised power in political affairs, sometimes directly and more often indirectly through their fathers, husbands, and sons. Elite women often experienced stronger ties with their fathers than with their husbands. Once Roman fathers decided to raise, rather than expose or abandon, their daughters, they granted them higher education as well as economic and political resources, strengthening the father-daughter tie. This tie continued even after the daughter's marriage, because marriage did not integrate wives into their husbands' households but left them legally under their fathers' control. A high divorce rate and the consequent separation of mothers from their children further reinforced this father-daughter tie. Through this tie, elite women were well integrated into the Roman elite society.[33]

Elite women thus possessed and exercised a significant measure of economic and social autonomy independently of their husbands. They wielded power over the majority of the populace, both men and women. For elite women, the concept of their household was extended to the larger institutions, such as entire cities or states. They were expected to take care of their extended households, to become patrons or benefactors of various municipal institutions, religious organizations, and *collegia*. Probably one-tenth of the influential benefactors of that time were women. It is basically these privileged people who would have sufficient education and free time to write with or without secretarial service. There were also women religious leaders and philosophers, and some women took an active part in the regular business of towns and cities.[34]

In the first-century Roman Empire, high-status Roman matrons started accompanying their husbands and participating in public banquets that were previously reserved for free males. Reflecting the general liberating milieu of the time, this came about as the expanded network of roads increased people's mobility and women increased their activities in business and religion. During the Greco-Roman time, public banquets of male elites had various cultural implications for the lives of both men and women, regardless of their social states.

In "high society," Greek-style formal banquets, or public meals, were held in private homes. A typical banquet included seven to eleven male guests. On such occasions guests reclined on couches arranged in the dining room. The host could use the seating order as an occasion for honoring or humbling certain guests, as well as to confirm or reward loyal connections (see, for example, Lk 14:7-11). These banquets were the most popular settings for upper-class male associations; they centered around various celebrations, discussions, poetry recitations, songs, music, and theatrical storytelling. Such public banquets consisted of two parts: a formal *deipnon* (the meal itself) and a following *symposion* (drinking party). For such banquets skilled artisans were hired—men for slaughtering and cooking of meat, women for preparing the sweet desserts. At a lavish *deipnon*, after eating heavy meat and poultry (or fish) courses, the dessert courses of cheesecakes, cookies, and honeyed fruit pies were offered before the serious drinking of the *symposion*.[35]

A *symposion* was typically the time for male entertainment, when dancers, flutists, and other slave entertainers were available for the guests' entertainment. It was customary that prostitutes or courtesans *(hetaerae)* would sit or recline along with each man. Certain of these courtesans were well known for their ability to participate in the male conversation with their wit and rhetorical skills.

When high-status Roman matrons accompanied their husbands and participated in the public male banquets, they usually withdrew after the *deipnon*, lest they be identified as prostitutes at the *symposion*. Young women were expected to remain quiet and not join in conversation with the men, in contrast to the behavior of witty courtesans. In such a social context women who joined in meals and conversations with men risked being labeled or denounced as sexually loose women.

There is a need to proceed with caution. Since ancient literature and history comes almost exclusively from privileged men, we have received a disproportionate amount of information about their lives and views. Information regarding women reflects an upper-class male desire for quiet and obedient women, rather than conveying accurate information about women's actual activities. This part of the lost history of women—a record of the activities of upper-class women—could yield valuable information. At the same time, however, we must remember that upper-class people were only a tiny segment of the entire population. Balance is very significant in developing our historical imagination of the ancient world as a whole.

### Religious Celibates

Some privileged women could and did choose lifestyles that were outside of these various forms of patriarchal households. Among them were the Therapeutrides, a group of Jewish women who lived in a contemplative community in Egypt during the first century. The Therapeutrides lived in rural isolation alongside the community of Therapeutae, their male counterparts. They devoted themselves entirely to prayer, the study of the scriptures, scribal activities involving the scriptures, hymn making, and a celibate lifestyle. In their festivals the Therapeutrides and the Therapeutae worshiped together and sang their hymns both independently and in chorus.[36]

It is also widely acknowledged that some women in the early Christian movements chose celibate lifestyles as virgins and widows, and that some of these women started living together creating non-patriarchal, non-kinship-based familial communities.[37]

## Women and Men in the Earliest Christian Movements

Unfortunately, the Christian Testament texts do not offer much information about people's occupations and ways of life in the earliest Christian movements. However, stories in the Christian Testament do yield clues about their possible occupations and life conditions that will help develop our historical imagination.

### Peasant Artisans and Fishers

First of all, the gospels introduce Jesus and his father as carpenters in Nazareth (Mk 6:3; Mt 13:55). Although they were not part of the earliest

Christian movements, their origins in the rural life of a peasant artisan family were certainly embedded in the complex first-century Roman political economy. The gospels tell us that Andrew, Peter, James, and John, the first male followers of Jesus, were fishermen in Galilee (Mk 1:16-20; Mt 4:18-22; Lk 5:1-11). While the gospels tell us that there were Galilean women who participated in the reign-of-God movement from the beginning (Mk 15:40-41; Mt 27:55-56; Lk 8:2-3; 23:49), they do not include any clear statements about their occupations. Given that Mary Magdalene was from a town renowned for its salted-fish trade, we can well imagine that some of the earliest women participants also worked in fishing and fish-processing trades.[38]

### *"Tax Collectors," "Sinners," and "Prostitutes"*

Scholars agree that the reign-of-God movement associated with those who were called "tax collectors," "sinners," and "prostitutes" from the very beginning (Mk 2:15; Mt 11:19; 21:31; Lk 7:34; 15:2). These people were likely the bearers of the movement and possibly the first members of the earliest Christian communities.

Tax collectors were frequently mentioned in the Christian Testament. Most notable are the stories of Zacchaeus, who was a rich chief tax collector (Lk 19:2), and the tax collectors Levi (Mk 2:14; Lk 5:27) and Matthew (Mt 9:9). While "chief" tax collectors might have been rich, most of the actual tax collectors, those who did the work, were impoverished or were slaves employed by a "tax agency." They were quickly dismissed if any problems arose. The agents of Rome as well as the client kings gathered two general kinds of tax: direct taxes (including taxes such as the head tax, soil or market tax, and toll tax) and indirect taxes (including import and export taxes). Jewish people were also required to offer tithes and sacrifices to the Jerusalem temple.[39]

In this context tax collectors were likened to robbers and thieves and treated with contempt, especially because the official taxation was heavy and tax collectors had to collect the money often by means of coarse harassment. Furthermore, working within the system, they had to take more than the official fee in order to make their own living. They were also associated with procurers, because for taxation purposes tax collectors kept lists of licensed prostitutes. Because of these connotations, the phrase "tax collectors" was also used as slander to label someone, regardless of the person's actual occupation, as immoral or associated with prostitution.[40]

The word "sinner" in the first-century Jewish context could be applied to anyone who did not keep the Torah (Jewish law) or who could not do so because of the limitations caused by occupation. This included a variety of people, criminals as well as those who worked in disreputable occupations such as swine-herders, garlic peddlers, fruit-sellers, bartenders, sailors, public announcers, tax collectors, pimps, prostitutes, servants, and people in other service occupations. Most of the employed "sinners" were not only badly paid but also often mistreated.[41]

As for the "prostitutes," we have observed that there must have been many women (and men) who had to work in prostitution, most of whom were slaves or impoverished and unskilled. It is likely that these women were involved in the reign-of-God movement, which intentionally included those who were marginalized in the patriarchal power-relations of the Roman Empire.[42]

At the same time it is important to note another dimension of the word "prostitute" as used in that society. As mentioned earlier, formal and public banquets of the upper class were typical occasions for male association that included a *symposion* (drinking party) where prostitutes and courtesans joined men for sexual as well as witty conversational entertainment. Women who participated in the public meal setting with men were often labeled as prostitutes by those who did not like this behavior of the "new" women.[43]

In the first-century Roman period many women started joining men in various kinds of public meal settings. Most of them probably engaged in the same occupational trades. Since such table fellowship was a central activity for various philosophical and religious groups, not only men but also women became active participants of table fellowship, or public meals. These "new" women, including those in the Cynics, Epicureans, the Dionysus religion, the Isis religion, and Judaism, were all accused by their adversaries as prostitutes or loose, promiscuous women. Women in the reign-of-God movement as well as in the earliest Christian groups were among them. Therefore, we can understand that the use of the word "prostitute" in referring to women in the reign-of-God movement was not necessarily a reference to their occupation or social status. Various women did participate in the reign-of-God movement, and many might well have become the core active members of the earliest Christian movements.

By saying this, I do not intend to claim that the reign-of-God movement was perfectly egalitarian, free from sexism and classism. In the Greco-Roman world, the patriarchal system and mind-set permeated all of society. Both the reign-of-God movement and the earliest churches were born and developed in such a world. We should not expect that any of them, including those of Jesus of Nazareth, was immune to the surrounding culture. Nevertheless, it is noteworthy that they did practice such egalitarian inclusiveness, given the broader social matrix, or more properly, patrix, of the Greco-Roman society.

### Misleading Presentation?

The Christian Testament presents other possible examples of the occupations of the earliest Christians. Anna is introduced as a temple prophet (Lk 2:36), Philip's four daughters prophesied (Acts 21:9), and a woman denounced as Jezebel (Rev 2:20) identified herself as a prophet. Stories also appear about Jairus, a ruler of a synagogue (Mk 5:22; Mt 9:18; Lk 8:40); a centurion/official in Capernaum (Mt 8:5; Lk 7:1-2; Jn 4:46); Joseph of Arimathea, a member of the council (Mk 15:43; Lk 19:2); an Ethiopian court official (Acts

8:27); Simon, a tanner (Acts 9:43); Cornelius, a centurion of the Italian Co-hort (Acts 10:1); Rhoda, a maid (Acts 12:13); Lydia, a seller of purple goods (Acts 16:14); a jailer in Philippi (Acts 16:27); Paul, Prisca, and Aquila as tentmakers (Acts 18:2-3); Erastus, a city treasurer (Rom 16:23); Luke, a phy-sician (Col 4:14); and Zenas, a lawyer (Tit 3:13). The overall picture in the Christian Testament is that the earliest Christians had various lifestyles rang-ing from those of fairly high to those of very low social status.

While this may be true, one crucial consideration is necessary. In the sec-ond century an elite male critic, Celsus, ridiculed Christianity as a religion of the lower classes that appealed only to the uneducated, slaves, women, and children. He contemptuously described the social origin of Jesus' mother, Mary, saying that she was a poor countrywoman who had to earn her living by needlework or spinning. Furthermore, Celsus was critical of the fact that these lower-class women and men were not governed by educated upper-class men. Origen, one of the "fathers" of the church, wrote a refutation. He did not deny Celsus's comment in substance. He asserted, rather, "Not only does the Gospel call these that it may make them better, but it also calls people much superior to them." He maintained that the ratio of the upper-class educated people to lower-class Christians corresponded to that of the population in Rome; that is, according to historians of the time, the ratio was 1 to 99. Even if these numbers are not exact, we should be aware that while the vast major-ity of the earliest Christians were lower-class people, their occupations and lifestyles are under-represented in the texts of the Christian Testament. It may be that the canonical writers tended to present Christians as coming from all ranks rather than mostly from the lower classes. Sometimes, however, it is not the Christian Testament texts themselves but later interpretations of them that render invisible lower-class occupations and lifestyles, as we will see in the following section.[44]

### The Earliest Missionary Leaders and Their House Churches

#### Tabitha

In the Christian Testament, Tabitha of Joppa is the only woman who is clearly introduced as a "disciple" (Acts 9:36). Joppa, today's Jaffa, is a town in Palestine on the eastern shore of the Mediterranean Sea. In the account in Acts widows who were mourning and weeping around the dead Tabitha showed Peter the *xiton* (inner garments) and the *himation* (outer garments) she had made during her lifetime. The *xiton* was a tunic, sewn at the top and the sides, leaving openings for the head and the arms. It was worn both by men (knee length) and women (foot length) as an inner garment and by itself at home and sometimes at work also. The *himation* is an outer robe, rectangular and of various sizes. While only Roman citizens wore the toga (large semicircular robe), the *himation* was the most common robe for both women and men. It was draped around the body, and could be girded with a cord or sash. Used as a cloak, the *himation* protected the body from heat, cold, and rain. It was also used as a blanket for sleeping and to wrap and carry things.[45]

Through a careful reading of the text, aided by multi-disciplinary research, Ivoni Richter Reimer has restored the historical figure of the woman Tabitha as a textile worker who wove and finished cloth for garments, earning her living by spinning and needlework. As mentioned above, this is exactly the scornful way in which elite male Celsus described Mary, the mother of Jesus. Tabitha lived with some people, possibly a group of widows who supported each other. This implies that the "disciple" Tabitha lived as an artisan, in a weak socioeconomic position as a widow without kinship ties.[46]

### Lydia

It is now known that the earliest Christian churches started as house churches as some Christians opened or offered their houses for Christian worship and gatherings. Lydia was one of the earliest leaders of such house churches in Philippi, Macedonia, on the northern shore of the Aegean Sea. There, Lydia lived in a riverside house where she was engaged in purple cloth dyeing. She is introduced in Acts as a seller of purple goods who traveled around on business (16:14). Apparently she worked as a traveling missionary as well as a traveling salesperson. Scholars have pictured her as a wealthy woman whose customers were aristocratic people who wore purple clothes. Recent feminist scholarship, however, offers a quite different picture of this leading woman.[47]

According to Ivoni Richter Reimer and Luise Schottroff, Lydia was most likely a former slave, as demonstrated by her being named by her place of origin rather than by a personal name. The city of Thyatira in Lydia was in West Asia Minor, the land to the east of the Aegean Sea (today's Akhisar, in Turkey). At the time of the story the city was an important center of the wool trade. Lydia might have learned her skills as an artisan while she was a slave girl in Thyatira. Now, in Philippi, she had a house close to the river, where she carried on her trade of purple dyeing and lived with women co-workers. This is an example of a woman-headed household, as might also have been the case with Tabitha.[48]

The use of purple cloth was not limited to aristocratic people. There were different types of color and different ways of purple dyeing: an expensive purple was extracted from sea snails, an inexpensive purple was extracted from plants, and in between, a variety of purple was produced or reproduced by mixing material of different qualities. The method used in Thyatira was plant dyeing for wool and for the clothes of slaves. It is highly likely that Lydia and her women co-workers engaged in this plant-dyeing method. Such work was poorly paid hard work. Since animal urine was used to set the dye, the process was also smelly and dirty. Even in producing the most expensive types of purple goods, the dyeing was a time-consuming, complex, and laborious process. Thus, Lydia and her women co-workers were likely to have belonged to a lower despised class because of the body odor caused by the dyeing work.[49]

**Paul, Prisca, and Aquila**

Paul, Prisca, and Aquila, the well-known leading missionaries who opened house churches in Corinth, Ephesus, and Rome, are introduced as tentmakers (Acts 18:2-3). Corinth was a well-known harbor city in Macedonia, on the western shore of the Aegean Sea. In Corinth shrines were dedicated to a variety of gods, including Aphrodite, Apollo, Asklepios, Athena, Demeter and Kore, Isis, and Palaimon. Ephesus was a large seaport city in Asia Minor, on the eastern shore of the Aegean Sea. Here, also, there were shrines dedicated to diverse gods, including Aphrodite, Apollo, Asklepios, Athena, Demeter, Dionysus, Isis and other Egyptian gods, the Mother Goddess, Poseidon, and Zeus, as well as huge temples for Roman imperial worship. Rome, of course, was the capital of the Roman Empire and the center of the Roman imperial worship.[50]

The house churches that Prisca and Aquila founded became the Christian centers in these cities, and scholars have portrayed their founders as a wealthy couple. But again, recent scholarship, especially that of Ivoni Richter Reimer and Jerome Murphy-O'Connor, offers a very different picture. Prisca and Aquila might have been freed slaves who were formerly owned by a great Roman family or families. Although Aquila was a Jew, he probably acquired this Latin name (meaning eagle) at the time of his manumission, as slaves often took their master's name on such an occasion. It seems Prisca (Priscilla is the diminutive) acquired her name similarly. Both Prisca and Aquila probably learned tentmaking skills while they were slaves.[51]

Around that time, tents were made of light linen, stronger linen, or leather, and they were used by the military, by wealthy travelers, for awnings in private houses and theaters, and for market stalls. The demand for tentmakers was high, as they not only made and repaired the wide variety of tents but also made and repaired various leather goods, including sandals, cloaks, gourds to carry water and wine, and other travel equipment. Since skill was more important than strength, women as well as men could find work. The work included heavy needle-and-palm work, or, in case of leather tents, cutting leather and washing hides. We read that they had to work "night and day" (1 Thess 2:9). Such hard work was despised and poorly paid.

## Pair Missionaries

If Lydia, Prisca, and Aquila were hard-working, poor artisans, and perhaps even despised, it is likely that many other traveling missionaries or house church leaders, as well as those gathered at their houses, were also part of the hard-working poor class. The names of two pairs of missionaries mentioned in Paul's letter to the Romans seem to support this interpretation. Paul sends greetings to "Philologus and Julia" as well as to "Nereus and his sister" (Rom 16:15). Julia was a common Latin name for a slave, and Nereus was a common Greek name given to a slave, particularly in Rome. These missionary pairs may well have been slaves or former slaves who traveled with their trade.[52]

### Tenement Churches

Recent archeological discoveries have demonstrated that some of the most likely areas for the earliest Christian house churches in Rome were slums. These slums were inhabited mostly by immigrants who lived as sailors, harbor workers, warehouse workers, brick and tile workers, potters, millers, tanners, leather workers, donkey drivers, carriers, and transport workers who worked at night. Such workers were considered to be the lowest on the ladder of social status.[53]

If the majority of the earliest Christians worked at trades or as manual laborers and lived in such neighborhoods, how should we imagine their house churches? Some stories in the Christian Testament tell of some conversions that encompassed an entire household, including slaves and clients (for example, Acts 10:1-48; 16:29-34). Such people's house churches were undoubtedly larger and more adequate, perhaps even luxurious. However, they were probably exceptions. It is more likely that most of the earliest house churches in urban areas were small houses or workshop/dwelling units in apartment buildings. They may be more properly called "tenement" churches, using space rented by their artisan/merchant leaders who opened their houses for the gatherings of ten to twenty people. In rural areas peasants' small houses, consisting of one or two rooms with a possible extension into the central common yard, were probably the prototypes of house churches.[54]

In such small and humble dwellings, with a few exceptions, women and men seem to have gathered together for praying, eating, healing, prophesying, and storytelling, crossing social boundaries of ethnicity, class (social status), and gender. They declared that all the people were "one in Christ," and that there were "neither Jew nor Greek," "neither slave nor free," and "not male and female" (an early baptismal formula, quoted by Paul in Galatians 3:28). For many impoverished or marginalized people, inclusive practices such as eating together and healing in communities would have been the activities that truly made the *basileia* (reign of God) tangible.[55]

### A Reflection on the Story of the Samaritan Woman

It has been said that the Johannine gospel was originally addressed to a community of relatively well-off people. Initially, it might seem that the Johannine communities were comprised of middle-class people, relatively free from poverty and concerned primarily with their spiritual quest. A careful study of the first-century social world, however, makes us question these assumptions. Furthermore, as we read the gospel with a critical awareness of gender and class issues, some stories in the gospel take on a different meaning.[56]

One such story is that of the Samaritan woman (Jn 4:1-42). Whereas the Samaritan man of a story in the Lukan gospel is known as "the good Samaritan," the Samaritan woman in the Johannine gospel is known as "the loose

Samaritan woman." It is not clear, though, that this was the most common image of her for the majority of the first-century audience. It is worthwhile to call attention to some nuances that her story might have had for many of the audience at that time.[57]

Samaria is a region sandwiched between Galilee (a northern region) and Judea (a southern region) in Palestine. Scholars assume that Samaritans were an integral part of the Johannine communities from the early period. There was, however, a long-standing conflict between the Samaritans and the other Jews, and the Samaritan people were generally hated or despised by other Jewish people. In any case, this story is told in the gospel as the occasion when the people of a Samaritan town were led to believe in Jesus through the testimony of a woman. Although we cannot assume that the story is historical, we can assume that there was a historical woman who was remembered in the Johannine communities as a representative missionary figure for the Samaritan people.[58]

Since her name does not occur in the text, let us call her Photini (meaning enlightened one), following the later practice of the Orthodox Church. The story in the Johannine gospel tells us that Photini married five men and now lived with a man who was not her husband. Why did she live with so many men? Many commentaries teach that she was a loose woman or was rumored to be such in the town, and that she went to the well around noon to avoid being seen because no other women would go to the well in the heat of day. If, however, she really was this sort of woman, is it plausible that the town's people, both women and men, would have listened to her and "believed in him [Jesus] because of the woman's testimony" (Jn 4:39)? Should we, perhaps, imagine Photini differently?[59]

When ordinary first-century women heard the story of Photini, in any of the versions in which it must have been told, how might they have imagined Photini? Undoubtedly, some women could immediately relate to her hard life of consecutive marriages, based on their own experience or that of their friends and neighbors. They might have imagined Photini as a very poor woman whose husband died early, perhaps a victim of war. Or, she may have been a daughter of a poverty-stricken family whose parents arranged her early marriage to an old man with money. When her husband died, regardless of whether she already had three children or not, she quickly had to remarry in order to survive. She likely had no professional skills to enable her economic independence and ended up marrying another old man. Such an experience of consecutive marriages might not have been so exceptional for poor women in the Roman colonies.[60]

Many women in the earliest audience probably "understood" that Photini had to visit the well around noon because she needed more water than the ordinary amount. Possibly she had someone sick at home to care for or perhaps she earned some money by carrying water. It is also possible that, while listening to the story, some women could almost experience Photini's back pain. She may have had a deformed back from carrying water repeatedly, which is still the experience of many poor women in the world, even at the beginning of the twenty-first century.[61]

In the story Jesus says to her, "You have had five husbands, and the one you have now is not your husband" (4:18). This has been interpreted as Jesus' denunciation of the Samaritan woman's loose sexual life. However, it is possible that some of the earliest storytellers told the story with a different emphasis and that their audiences heard the words quite differently. In just one sentence Jesus showed his understanding of the depth of the hardship she had gone through in her life. Even if others had spoken the same words with contempt, Jesus' words, when spoken by some women storytellers, may have conveyed his compassion and understanding of her life. To this, Photini immediately replies, "Sir, I see that you are a prophet" (4:19): a prophet, a true prophet, someone she could trust, after all the pain and despair she has experienced. She leaves her water jar at the well and goes to testify to what she has experienced with Jesus.

Indeed, in the story, Jesus and Photini experience a profound encounter at the well, a traditional story setting for the meeting of future spouses. We may assume that their conversation, even given the various theological implications pointed out by scholars, did not necessarily sound to the earliest audiences as a righteous Jewish male's denunciation and a sinful Samaritan woman's surrender. Some women and men who heard a version of this story must have thought the conversation of Jesus and Photini sounded more like mutual recognition and hope for shared worship. It crossed the religious and social boundaries between the two people: between a Galilean Jew and a Samaritan Jew, as well as between a male teacher with disciples and a poor woman without a legal husband.

Why is it that we have never before been sensitive to the possible nuances of this story? Does our indifference to and ignorance of the daily experiences of first-century ordinary women prevent us from noticing many signs of their concerns and desires? Do we miss hearing the many different voices contained in the gospel? It is crucial to pay much more attention to the first-century world in which people of the early Christian communities lived if we wish to appreciate their experiences, their suffering and hope, and their different voices.

# 3

## Deities and Religious Leadership

The previous chapter focused on the daily experiences of first-century people, paying more attention to ordinary women, in order to expand our historical imagination. This chapter will turn to the various deities and religious leadership in the Greco-Roman world—again with the purpose of gaining a more inclusive understanding of the earliest Christians' lives. The term "Greco-Roman world" refers to the vast Roman provinces characterized by Roman political and economic rule and Hellenistic culture. The term "Hellenistic" refers to the culture that was created by the interaction of Greek culture with various other ethnic cultures, starting from the time of the Greek emperor Alexander and continuing through the Roman emperor Constantine, 330 C.E.[1]

Most Christians have been taught that Jews and Christians believed in the one and the same God from ancient times, while "pagans" (all remaining people of other faiths) believed in many gods. We have also learned that from the earliest Christian origins men, not women, held leadership roles in churches. At the same time we have commonly been taught that Jesus was uniquely open-minded to women and that only Christian communities were outstandingly egalitarian, over against more conservative Jewish communities as well as the broader patriarchal world. Furthermore, it has often been emphasized that the primary concern of the church is for faith or spiritual matters and that the political and social issues should be the concerns of secular organizations. However, things look different as we look at Jewish and Christian communities more carefully and locate them in their broader historical contexts.

## In the Greco-Roman World

### Heaven and Earth

An understanding of how the Hellenistic people pictured the universe, their heaven and earth, will be helpful, as our modern view of the universe is very different. We know that the earth is not located at the center of the universe, that it is not flat, that the sun does not go around the earth, and that our solar system is not the center of the universe, which is an endlessly vast cosmos. From ancient times through the medieval period, the earth was viewed as a flat sphere located at the center of the universe and surrounded by the sun, moon, and other planets, which traveled around the earth. This universe was covered by a firmament, and in the firmament was a hole or an opening to the other side. The gods as well as various kinds of angels and other spiritual beings lived on the other side or layers of the heaven/sky *(ouranos)* above. As the heaven/sky was the dwelling place for divine beings, astronomy or the reading of signs in the sky was an important means to know the divine will, which directly intervened in human lives.[2]

Some gospel texts indicate that first-century Jewish people shared this basic view of the heaven and the earth with their Greco-Roman contemporaries. They also imaged the *sheol* beneath the earth where the dead go down and then either were raised or were moved further down to hell. The gospels tell that when Jesus was born the *magi,* or wise men who read signs in the heaven/sky, came from the East to greet him (Mt 2:1-12) and that an angel and a multitude of the heavenly host told the good news to the shepherds (Lk 2:8, 15). When Jesus was baptized, he saw "the heavens torn apart and the Spirit descending like a dove on him" (Mk 1:10; Mt 3:16; Lk 3:21-22). The gospels also tell that Jesus spoke of heavenly signs: "the sun will be darkened, and the moon will not give its light, and the stars will be falling from heaven, and the powers in the heavens will be shaken" (Mk 13:24-25; Mt 24:29-31; Lk 21:25-26).

In the Matthean gospel Jesus speaks of the throne of God, "whoever swears by heaven, swears by the throne of God and by the one who is seated upon it" (Mt 23:22), and in the Johannine gospel Jesus tells of the house of God, "In my Father's house there are many dwelling places" (Jn 14:2). At the first resurrection appearance of Jesus, he tells Mary Magdalene, "I am ascending to my Father and your Father, to my God and your God" (Jn 20:17). With this basic image of the heaven/sky above and the earth beneath, let us examine the world of Greco-Roman religions.

### Popular Religions

A variety of popular religions coexisted in the Greco-Roman world, and it was taken for granted that women took leadership roles, as they had in earlier times. Ross Kraemer wrote, "It was commonplace in Greco-Roman antiquity that religion was women's business." Numerous inscriptions and ancient writings testify to women's leadership in serving a diversity of deities, both female and male. The gender of the leaders seems to have generally correlated with that of the deity, but not exclusively, nor without exceptions.[3]

It is important to note that the female gender of a god did not mean that the god's attributes were what we would call feminine. For example, many ancient female gods were viewed not only as fertility gods who would assure human and agricultural fertility and prosperity, but also as warrior gods who would bring victory and peace. Again, it is doubtful that modern concepts of so-called femininity and masculinity were relevant to the majority of the ancients. Actually, many gods had similar attributes, which may reflect the similar concerns shared by people in agrarian societies in the Greco-Roman world. It may also reflect their syncretistic activities, mutually learning and appropriating attractive features of the gods of their neighboring peoples.[4]

At the same time, each regional and ethnic god had particular aspects that appealed to people in particular situations. For example, the triad of Greek female deities—Kore, Demeter, and Hecate—seems to have functioned to meet the particular needs of Greek free women in their life stages of daughter, mother, and widow. These deities affirmed and ensured the transition of free women from one stage to the next in Greek society. At the same time, some of their festivals had subversive elements. They strengthened the mother-daughter bond beyond their separation by patriarchal marriages. Women also reconfirmed their power for both human and agricultural fertility, ridiculing men's concept of mighty male power. Restricted to Greek free women, the rites and festivals dedicated to female deities seem to have offered women occasions of autonomy and solidarity, while at the same time serving to maintain the patriarchal Greek society.[5]

While ancient religions had their origins in particular regions and ethnic groups, in the Hellenistic and Greco-Roman period some universalizing social changes made many religions more open, crossing the boundaries of regions, ethnicity, class, and gender. In such a milieu many religions competed to attract diverse people, and some deities obtained broad and strong popularity beyond their original regions.

The religion of Dionysus was one of the more popular Greco-Roman religions, and women's devotion to the Greek male deity was legendary. The famous *Baccae* or wine-drinking festivals of Dionysus seem to have originated from women's private rites in Athens in the late fifth century B.C.E. Gradually, these became public rites for women in many cities of western Asia Minor, and men also became involved. In the second century B.C.E., the cult of Dionysus was widespread. At that time the Roman government carried out a harsh persecution, and some people committed suicide rather than submit to the punishment. Such persecution, however, did not diminish the attraction to the religion.[6]

In the first century C.E. the Dionysus religion was quite popular among both women and men. One of its features was the elimination of social and cultural boundaries, such as male/female, young/old, and life/death. In their *Baccae* festivals adherents abolished the barriers of social status. There was also a festival when women enjoyed a wild ritual in which they disregarded gender expectations in the "blessings of madness." The licensing of the departure of women from their homes and gender roles might explain the particular attractiveness of this male deity for many women devotees.

While this temporal and ritual reversal of social and cultural norms was not revolutionary, these activities seem to have offered both male and female participants occasions of spiritual emancipation and relief from the oppressions they had to bear in their daily lives. Similarly known for wild rites was the religion of the Great Mother Cybele, originally a Phrygian deity in Asia Minor. This religion also spread broadly throughout the Greco-Roman world.

Isis, the Egyptian female deity from archaic times, became probably the most powerful and universal god in the Hellenistic and Greco-Roman world. She was renowned for her power especially in regard to childbirth, fertility, and healing. These features corresponded to the basic needs of agrarian families, especially the needs of women. The historian Diodorus of Sicily (first century B.C.E.) writes that Isis was honored by all of the inhabited world for revealing herself and her powers to those in need.[7]

Archeological discoveries show that there were numerous Isis revelations and *aretalogies* (praising hymns). In them, her devotees proclaimed that Isis the "lord" (*kyria*; sometimes *kyrios* in the masculine form) created the cosmic order; made laws against injustice, tyranny, and wars; and upheld peace and justice as well as gender equality. They even claimed that all the other names of both female and male gods were only variant names of Isis. Isis temples were found everywhere in the vast Roman provinces, and they commanded the popular devotion of both women and men. Women seem to have outnumbered men not only as devotees but also as priests and other officials. The universal popularity of Isis was such that even some Roman emperors alleged the assurance of Isis in support of their ascendancy.

Followers of the official Roman religion worshiped many traditional gods, including such famous female deities as Bona Dea, Matuta, Roma, and Vesta. Numerous official Roman festivals involved significant participation by aristocratic women, but women from lower classes, especially freedwomen, were not excluded. Active participation of freedwomen may reflect the relatively high financial means some of the former slaves acquired in the complex Roman slavery system. Both men and women assumed official roles, but one of the most prestigious of all priestly roles was held exclusively by women. These women, originally the daughters of Roman kings, served the female deity Vesta and were called vestal virgins. The prestigious role of vestal virgin may be one example of the connection between religious leadership roles and higher financial status. This is understandable, especially since religious leaders were often expected to maintain religious offices and activities with their own financial resources. Gender was not a detrimental factor in the area of religion, and women's religious leadership in one way or another seems to have been commonplace in the first-century Greco-Roman world.[8]

### Hellenistic and Greco-Roman Imperial Worship

An understanding of imperial worship is key to understanding the religions operating in the Greco-Roman world. In these societies, where only a few elite people had tremendous economic and political power over the rest of the population, who could barely survive, it would have been rather easy for monarchs to think or act as though they were divine representatives. Indeed, imperial worship, the deification of monarchs, was quite common in the ancient Near East. Hellenistic Egypt and the Roman Empire offer good examples.

In Hellenistic Egypt both queens and kings were worshiped as the earthly representatives of deities or even as deities themselves. The Hellenistic period began in Egypt when Alexander the Great conquered Persian Egypt (332 B.C.E.). He was hailed as liberator as well as the "son of Zeus" and a descendant of Heracles, "the savior of the world and of humanity." The primary meaning of the word "savior" *(soter)* was political rather than religious, designating the one who had control of the security *(soteria)* of the city state. And the one who had such power was considered divine.[9]

After the death of Alexander the Great, King Ptolemy I (305-282 B.C.E.) was called Soter (savior). He and his wife, Bernice I, were worshiped as Zeus and Aphrodite. Ptolemy II (285-46 B.C.E.) was called Philadelphus (one who loves a sibling), and his elder sister-wife Arsinoe II was called Aphrodite of the Western Shore and King of Upper and Lower Egypt. The couple followed the model of Zeus and Hera and were worshiped as "Gods Adelphi" (sibling gods). Ptolemy III (246-22 B.C.E.) was given the divine title Euergetes (benefactor), while his wife, Bernice II, was worshiped as the "pharaoh." Ptolemy IV (222-205 B.C.E.) was called Philopater (father-loving).

Ptolemy V (204-180 B.C.E.) and Cleopatra I were worshiped as Epiphanes (gods-manifest). Cleopatra II (170-16 B.C.E.) and her husband Ptolemy VI, who was her fourteen-year-old brother, were worshiped as Philometor (mother-loving) gods. Cleopatra III (142-101 B.C.E.) was worshiped as Isis or Isis incarnate, and her titles included "savior," "the saving one," "great mother of the gods," "mother-loving god," and "justice." Similarly, Cleopatra VI (58-57 B.C.E.), the famous Cleopatra VII (51-30 B.C.E.), and her daughter Cleopatra Selene (although she was under Roman control) were all worshiped as Isis. Egyptian kings, on the other hand, were regarded as the sons of Isis.

Throughout the Hellenistic and Greco-Roman period, the images of monarchs were stamped on coins to signal their immortality. Some of the coins picture these queens as Isis and glorify them as the "new goddess," "new Isis," and "queen of kings." In this milieu it is noteworthy that the Jewish Hasmonean Queen Salome Alexandra ruled Israel as sole monarch from 76 to 67 B.C.E., and coins issued at that time pictured her as Isis. As we will see in the next chapter, it was during this Hellenistic period that the Jewish divine female imagery of Wisdom/Sophia was profoundly developed to become coterminous with Yahweh.

During the period of both the reign-of-God movement and the earliest Christian communities, powerful Roman emperors emerged. They were deified and worshiped mostly after death, but some during their lifetime, as sons of god or children of Roma, the female protective deity of Rome. Augustus (30 B.C.E.-14 C.E.) made it clear that he was not to be worshiped as "god" during his lifetime, but he did not hesitate to be worshiped as "son of god," "father," "ruler," "the real savior of human beings," and as the earthly counterpart of Jupiter or vice-regent of Jupiter over human beings. Tiberius (14-37 C.E.), following Augustus, also resisted being deified during his lifetime, but he was also called "son of god."[10]

On the other hand, Gaius (37-41 C.E.), nicknamed Caligula, declared that he was to be worshiped as "god" (as the incarnation of Jupiter) and as "savior and benefactor," even during his lifetime. Claudius (41-54 C.E.) was called "lord" and "savior of the world." Nero (54-68 C.E.) was called "our Apollo," "Heracles," "savior and benefactor of the world," "lord of the whole world," "lord," and "god." He also deified his wife, Poppaea, and his daughter. Vespasian (69-79 C.E.) was called "lord" and "savior." Titus (79-81 C.E.) was hailed as "savior of the world" and deified his sister Domitilla.

Domitian (81-96 C.E.) deified himself during his lifetime and was worshiped as the vice-regent of the supreme father-god Jupiter/Zeus. He demanded that he be addressed as "our lord and god" and that all who refused should be punished. Trajan (98-117 C.E.) rejected deification in his lifetime, but he was linked to Jupiter. Statues of these emperors were erected throughout the empire, and their images on Roman coins celebrated their divine immortality.

## In the Jewish Communities

Christians have usually been taught that the Jewish religion was a strict and changeless monotheistic faith in Yahweh for more than four thousands years. However, recent scholarship has found ample strong evidence to the contrary. It is important to recognize that not only the Jewish people's conception of their God went through various changes throughout history, but also that their faith was not monolithic but diverse. Of particular interest are several female images of the God of Israel that illustrate the transformations (or changes in emphasis) and diversity of the Jewish faith.

During the tribal period Jewish ancestors imaged their God as a tribal god such as the God of Abraham, the God of Isaac, and so on. There might also have been the God of Sarah and the God of Hagar, although they are not found in our Hebrew Bible. When the tribal confederacy of Israel was established in the twelfth century B.C.E., all of these tribal gods were identified as one and the same God, YHWH or Yahweh, who led them out of Egypt and throughout the wilderness (Deut 29:1-6). This God was also identified as El, the high god or the head of the gods in the ancient Near East pantheon, hence the name of their confederacy, *Israel* (meaning, El founds). Some texts in the Hebrew Bible indicate that the God of Israel, or Yahweh, was once a chief member of a pantheon (or a heavenly court, or a divine assembly) where the "sons of god(s)" and "gods" were present (Gen 6:1-4; Job 1:6; 2:1; Ps 82:1).[11]

The Hebrew word *yhwh* is a verb form of *haya*, the word that corresponds with *hay* (life/living), *hawwa* (Eve: the mother of all living, probably a mother-deity in origin), and the Aramaic *hiwya* (snake/life). Scholars assume that the "name" YHWH, or Yahweh, means "I am the one who is always present and active," "I am who I am," or "I will be who I will be," with the connotations of both the impossibility of naming as well as an abiding and continuing presence. This God of beyond naming was referred to not only in male images but also in female images and in nonhuman images. In the Hebrew Bible some of the female images are reflected especially in the use of words such as "breasts" (e.g., Gen 17:1) and "womb" (e.g., Isa 46:3) in connection with Yahweh.[12]

The Hebrew Bible employs various ways of naming El, such as El Elyon (the God most high: e.g., Gen 14:18-19); El Olam (the eternal God: e.g., Gen 21:33); El Berith (the God of covenant: Judg 9:46); and El Shadday.

El Shadday is now usually translated as the "God of almighty." Translation of this Hebrew word depends on how vowels, which the ancient Hebrew texts do not have, are added, so it can be read equally as "God of the mountains" or "God of the breasts." The most likely grammatical derivation of *shadday* is from the word *shad* (breast), mostly occurring in the dual form *shaddaim* or *shadayim* (breasts). Moreover, the word *shadayim* often appears together with the word *rehem* (womb), in connection with reproduction, such as in "make you fruitful" or "be fruitful and multiply," (e.g., Gen 28:3; 35:11; 48:3; 49:25; Ex 6:3; Num 24:16; Ps 68:14). Thus, although the last translation of El Shadday seems closer to the root meaning, it is also the most likely one to be obscured or suppressed in later translations. "May the God of the breasts bless you and make you fruitful and numerous, that you may become a company of peoples" (Gen 28:3; my translation).[13]

The creator God of Israel is also imaged as the shaper, maker, and mother God who formed Israel in the womb and birthed Israel with labor pains (Deut 32:18; Ps 90:2; Prv 8:24-25; Isa 43:1, 7, 15; 44:2, 24; 45:9, 11; 51:13; 54:5). From the word "womb" *(rehem)* comes the verb "to have compassion" *(raham)*, and the phrase "Yahweh compassionate *(rahum)* and gracious" repeatedly appears in the Hebrew Bible to describe the merciful and saving acts of God in history (Deut 4:31; 2 Chr 30:9; Neh 9:17; Jl 2:13; Pss 78:38; 86:16; 103:8; 111:4; 112:4; 145:8; Jon 4:2). These verses show images of God who demonstrates "womb-like compassion" for her child Israel.[14]

> Like a travailing woman I will groan; I will pant. I will gasp at the same time. (Isa 42:14, Trible)

> Can a woman forget her sucking baby that she should have no compassion on the child of her womb? Even these may forget, yet I will not forget you. (Isa 49:15, Trible)

On the other hand, some texts of the Hebrew Bible indicate that ancient Jewish people worshiped a mother-god Asherah together with Yahweh, although they are written from later strict Yahwistic perspectives and denounce such practices. According to the study of Susan Ackerman, however, the worship of the mother-god Asherah was connected to official roles of the queen mothers of Israel. In the Israelite and Judean monarchies through the ninth to seventh centuries B.C.E., the queen mother *(gebira)*, the mother of the king, had an official political position as counselor in her son's court. She also had a religious role, that of devoting herself to the worship of Asherah as Asherah's earthly representative. The king seems to have been regarded as the adopted son of Yahweh.[15]

The Hebrew Bible mentions four queen mothers: Maacha, queen mother of Abyam and Asa (1 Kgs 15:1-2, 9-10); Jezebel, queen mother of Ahaziah and Jehoram (1 Kgs 22:51; 2 Kgs 3:1; 10:13); Athaliah, queen mother of Ahaziah (2 Kgs 8:25-26); and Nehushta, queen mother of Jehoiachin (2 Kgs 24:8). Their worship was performed in Yahweh's temple in Jerusalem, both as part of the official religion of the Yahwistic cult and as part of the so-called popular religion. It appears that people worshiped Yahweh and Asherah side by side in the Jerusalem temple, as well as in the towns and villages of both monarchies, but more so in southern Judah.

The Hebrew Bible also contains texts referring to a female deity called the queen of heaven (Jer 7:16-20; 44:15-19, 25). According to these biblical texts, when the prophet Jeremiah denounced women and men who engaged in the worship of the queen of heaven, the women and men challenged Jeremiah, saying,

> As for the word that you have spoken to us in the name of the LORD, we are not going to listen to you. Instead, we will do everything that we have vowed, make offerings to the queen of heaven and pour out libations to her, just as we and our ancestors, our kings and our officials, used to do in the towns of Judah and in the streets of Jerusalem. We used to have plenty of food, and prospered, and saw no misfortune. But from the time we stopped making offerings to the queen of heaven and pouring out libations to her, we have lacked everything and have perished by the sword and by famine. (Jer 44:16-18)

These texts were written from a perspective that viewed Jeremiah's faith as authentic and the people's faith as idolatrous. Therefore, we need to be cautious not to read the texts as objective descriptions of these conflicts. However, we still find that in the seventh century B.C.E., the worship of the queen of heaven had been widespread throughout the nation for generations. It seems that a great assembly of women and men first respected the prophet Jeremiah and followed his words but then questioned whether this was right. Or, they may have come to the conclusion that Jeremiah's judgment about worshiping the queen of heaven was not right in the eyes of Yahweh or in the eyes of their ancestors.

Women took the lead in challenging Jeremiah and expressed their confidence that worship of the queen of heaven was not only compatible with their faith in Yahweh but also an important continuation of their ancestral tradition, which had involved family members for generations. Moreover, they critically questioned Jeremiah whether or not his understanding of God and the lifestyle derived from such a faith were actually inviting the perils of war and famine.[16]

The nature of their worship of the queen of heaven was described thus: "The children gather wood, the fathers kindle fire, and the women knead dough, to make cakes for the queen of heaven" (Jer 7:18). Susan Ackerman's study of various archeological evidences from the ancient Near East illuminates certain aspects of these practices. The people seem to have appropriated and developed their images of the queen of heaven from the divine images of the east Semitic Ishtar and the west Semitic Astarte. For worship, the people gathered together to bake certain kinds of bread-cakes that were probably the staple food for shepherds, and they baked them in the image of the queen of heaven. There was undoubtedly worship and a meal enhanced with sweet flavor and shared in warmth in the midst of poverty and the threat of wars. Such a practice of worship and the sharing of bread-cakes might have offered the poor ordinary people an occasion for confirming their generations of kinship/religious ties and for sharing hope under the protection of the queen of heaven. It is tempting to see some relationship between this popular familial worship of a female deity and the longer survival of the southern kingdom of Judah.[17]

It is intriguing to see relationships between the popular worship of these female deities and the female statues found in almost every household throughout the history of ancient Israel. It is also intriguing to see relationships between the disappearance of such figurines in the sixth century B.C.E. and the appearance of the Jewish divine female imagery of Wisdom/Sophia in the Hebrew Bible around the sixth century B.C.E. Although the God of Israel transcended human genders, Yahweh was referred to by the male personal pronoun and was imaged predominantly as a male figure in the Hebrew Bible. Within this tradition the personified female imagery of Sophia, the Wisdom of God, appeared in the Proverbs that were written in the sixth century B.C.E.:[18]

> Wisdom cries out in the street;
>> in the squares she raises her voice. (Prv 1:20)

> By me kings reign,
>> and rulers decree what is just. (Prv 8:15, Camp)

> Come, eat of my bread
>> and drink of the wine I have mixed
> . . . and live. (Prv 9:5-6)

The divine imagery of Wisdom/Sophia was gradually developed, and by the first century C.E. not only were her functions coterminous with Yahweh, but she had also obtained very rich and attractive images, appropriating elements from various Greco-Roman female deities, especially those of Isis. Some scholars believe that a Jewish Wisdom/Sophia hymn lies behind the prologue of the Johannine gospel, although the word *sophia* (wisdom) is replaced with the word *logos* (word) in the prologue. There is no extant text of such a Sophia hymn, but we can still infer it from some texts in the Hebrew Bible and intertestamental literature, such as Job 28, Proverbs 1—9, Sirach 24, Baruch 3-4, 1 Enoch 42, and the Wisdom of Solomon. The hymn proclaims that the divine Sophia is the preexistent being and the partner of God in creation. She called to people to listen to her and sent messengers to every generation to reveal her, so that the people would have knowledge for life and, by loving her, become friends of God. When she sought a place to dwell in her own created world and found no place, she returned to her heavenly world. Nevertheless, she dwells among the people of God.[19]

Many Jewish people, as minority groups or communities of resident aliens in the Greco-Roman world, seem to have conceived of themselves as the children of Sophia, gathered under her wings and sent out to the world as her messengers: "Jerusalem, Jerusalem, the city that kills the prophets and stones those who are sent to it! How often have I desired to gather your children together as a hen gathers her brood under her wings, and you were not willing!" (Mt 23:37; Lk 13:34; 11:49).[20]

These deities or images of deities compose but a small part of a much larger picture of complex and diverse ancient Jewish traditions. Recent scholarship increasingly demonstrates more and more nuanced differences within ancient Jewish traditions. Although such diversity seems to have been mostly filtered out in the canonization processes of the Hebrew Bible, it appears to have been firmly embedded and accepted among the ancient Jewish people.

### Jewish Diversity in the First Century

The great diversity among the Jewish communities was acknowledged in their religious visions, beliefs, and practices both within Palestine and among the various diaspora in the Greco-Roman world. A good example of Jewish diversity is demonstrated in the various practices related to purity laws, those laws that prescribed people's religious and daily lives. Many rabbis spoke about the observance of purity laws. Oftentimes, however, their interpretations of laws differed, yet they coexisted within various Jewish communities. Furthermore, it is said that "because impurity was so common, Jews in general were not afraid of it." There seems to have been no room for the monolithic conception of Jewish legalism.[21]

Many purity laws specifically restricted women's activities, especially during the menstrual period. Considerable evidence indicates, however, that poor women could not observe or did not care about purity laws or ritual purity/impurity but had to continue working to survive. It appears that, while there were women who cared or strictly observed purity laws, most ordinary women thought it more important for their faith, and for their life, to continue their daily activities. During the menstrual period most women helped and socialized with each other as usual, even if that meant being contaminated by someone with impurity or by contaminating others around her, knowingly or not. Undoubtedly, there were both obvious and nuanced differences among women regarding this matter, depending on the different communities and classes to which they belonged.[22]

Furthermore, archeological sources, among others, have demonstrated "the astonishing degree to which many Torah-true Jewish people were involved in the syncretism that pervaded the Mediterranean world in the Greco-Roman period." Many Jewish people appropriated various symbols from other religions, including bulls, lions, cupids, birds, rosettes, cornucopias, and astronomical symbols, and also images of gods from other religions. It may be that many Jewish people appropriated the most appealing parts of other religions, finding in them their own meaning in their faith, as was also the case for Greeks, Romans, and other neighboring people.[23]

A Hebrew text written by a man "steeped in the Torah" in the first century contains prescriptions for making images as well as prayers to deities of other religions. Scholars assume that the Jewish people probably perceived these deities as subordinate to Yahweh. The image of Helios on the floors of some synagogues, for example, may represent a minor deity to whom the congregations prayed for practical purposes. There were also many Jewish people who engaged in popular magical spells for both love and curses, which invoked not only the spirit of Yahweh but also many other spirits, both angelic and demonic, of various religious origins. The earliest Christian communities were among these diverse Jewish communities and at least one piece of archeological evidence in Philippi points to the high probability that many Christians in the early centuries did not see any conflict in participating in other religious practices or syncretistic activities. There is no certain way to speak about *the* Judaism, *the* Jewish community, *the* Jewish man, or *the* Jewish woman in Greco-Roman times.[24]

At the same time we should remember that most Jewish synagogues were very small, and many of the religions of their neighboring communities were more popular and powerful. Surrounded by various attractive gods, both male and female, many Jewish people conceived the God of Israel not only as Yahweh but also as Sophia. Of the many proselytes or those who converted from other religions to the Jewish faith, women outnumbered men. Many of these women may well have been accustomed to leadership roles, and they would have expected the same in Jewish synagogues.[25]

### Women's Leadership at Synagogues

In spite of great diversity the Jewish communities that gathered at synagogues also had much in common. In the first century c.e. the nascent Jewish synagogues were located mostly in private houses or in certain spaces in public buildings. Synagogues often had three major functions: to hold services, to facilitate religious education, and to offer hospitality to fellow Jews in need or traveling. In this way Jewish communities, as an ethnic minority group, pre-served their religious and cultural traditions and consolidated their practical support network.[26]

How might women have participated in the house synagogues? The major functions of the synagogues included activities that would have been a con-ventional part of a faithful and hospitable Jewish home. Indeed, the nascent house synagogues looked like hospitable homes or regional community cen-ters. Given the Greco-Roman religious context in which women's leadership was commonly practiced, it seems plausible that Jewish women also assumed leadership roles at these house synagogues.

Earlier scholarship indicated that Jewish women did not and could not take leadership roles since women sat separately from men at synagogues. Such an assumption, however, was based on the example of much later syna-gogues. Through critical and meticulous analyses of ancient Jewish inscrip-tions and literature, as well as archeological artifacts, Bernadette Brooten has uncovered firm evidence of women's leadership practiced in the ancient syna-gogues in diverse regions. Women's galleries or separate sections for women did not exist in the ancient synagogues, neither in the house synagogues nor in those found in public buildings. Women and men sat together at wor-ship. There, women served as "synagogue heads," "leaders," "elders," "mothers of the synagogue," and "priests." Some wealthy Jewish women were donors of synagogue buildings, as they also were sometimes donors of municipal buildings. In return, they received honor and privilege in their communities.[27]

Thus, contrary to earlier scholarship, it should be acknowledged that Jew-ish women were exercising various religious leadership roles in their commu-nal synagogue settings in the first century C.E. We may also safely assume that perceptions of the divine world for the majority of ordinary Jewish women and men were not exclusively male but inclusive in many ways of both male and female images.

## In the Earliest Christian Communities

### *Women's Crucial Roles at the Origin*

If women widely practiced leadership not only in the variety of Greco-Roman religions but also in the Jewish synagogues, it should not be surpris-ing if women also assumed leadership roles in the reign-of-God movement and in the earliest house churches. First of all, not only was the reign-of-God movement part of the Jewish prophetic movements, the earliest Christians were also Jewish people, both ethnically and culturally, firmly embedded in the diverse traditions of Judaism in one way or another. The earliest house churches were actually part of the diverse Jewish synagogues, and they were indistinguishable from other synagogues.

In her book *In Memory of Her* Elisabeth Schüssler Fiorenza has demonstrated convincingly how significant were women's contributions in the shaping and developing of both the reign-of-God movement and the earliest Christian movements. The extant gospels designate only men as disciples; nevertheless, the gospels describe women participating actively from the beginning of the reign-of-God movement. Furthermore, it was Mary Magdalene and some other women with her who were the first to proclaim the resurrection of Jesus to other members of the movement. These women played crucial roles "for the very continuation of this movement after Jesus' arrest and execution." That is, they gathered together those who fled to Galilee in fear and despair, and they re-inspired them to pursue the realization of the reign of God in the midst of political injustice. The gospels also contain stories that imply that women played decisive roles for the extension of the movement to gentiles (Jn 4:1-42; Mk 7:24-30; Mt 15:21-28).[28]

Many scholars agree that the major activities of the reign-of-God movement were prophecy, open table fellowship (communal eating together), and healing. All of these were activities in which women could easily take leadership roles. First of all, prophecy was an activity in which any person regardless of their gender, ethnic, and class background could participate. (The following chapter will describe some of the participation of Greco-Roman women in a variety of prophetic activities.) Furthermore, women have traditionally been responsible for the preparation, preservation, and distribution of food. Similarly, care of babies, children, the aged, and the sick was primarily borne by women. Practical knowledge of herbal plants and drugs for medication was conventionally handed down from grandmothers to mothers to daughters. Women, rather than men, held the accumulated practical wisdom in eating and healing activities: how to utilize scarce provisions and means, and how to ease the pain and fear of the sick. Thus, it seems plausible that women would show resourcefulness and take the initiative in these activities at various communal gatherings. These were the core activities of small minority groups of the reign-of-God movement, which eventually became the earliest Christian communities.[29]

Women's active participation in leadership roles and the egalitarian inclusive ethos seem to be reflected in an early baptismal formula quoted by Paul: "There is no longer Jew or Greek, there is no longer slave or free, there is no longer male and female; for all of you are one in Christ Jesus" (Gal 3:28). This does not mean that all the earliest Christian communities practiced perfect egalitarianism. It does tell us, though, that women's leadership activities must have been much more common than the impression generally given by the Bible, which tends to mean a collection of male-authored versions of biblical stories.[30]

### Women as Leaders at House Churches

The Christian Testament offers many stories of the earliest house churches. It is also noteworthy that house churches are called by women's names, suggesting the leadership of many women. These include the house churches of Mary, the mother of John Mark, in Jerusalem (Acts 12:12-17); of Nympha in Laodecia (Col 4:15); of Aphia in Colossai (Phlm 2); of Lydia in Philippi (Acts 16:14); and of Prisca in many places (Acts 18:2, 26; Rom 16:3-5). Prisca and Aquila founded house churches wherever they went on business; among them were missionary centers in Corinth, Ephesus, and Rome. It is not surprising to see that many house churches were also called by men's names (Acts 10:1ff.; 16:3ff.; 18:8ff.; Rom 16:23; 1 Cor 1:14, 16; 16:15ff.), since it was customary to use men's names rather than women's names for references. However, we should not automatically assume that women did not take leadership roles at these house churches.[31]

In their communities they continued using familial terms, such as sister and brother, as was customary among Jewish people. In their use of familial terms, however, they included mother but not father (Mk 10:29-30; Mt 23:9). In other words, they were creating a house of sisters and brothers in faith, rejecting patriarchal relations among them, while affirming strong familial and affectionate bonding. This would have been a direct challenge to the elite male ideology of benevolent patriarchy. In a society where sons were socialized to become patriarchs, dominating not only wives and other women but also as many other men as possible, the strongest affectionate bonding was experienced among brothers and sisters. Making their communities a family of sisters and brothers in faith was a radical, alternative vision. Such an antipatriarchal ethos and practice, combined with the church location in houses, must have worked to support women's leadership roles. At the same time, such a practice may have offered comfort and new identities to those who had lost their own familial or kinship ties because of their faith or other causes.[32]

### Women as Traveling Missionaries

Traveling preachers and missionaries in the reign-of-God movement and in the earliest Christian movements seem to have moved about in pairs. The term "pair" does not necessarily mean husband and wife, nor man and woman. There also were male pairs (for example, Paul and Barnabas: Acts 13:1-3; 1 Cor 9:5-6) and female pairs. Paul's letter mentions a variety of pair missionaries. The first among them is Prisca and Aquila (Rom 16:3-5), who are also mentioned as co-workers with Paul. They even risked their own execution for the sake of Paul's life (Rom 16:4). It is noteworthy that Paul abandons the customary order of identification and mentions Prisca first, rather than her husband. Prisca is also a teacher and the person who taught scripture to Apollos, a well-known and well-educated missionary (Acts 18:24-27).[33]

Paul comments that Andronicus and Junia were "outstanding among apostles" and co-prisoners with Paul (Rom 16:7,15). Until recently, Junia was identified as a man, based on the reference to her as "outstanding among apostles." Brooten's study recovered the lost history of this woman apostle after centuries of misidentification. Others mentioned as pair missionaries are

Philologus and Julia (Rom 16:15), and Nereus and his sister (Rom 16:15). These two pairs are mentioned only in passing, but their very names imply that these pairs may well have been slaves or former slaves who led house church gatherings. Tryphaena and Tryphosa (Rom 16:6, 12), and Euodia and Syntyche (Phil 4:2-3) probably represented a pair of female missionaries, evangelizing and teaching in Rome and in Philippi, respectively.[34]

Paul's letter provides even more names of women leaders. Phoebe was an official teacher and missionary in the church of Cenchreae (Rom 16:1ff.). Both Mary and Persis worked in evangelizing and teaching in Rome (Rom 16:6, 12). Lastly, we should note that women were also among those whom Paul greeted as "brethren" and "saints" in Rome (Rom 16:15).[35]

All of these references stem from one man's missionary activity. How many more women's names and diverse information would be available if only women's missionary records had survived the male-centered history? We may safely conclude that women participated in leadership roles in the earliest Christian churches as well as in the reign-of-God movement, and that such a practice was not one of regional exceptions but was commonly practiced in diverse districts. This was also the case in the broader Jewish communities as well as in other Greco-Roman religions in the first century C.E.

### Christian Appropriation of Imperial Titles

One important practice of the earliest Christian communities was their resistance against Roman imperial and political power. As we saw above, Greco-Roman practices of imperial worship were widespread. It seems that in referring to Jesus the earliest Christians intentionally appropriated many Roman imperial titles. Many scholars have pointed out that the Christian gospels appropriated for Jesus such Jewish terms and titles as "son of human being," "son of God," "holy one of God," "lamb of God," "messiah," and so forth, attaching their own meanings to these terms. At the same time, we should not overlook the significance of their practice of also appropriating Roman imperial titles. This represented a strong form of resistance used by a small minority of colonized people against their enormously powerful rulers.[36]

These early Christian communities claimed that none of the Roman emperors would be called "father." Nor would Jupiter/Zeus be "father in heaven." They would "call no one father on earth," for it is only the God of Israel who is "our Father in heaven" (e.g., Mt 6:9). Furthermore, they declared that their loyalty was to the executed Jesus and not to any one of the deified Roman emperors. Only Jesus was the king *messiah*.[37]

In the Johannine gospel the Samaritan people say, "This is *truly* the Savior of the world" (Jn 4:42, emphasis mine), as if countering the Roman imperial claim. Similarly, Thomas's confession to Jesus, "my Lord, my God" (Jn 20:28), echoes and directly counters Domitian's self-designation as "lord and god." The Johannine depiction of Jesus as a kingly figure (1:49; 6:15; 12:13, 15;

18:33, 37x2, 39; 19:12, 14, 15, 19, 21x2) may also imply a subtle form of political resistance.[38]

In other words, the gospels proclaimed the good news of Jesus in a way that could be seen to directly challenge Roman imperial "benefaction." Indeed, such a practice involved very daring political elements. In the highly patriarchal Roman society, all subjugated people survived only by receiving benefactions from their divine rulers through the layers of the patron-mediator-client system. But the earliest Christians were determined to have Jesus as their only mediator to the God of Israel, the only Father in heaven, and the only true patron of the universe. In the gospels Jesus the mediator assured believers of the true benefaction of God, the only true patron, and taught them how to pray to "our Father in heaven" (e.g., Mt 6:9) and to ask for everything "in my name" (e.g., Jn 15:16, 16:24).[39]

At the same time, we notice that the Johannine gospel mentions often that what the reign-of-God Jesus proclaims is "not of this world" (e.g., Jn 18:36; cf. 17:14, 16). This might have been a means to avoid a direct clash with the imperial power, implying that kingdom being foretold by Jesus did not represent a political threat. Notice, however, that according to the Johannine gospel it was the Roman and Jewish authorities and their men who arrested Jesus, and the ordinary people, the "crowd," were not involved (Jn 18:3, 12). On the other hand, the synoptic gospels of Matthew, Mark, and Luke have their own ways of avoiding direct clashes with the authorities. For example, Pilate is presented as reluctant to convict Jesus, in contrast to the Jewish authorities and crowd who are eager to arrest and kill him (Mk 14:43; 15:14-15; Mt 26:47; 27:19-26; Lk 22:47; 23:13-25).[40]

Therefore, it is likely that by appropriating various titles of Greco-Roman imperial worship to the God of Israel and to Jesus, while making use of subtle devices to avoid direct clashes, the earliest Christian communities practiced a strong form of nonviolent and savvy resistance against Roman imperial worship. This, combined with their creation of sibling communities without a father, must have served as an effective challenge to the Roman patriarchy.[41]

The above observation indicates that the divine or "divinizing" language of the Greco-Roman context is different from the language of divinity used in later doctrinal statements. The understanding of divinity of people in the Greco-Roman world was not opposite to or totally alien from humanity. Rather, it was the divinity people recognized in great humans or the gods' divinity at work, residing, or manifested in human persons. In the Johannine gospel Jesus himself employs this language, "Is it not written in your law, 'I said, you are gods'? If those to whom the word of God came were called 'gods'—and the scripture cannot be annulled—can you say that the one whom the Father has sanctified and sent into the world is blaspheming because I said, 'I am God's Son'?" (Jn 10:34-36; cf. Ps 82:6). In summary, there were many differences among the various Jewish communities during this time, including the earliest Christian communities. One important aspect of these communities is that they practiced various forms of religious and political resistance against the Roman imperialism and pointedly reserved the title of father for their God in heaven; they saw this divinity manifested in Jesus and not in any of the Roman emperors.

# 4

## Prophecy and "I Am" Revelation

The previous chapter expanded our historical imagination of this period of history by looking at various deities and religious leadership in the Greco-Roman world. We now turn to prophecy, one of the central activities of both the reign-of-God movement and the earliest Christian communities. The reign-of-God movement itself was a Jewish prophetic movement. All the gospels in the Christian Testament present Jesus as a prophet, and the earliest Christian teachings or christology describe Jesus as a prophet of Wisdom/Sophia.

### Greco-Roman Prophetic Movements

In the Greco-Roman world, as *koiné* Greek became widespread as a common language and people's mobility was increased, some regional and ethnic religions spread widely. Prophecy, a major method of making deities known, was an activity in which uneducated women as well as highly educated men could participate equally. As we have seen, there were many Greco-Roman deities, both male and female, and women prophets seem to have been especially active in revealing female deities, although they did not exclude male deities.[1]

Jewish people were not exempt from participating in these vigorous prophetic movements. The various Jewish reign-of-God movements, including the one that later became the Christian movement, were part of such prophetic movements. As Migaku Sato puts it, "Without this rebirth of prophecy, there would have been no Jesus movement, no Gospels, and thus no Christianity."[2]

For many Jews, the beginning of our Common Era was a time of re-visioning the past for the purpose of transforming the present. The emergence of the great Roman Empire and its ever-growing prosperity in the Pax Romana led the first-century Jewish historian Josephus to think that if it were not the divine will even the Romans could not have prospered to such an extent.[3]

While Josephus and others decided to become supporters of the Roman conquerors, other groups of people appear to have made different interpretations. As mentioned before, much political and religious resistance occurred among the Jewish people. It took various forms, including messianic movements and prophetic movements, each with its own vision of the *basileia* (reign of God). While messianic movements often had a military orientation, the prophetic movements were non-militaristic. Even so, popular Jewish prophetic movements were usually inseparable from political resistance to Roman imperial power.

Josephus, who served the Roman government and attempted to elevate the status of Jewish communities under Roman rule, left a very hostile written record of these anti-Roman popular Jewish prophets. According to him, these prophets were "fostering revolutionary changes" and were "deceivers and impostors, under the pretense of divine inspiration . . . [who] persuaded the masses to act like madmen." Nevertheless, Josephus applied the same terms to the activities of these prophets as he did in his account of the Exodus—the "wonders and signs" of deliverance. So, to use Richard Horsley's rephrasing of Josephus's statements, "these prophets, filled with the Spirit of God, inspired their followers with the conviction that they were called to participate in God's imminent liberating action."[4]

## Prophecy in the Corporate Personality

It is important to begin with a look at the culture of a "corporate personality" in place at this time, because such a concept of personality is very different from our contemporary individualistic understanding. The term "corporate personality" was coined by H. Wheeler Robinson to designate the ancient concept of personality in which a household or a social unit, however broadly conceived, is perceived as a single person, or a psychical whole, representing the extended personality of the head of the hierarchy. So, in ancient patriarchal societies, a patriarchal figure was thought to have a variety of extensions of his personality. A servant sent by the master could act and speak as an extension of the master's personality, and through the agency of the servant the master was regarded as being present. That is, the agent/messenger "is treated as actually being and not merely representing" the master.[5]

This conception of the extension of a god's personality is present in the Hebrew Bible. In the Third Commandment, God's name is taken as an extension of God's personality: "You shall not take the name of Yahweh your God in vain" (Ex 20:7). There is also a fluidity in references to the divinity, both in the singular forms *el/eloah* and in the plural forms *elim/elohim*. One example reads:

> In the beginning gods created the heavens and the earth. . . . And gods said, Let us make adam [i.e., earthling] in our image, according to our

likeness, and let them rule over. . . . And gods created the adam in his image; in the image of gods he created him, male and female, he created them. (Gen 1:1-27, bracketed note is mine)

In the same vein, the spirit of God, as an extension of God's personality, was perceived as manifested in various "servants" of God. The prophets in particular were commonly thought of as messengers of God and were held to be more than mere representatives. They were, in their active agency, God in person. In Exodus, God tells Moses, "He [Aaron] shall be a mouth for you, and you shall be *Elohim*/God for him" (Ex 4:16).

Some prophetic utterances show a lack of differentiation between the prophet's speech and his or her speaking in the person of God, as well as a fluid switching between the two. It seems that prophets occasionally inserted phrases such as "thus says Yahweh" in order to make it clear to listeners that the "I" of the speech was not the prophet but God speaking directly through God's servants. Some examples read:

And Moses called to all Israel, and said to them, You have seen all that Yahweh did before your eyes [Moses is speaking]. . . . I have led you forty years in the wilderness [who is speaking? Moses?] . . . so that you might know that I am Yahweh your God [God is now speaking, but when did the switch occur?]. (Deut 29:1-5, bracketed notes are mine)

Behold, Yahweh hurls you [Isaiah is speaking]. . . . And I will drive you from your position [Yahweh is speaking]. And he will pull you from your station [Isaiah's speech]. And on that day, I will call my servant [Yahweh again]. (Isa 22:17-20).[6]

This concept of a corporate personality was still relevant in the time of Christian origins. For example, some words of Jesus in the gospels illustrate the shared assumption of various extensions of God's personality, such as name, finger, and spirit, as well as the fluid border between the prophet's own words and those of God in person. Jesus teaches his disciples to pray, "hallowed be your name" (Mt 6:9; Lk 11:2). To those who are suspicious, Jesus says, "But if I cast out the demons by the finger of God" (Lk 11:20). Jesus also tells his disciples, "But say whatever is given to you at that time, for it is not you who speak, but the Holy Spirit" (Mk 13:11; Mt 10:19-20; Lk 21:15).

At the same time, there is no external guarantee whether "the finger" and "the spirit" are extensions of God or of "the demons" (Mt 12:24, 27; Lk 11:15, 19), or whether a prophet is true or false (Mk 13:22). Hence, many controversies and much suspicion arose among the audience of Jesus or any other prophet.

In the gospels at times Jesus speaks as if the divine Sophia herself is speaking in person:

Jesus said, "I praise you, Father, lord of heaven and of earth . . . [Jesus]. Come to me, all those laboring and being laden, and I will give you rest [Jesus?]. Take my yoke upon you, and learn from me. . . . For my yoke is easy, and my burden is light [Sophia speaking]. (Mt 11:25-30, cf. Sir 51:23-26; 6:23-31; Prv 3:13-18; 9:5, bracketed notes are mine)

Jerusalem, Jerusalem, the one killing the prophets and stoning those who are sent to her! How often I desired to gather your children in the way a bird gathers her chicks from under her wings. . . [Sophia speaking?]. For I say to you, in no way shall you see me from now on, until you say, "Blessed is the one who comes in the name of the Lord" [Jesus speaking?]. (Mt 23:37-39; Lk 13:34-35; see also Mt 23:34; Lk 11:49)[7]

It is often difficult to distinguish between the prophets' own voices and their speaking in the person of Yahweh, Sophia, the Spirit, or the Christ, without being given clear reminders.

In a culture of a corporate personality—where a servant sent by the master speaks, acts, and is treated as the master in person—a son sent by his father is regarded as the most authentic agent. In the field of commerce, where trade is hereditary and is handed down from father to son, it is customary for a father to commission his son, and for the son to travel and make contracts for his father. When it comes to legal issues, the son functions as the most fully qualified agent of the father. In such a society, the father and the son are one, although they are definitely not identical, and the son is totally subordinate to the father.[8]

This conventional relationship between the father and the son is found in the Johannine gospel: "Very truly, I tell you, the son can do nothing on his own, but only what he sees the Father doing" (5:19); "Very truly, I tell you, anyone who hears my word and believes him who sent me . . . " (5:24); "I and the Father are one" (10:30); "My Father is greater than I" (14:28); "the word which you hear is not mine, but of the Father who sent me" (14:24). In the Johannine gospel Jesus speaks in the person of God, including the many "I am" sayings, following this conventional prophetic practice.

One caution is important, however. A recent study by Kathleen Patricia Rushton shows that the father-son traditions constitute a particular strand of the Johannine traditions (see, for example, Jn 5:19-27) and that there are other strands in the gospel, including those of the Wisdom/Sophia image (1:1-18) and others (for example, 3:3-8; 16:21-22) in which the father-son traditions do not feature. Rushton points out that later interpretations accentuated the divine male images while marginalizing and obscuring female images in the gospel. It is important to pay careful attention to these neglected strands in reading the gospel texts.[9]

Another ancient practice likely related to the concept of corporate personality is the attribution of disciples' words to their teachers. In Greco-Roman times it was a standard practice in writing biographical and historical works to compose appropriate speeches and place them in the mouths of protagonists. No clear distinction was made between the actual sayings of historical teachers or philosophers and posthumous sayings that were composed by their students or disciples or delivered through dreams or seances. Posthumous sayings were often included in the body of those teachers' sayings and received the same authority.[10]

In accordance with the customary practices of the time, early Christians also composed "Jesus' sayings" in their narratives so that the protagonist Jesus would be presented in ways more appealing to their audiences. They used the name Jesus and the later christological titles such as "Christ" or "Lord" in referring both to the historical Jesus of Nazareth and to the resurrected Jesus of their faith. Accordingly, the distinction between the "sayings of Jesus" and the "words of the Lord" was ambiguous from the beginning, yet the use of such sayings and words expanded in the various faith-communities.[11]

Seen against a background of a corporate personality, it seems likely that Jesus as a prophet could speak fluidly in his own person and in the person of God, whether Yahweh or Sophia. Or, Jesus could be imaged easily in this way by the earliest Christians. It is also likely that some of the earliest Christian prophets delivered their prophetic speeches as the "sayings of Jesus" or as the revelations of the Christ.

## The "I Am" Revelation and Women

Among various forms of prophecy, first-person revelations were particularly used in legitimating oracles in which "the speaker claims to be an authentic vehicle of divine revelation." The "I (am)" revelation was used to demonstrate the attractive personality of the divine and also to form a new communal identity in relationship to a certain deity. Many prophets used this form in the ancient Near East, from archaic times to Greco-Roman times. Jewish and Christian traditions were no exceptions.[12]

In the church the imaginative world of Jesus' "I am" sayings has been thoroughly male. They have been read predominantly as Jesus' divine self-revelation in relation to the sayings of Yahweh in the Hebrew Bible. A look at the "I am" sayings in a broader context, however, shows that the world of "I am" sayings was not dominated by males; rather, female figures also emerged large.

### In the Ancient Near East

Extant texts from the ancient Near East include many oracles and aretalogies (praising hymns) uttered in the first person singular "I," as well as hymns uttered in the third-person singular "s/he." From the distant past of the Near East, probably from the second to first millennia B.C.E., the Egyptian Isis, the east Semitic Ishtar, and the west Semitic Astarte were known as great female gods. There were others as well. The Egyptian god Isis became a universal god in the Greco-Roman period, and there are numerous Isis aretalogies. Both Ishtar and Astarte were popular gods and they seem to have strongly influenced the image of the queen of heaven, worshiped by generations of the people of Judah (Jer 7:16-20; 44:15-19).

The oracles of Ishtar, delivered through women prophets in the "I am" sayings, were written in seventh century B.C.E.:

> [Esarhad]don, king of the lands, fear not! . . . I am the great Belet—I am the goddess Ishtar of Arbela, she who has destroyed your enemies at your mere approach. . . . I watch over your inner heart as would your mother who brought you forth. . . . I am Ishtar of Arbela. . . . I am the great midwife, the one who gave you suck, who has established your rule under the wide heavens. . . . I will not abandon you. . . . I am . . . for you. I am your good shield.[13]

Also from the ancient Near East come the famous Sibylline oracles, a large collection of oracles uttered by the Sibyl that includes "I (am)" sayings. Some scholars assume that a historical woman existed behind this phenomenon, and by the fifth century B.C.E. she was already a legendary figure. The extant texts come from the second century B.C.E. to the seventh century C.E. and encompass Asian, Greek, Jewish, and Christian traditions.

The proliferation of the Sibylline oracles among various religious traditions for several centuries seems to attest to a long-term and wide recognition of women's prophetic abilities as well as vigorous cross-cultural or interreligious borrowings in the ancient Near East. Interreligious appropriations of divine images were probably used to enhance the wonderful and mighty images of deities, given the vigorous competition among deities in the ancient Near East. It is reasonable to assume that the "I" style aretalogies and oracles, including "I am" sayings, were inclusive of both genders.[14]

### In Ancient Jewish Traditions

The "I am" sayings in the Hebrew Bible, emphasizing Yahweh's creating and saving actions, demonstrate the exclusive claims of Yahweh as the only God for Israel. The so-called absolute "I am" sayings of Yahweh—those without predicates—are grounded in the exclusive caring relationship that Yahweh had with the people of Israel.

> I am Yahweh your God, who has brought you out from the land of Egypt, from the house of bondage. (Ex 20:2; see also Isa 43:3, 10; Hos 13:4)

> And God said to Moses, I am that I am; and God said, you shall say this to the sons of Israel, I am has sent me to you. (Ex 3:14)

These "I am" sayings of the God of Israel demonstrate Israel's claim of Yahweh as its exclusive and only God and savior for Israel, and they also make relational claims in the context of a communal faith confession. This is important to remember, because in later periods such claims were often interpreted as objective or absolute truth-claims.

Given the religious context of the "I am" sayings and their revelation of both male and female deities, each with a variety of extensions in the corporate personality, it is not likely that these "I am" sayings of Yahweh would have been understood as exclusively male images. Furthermore, in the Hebrew Bible, in some of the "I am" sayings Yahweh can be perceived more clearly in a female figure:

Yahweh appeared to Abram, and said to him, "I am El Shadday [the god of the breasts]. . . . And I will make my covenant between you and me, and will multiply you exceedingly." (Gen 17:1-2, bracketed comments are mine)

So says Yahweh, your redeemer and your former from the womb; I am Yahweh who makes all things. (Isa 44:24)

Listen to me, O house of Jacob, all the remnant of the house of Israel; who are borne from the belly, who are lifted from the womb; even to old age I am the one; and I will bear you to gray hair; I made, and I will bear; and I will carry and deliver. (Isa 46:3-4; cf. Ps 22:8-11; 71:5-6, 18)

There are also "I (am)" sayings in the voice of Sophia, the Wisdom of God. Some of the "I" sayings in the Jewish wisdom traditions read:

Wisdom cries aloud in the plaza; she gives her voice in the square; . . . Turn at my warning; behold, I will pour out my spirit [breath] to you; I will make my words known to you. (Prv 1:1, 23)

I am the mother of beautiful love, of fear, of knowledge, and of holy hope; being eternal, I am given to all my children, to those who are named by the one. . . . Yahweh-Shadhay alone is the God, and besides the one there is no savior. (Sir 24:18, 24, omitted from the text of the NRSV but kept in footnotes)

### In the Greco-Roman World

A variety of ethnic and regional gods, both male and female, coexisted in the Greco-Roman world. Isis was extraordinarily powerful and was acclaimed for her wisdom in giving laws and in ending injustice, tyranny, and wars. Her devotees claimed that all other names of both female and male gods were only variant names of her own. Corresponding to the imagery of Isis as wisdom, women prophets played a crucial role in revealing her. Numerous Isis aretalogies contain the "I (am)" sayings. Some of them eloquently express her eternal and universal authority, while using the language of relationships.

> I am Isis, the lord *(kyria/os)* of every land, . . .
> I gave and ordained laws for men, which no one is
>     able to change.
> I am eldest daughter of Kronos.
> I am wife and sister of King Osiris. . . .
> I divided the earth from the heaven.
> I showed the paths of the stars.
> I ordered the course of the sun and the moon.
> I devised business in the sea.
> I made strong the right.
> I brought together woman and man.
> I appointed to women to bring their infants to birth
>     in the tenth month.
> I ordained that parents should be loved
>     by children. . . .
> I broke down the governments of tyrants. . . .
> I established penalties for these who practice
>     injustice.
> I decreed mercy to suppliants.
> With me the right prevails. . . .
> I set free these in bonds. . . .
> I overcome Fate.[15]

### In the Greco-Roman Jewish and Christian Traditions

As if to compete with such powerful and attractive female deities, such as Isis, a personified female imagery of the Jewish wisdom of God, Sophia, was fully developed by the first century B.C.E. In her creating and saving relations with the people of Israel and with the world, she was coterminous with Yahweh. Some of Sophia's "I (am)" sayings appear in early Jewish and Christian documents. Among them, "I am" sayings in *The Thunder, Perfect Mind* and the *Odes of Solomon* deserve special attention in connection with Jewish and Christian women's prophetic activities and their divine visions.

*The Thunder, Perfect Mind* is a document of a revelation discourse. A striking feature of it is a series of "I am" sayings that include opposing images. These sayings are uttered by a female divine figure who proclaims "I am the wisdom [of the] Greeks and the knowledge of [the] barbarians." The sayings begin:

> I am the first and the last.
> I am she who is honored and she who is disgraced.
> I am the harlot and the holy one.

I am the woman and the maiden.
I am [the mother] and the daughter. . . .
I am the barren one and many are her children. . . .
I am the solace of my labor pains. . . .
I am the bride and the bridegroom.
The one who begot me is my husband, and
I am the mother of my father,
And the sister of my husband, and he is my
    offspring. . . .
I am the silence which is unattainable. . . .
I am she who is called Law and you have called me
    Lawlessness. . . .
I am unlearned, and they learn from me. . . .
I am the audibleness which everyone receives and the
    word which cannot be understood.
I am a mute unable to speak, and great is the
    quantity of my words.
Hear me gently and learn about me rigorously.[16]

There are numerous similarities as well as contrasts between the "I am" sayings in the Thunder and Isis aretalogies. On the one hand, the "I am" of Isis inclusively appropriates and attributes all the attractive and good things to Isis. On the other hand, the "I am" of the Thunder attributes both positive and negative qualities to Sophia. It seems that in competing with the all-inclusive universality of Isis, the Thunder's "I am" sayings intend to express the transcendence of Sophia. By attributing both good and bad things as well as the male and the female to one female deity, Sophia, the sayings transcend the dualistic values of good/bad and masculine/feminine.[17]

As Anne McGuire notes, recitations of the "I am" revelations of the Thunder may have had a strong influence on imaging both the divine and the self very differently from the way they are imaged in the world of patriarchal values. Some scholars speculate that the "I am" sayings of the Thunder were survivals of some very old Jewish views of the deity. If so, the sayings seem to present female images of their God, not only as competing with the attractive Greco-Roman female gods but also as functioning subversively in the midst of more patriarchally oriented divine language in the Hebrew Bible.[18]

### In the Odes of Solomon

"I" sayings in the Syriac manuscript of the *Odes of Solomon* provide other information about women's prophetic activities and divine visions in the Greco-Roman time. The title of this document, which attributes its hymns to King Solomon (tenth century B.C.E.), may be an example of the custom of attributing authorship to teachers or other prominent figures.

The prophet/odist of the *Odes of Solomon* freely imagines the Christ and God in both male and female images, switching back and forth in the way the prophets switched between speaking as the human and speaking as the divine. The hymns below present the Christ and God in the imagery of lactation.[19]

I fashioned their members, and my own breasts I prepared for them, that they might drink my holy milk and live by it. (*Odes*, 8:14)

A cup of milk was offered to me, and I drank it in the sweetness of the lord's kindness. The son is the cup, and the father is he who was milked; and the holy spirit is she who milked him; because his breasts were full, and it was undesirable that his milk should be released without purpose. The holy spirit opened her bosom, and mixed the milk of the two breasts of the father. Then she gave the mixture to the generation [world] without their knowing, and those who have received [it] are in the perfection of the right hand. (*Odes*, 19:1-5)

The mother and the holy spirit whose breasts are full is God the Father as well as the Christ. Susan Ashbrook Harvey analyzes, "Male is more than male—it is also female; female is more than female—it is also male; the divine exceeds any clear boundaries; even the human is more than human. . . . One gender does not and cannot suffice even as metaphor to express identity, especially in the divine persons." It seems reasonable to speculate that other sources from the ancient oral world would reveal additional images of both God and the Christ speaking to us in both male and female figures.[20]

### *The Prologue of the Johannine Gospel*

A hymn in the prologue of the Johannine gospel presents another example of the images of God and the Christ that go beyond male or female boundaries. As noted in the previous chapter, scholars assume that a Jewish Wisdom/Sophia hymn lies behind the prologue of the Johannine gospel, although the word *sophia* (wisdom) is replaced with the word *logos* (word). The divine Sophia, a preexistent being and partner of God in creation, called people to listen to her and sent messengers to every generation so that people would have knowledge for life and, by loving her, become friends of God. Sophia sought a place to dwell in her own created world but found no place and returned to her heavenly world. Nevertheless, she dwells among the people of God. Elizabeth A. Johnson says, "The figure of divine Sophia shines through the Logos terminology."[21]

The prologue of the Johannine gospel begins with the words, "In the beginning was the Logos, and the Logos was with God, and the Logos was God" (Jn 1:1). When the first-century audience heard this passage recited, it would have immediately heard echoes of the opening words of Genesis, "In the beginning created God (Elohim) . . . and said God . . . and said God . . . " (Gen 1:1-26). As the prologue proceeds, the echoes of Sophia hymn(s) emerge more and more clearly. On the one hand, the word *logos* (word, reason) was one of the key terms in Greek philosophy. Here, this *logos* (masculine) is reinterpreted in the matrix of Jewish Sophia and is introduced as a manifestation of the divine Sophia (feminine).

In the overlapping imageries of *logos* in Greek philosophy and the words of God in creation, integrated into the Jewish Sophia hymn, the prologue introduces the story of the Christ, who is a revealer of Sophia, or, as a revealer/ prophet, Sophia herself. Thus, this prologue may be an example of prophetic hymns in which the images of the person as well as the divine are fluid and inclusive, crossing the boundaries of male or female.[22]

### *Reflecting on the Johannine "I Am" Revelations*

In the Johannine gospel in twenty-five instances Jesus' words use the emphatic "I am" phrase followed by different predicates, images, and states of being, some vague and some more specific. Some imply a predicate, as in "But he said to them, 'I am. Do not fear'" (6:20), or "I told you that I am; then if you seek me, allow these to depart" (18:8, and similarly in 18:5, 6). Four of these "I am" sayings are termed "absolute," having no predicates at all.[23]

8:24: . . . For if you do not believe that I am, . . .

8:28: . . . then you will know that I am, and from myself I do nothing, . . .

8:58: . . . before Abraham came into being, I am.

13:19: . . . when it happens you may believe that I am.

This use of the "I am" phrase echoes back to "direct" speeches of God in the Hebrew Bible, such as "I am the one" and "I, Yahweh." Some of them read as follows:

And the God said to Moses, I am that I am; and God said, you shall say this to the sons of Israel, I am has sent me to you. (Ex 3:14)

. . . that you may know and believe me, and understand that I am the one. (Isa 43:10)

Mainly because of this echo of Yahweh's "I am" sayings, scholars' opinions differ as to who is revealed in Jesus' "I am" sayings. There are two main interpretations: the first takes Jesus' "I am" sayings as Jesus' divine self-revelation; the other takes Jesus as not revealing himself but as revealing God. The first view was established in the mid-twentieth century by the German theologian Rudolf Bultmann, who stated that Jesus' words are utterances about

Jesus and that Jesus is "the absolutely transcendent one whose place is at the side of God." This interpretation became the basis for the dominant understanding of Jesus' "I am" sayings as divine self-revelation.[24]

Recently, however, more Johannine scholars take the second view, that Jesus' "I am" sayings point not to himself but to God. They interpret these sayings as expressing the mystical unity of Jesus with God, not the deity of Jesus. For example, Charles K. Barrett points to the basic scheme of the gospel as not christocentric but theocentric—it is God who is at the center of Jesus' presentation. God is revealed, and Jesus is the revealer (1:18; 14:9). Paul Trudinger basically agrees and asserts that the Johannine Jesus' "I am" sayings reveal God, using mystical language, and argues that the Johannine gospel is "consistent in its testimony to the non-deity of Jesus."[25]

Even this shift of scholarly interpretation, however, remains very male and individualistic. It is important to see the culture of corporate personality behind the Johannine Jesus' "I am" revelations. At the same time, it is worth noting that some of the Johannine Jesus' "I am" sayings also evoke Sophia imagery. These include "I am the bread of life" (6:35, 41, 48, 51), "the light" (8:12), "the one witnessing myself" (8:18), "from above" (8:24), "not of this world" (8:4), "the door" (10:7, 9), "the good shepherd" (10:11, 14), "the resurrection and the life" (11:25), "the way" (14:6), and "the true vine" (15:1, 5). Martin Scott points out that the Johannine Jesus' "I am" sayings are "thoroughly rooted in Sophia speculation." Scott asserts that by the first century C.E., not only was the image of Sophia developed into "a full-blown expression of the God in female terminology," but the concepts of *sophia* and *logos* (word) became interchangeable in some Jewish circles. Thus, Jesus was introduced by the male term *logos* in the prologue but by the image of Sophia in the Jewish Wisdom traditions. Then, in the body of the gospel the theme of Jesus Sophia, or Jesus revealing Sophia, was expanded, most distinctively in the "I am" sayings of Jesus.[26]

The Johannine Jesus' "I am" sayings reveal Sophia as the provider of sustenance, bread and water (or wine) (Prv 9:5; Sir 24:21), as well as the vine (Sir 24), the door or access to knowledge to life (Prv 3:16-18; 8:34-35; Sir 4:12), the way to salvation (Sir 24:16-19), the everlasting light (Eccl 2:13; Wis 7: 26-30), and the giver of eternal life (Prv 3:16-17, 8:25, 32-35, 9:11; Sir 6:26; Wis 8:13). These sayings probably carried strong echoes of Sophia for the audience in the Greco-Roman world. Today, by contrast, we are used to hearing only male imagery of Yahweh.[27]

## Women Prophets in the Jewish and Christian Traditions

### *In the Hebrew Bible*

As noted above, it seems likely that ancient Jewish women actively participated in prophecy. When it comes to historical Jewish women, however, the literary evidence is scant. In the Hebrew Bible the word "prophet" in the male form appears 309 times, but in its female form only six times. The women introduced as prophets are Miriam (Ex 15:20), Deborah (Judg 4:4), the wife of the prophet Isaiah (Isa 8:3), Huldah (2 Kgs 22:14; 2 Chr 34:22), and Noadia (Neh 6:12-14).

It seems noteworthy that at a crucial time in the history of Israel, King Josiah consulted Huldah rather than the contemporary male prophet Jeremiah. That is, according to some texts in the Hebrew Bible, Josiah made his final decision to undertake a program of reform based on Huldah's validation of the newly found book of the covenant. Huldah must have been a prophet of the highest official rank in Jerusalem. Furthermore, in the Hebrew Bible, Miriam marked the beginning of the era of prophecy, and Noadia stood at the end of it. Solomon D. Goitein states that "the whole time there were prophets in Israel, prophetesses were active as well."[28]

Other Jewish sources list Sarah, Hannah, Abigail, Esther, and Rebecca as prophets. Various Sibylles and the Therapeutrides are also mentioned as circles of Jewish women involved with prophetic activities. These brief references come from very different time periods in Jewish history and may represent other Jewish women prophets whose historical memories have been filtered out in the later androcentric editing processes.[29]

On the other hand, there are numerous vehement denunciations of false prophets, diviners, spirit-raisers, soothsayers, and the like throughout the Hebrew Bible (see, for example, Ex 22:18; Lev 20:27; Num 24:24; Deut 18:9-14; 1 Sam 15:23; 28:6-9; Jer 14:14; 29:8-9; and Ezek 13:1-7, 17-23). Thomas Overholt has concluded that both "prophets" and "diviners" facilitated the communication between the divine and human spheres, and that the different labeling was decided by the vested interest of those in power.[30]

The prophets who were specialized as spirit-raisers or soothsayers were not limited to women. Nonetheless, it is probable that, outside the male-dominated institutional settings, there were more women prophets, or spiritual intermediaries, including those specialized or labeled as false prophets or diviners. It seems safe to speculate that the continuous denunciations leveled at such prophets/diviners in the Hebrew Bible testify to the activities of dissenting or different prophets throughout the time of the Hebrew Bible.

### In the Christian Testament

The Christian Testament mentions only one woman as a prophet: Anna, the widow who stayed in the temple (Lk 2:36). Other than Anna, only a few women are introduced in relation to prophetic activities. This is true of Elizabeth and Mary (Lk 1:5, 41-55), Philip's four daughters (Acts 21:9), and a woman in the church of Thyatira (Rev 2:20-23). In this way the Christian Testament texts marginalize women's prophecy.

For example, the Lukan gospel refers to Elizabeth as "one of the daughters of Aaron" (Lk 1:5) and introduces her prophetic speech together with Mary's, but neither is referred to as a prophet. Anna is the only woman specifically labeled "a prophet" (Lk 2:36), and the gospel tells that, while the male prophet Simeon prophesied in front of the baby Jesus and his parents, Anna prophesied not only to them but in front of the entire congregation. While the figure of Simeon is highlighted and his words quoted (Lk 2:25-35), Anna's prophecy is summarized in a single verse (Lk 2:38).

Philip's four daughters are mentioned only in passing as "prophesying" (Acts 21:9). Their names are not given nor are they identified as "prophets." According to the fourth-century church father Eusebius, however, Philip's daughters were so famous that the churches of the province of Asia Minor derived their apostolic origin from them.[31]

Other feminist studies have reconstructed historical figures of some women prophets through critical and careful reading of some Christian Testament texts, such as those describing communities in Corinth. Corinth, a Greek harbor city in Macedonia, on the western shore of the Aegean Sea, was known from the fifth millennium B.C.E. It had a long and complex history and in the second century B.C.E. was destroyed and rebuilt as a Roman colony. The new settlers were mostly freed slaves from Greece, Syria, Judea, and Egypt. By the first century C.E. Corinth had become an important commercial and financial center, with shrines dedicated to many gods, including Aphrodite, Apollo, Asklepios, Athena, Demeter, and Isis.[32]

The earliest Christian communities in Corinth consisted mostly of slaves and freed slaves. Some among them were women who prophesied and served their community. Through a critical analysis of Paul's rhetoric in his first letter to the Corinthians, Antoinette Wire has reconstructed the historical figures of these women prophets. According to Wire, the Corinthian women prophets understood that they were no longer constrained by the old identity of "male and female"; they obtained their new identity by putting on Christ, the human image of God. These women considered themselves "already filled, already rich, already ruling," and were "eager for manifestation of the spirit" (1 Cor 4:8; 14:1, 12, 39).[33]

Paul had a different opinion. In his view these women should behave appropriately, according to the conventional concept of femaleness, for the sake of evangelizing the gospel. In his letters he attempted to dissuade these women, although his repeated arguments imply that he was not so successful. For those poor women and their community, putting on Christ and being freed from the old identity was the source of their hope and pride, the gospel itself.

Elisabeth Schüssler Fiorenza has critically analyzed rhetoric of the Revelation to John and has reconstructed the historical figure of the woman prophet in Thyatira, whom the author of Revelation called Jezebel. Thyatira was a city in Lydia in western Asia Minor, an important center of the wool trade. It had shrines dedicated to the worship of Apollo, Helius, and also to Roman emperors. A lively issue in the church of Thyatira was who would participate in eating the meat that had been used as sacrificial offerings at the Roman imperial worship. For poor people participation was an issue of survival, not only because it supplemented their otherwise inadequate diet but also because it provided opportunities for finding and maintaining trade connections.[34]

A woman prophet and her group argued on behalf of the poor Christians who participated in eating this meat, saying that such participation would be harmless for spirit-filled Christians. The author of Revelation had a different opinion and fiercely denounced the woman prophet, naming her Jezebel, with all the associated pejorative sexual connotations of that name (2 Kgs 9:22; 1 Kgs 18:19). There is no textual evidence, however, that the woman prophet and her group were dissuaded by the author of Revelation.[35]

Thus, there is strong evidence in both the Hebrew scriptures and the Christian Testament that both Jewish and Christian women actively participated in prophetic activities and that there were diverse theological opinions about their participation. This was true of the Johannine communities as well. These prophets made use of the divine "I am" revelation to reveal their gods, including the God of Israel. Some or many of these people would have conceived of themselves as Sophia's children and co-workers with Jesus, and some of their prophecies might have been included in some form in the "I am" sayings and farewell discourses of the Johannine Jesus.

# 5

## Healing and Sign-Working

Along with prophesying, healing was a central activity of both the reign-of-God movement and the earliest Christian communities. Powerful healing activities were seen as divine signs and nearly two-thirds of the signs recounted in the Christian Testament are healings.[1]

### World of Divine Humans

For many people in modern times, the so-called miracle stories in the Christian Testament do not function to generate faith. Instead, they may often function as obstacles to faith, and as a result many scholars attempt to give scientific explanations for these "miracles." In contrast, stories of miraculous events were very important to the Greco-Roman audience, who interpreted them as divine signs *(semeia)* or signs of divine intervention.[2]

Each of the synoptic gospels recounts more than twenty sign stories of Jesus. In the Johannine gospel the total number of Jesus' sign stories is reduced by half, but the Johannine author/s clearly state the importance of including sign stories—the intent is to generate life-giving faith: "Now Jesus did many other signs in the presence of his disciples, which are not written in this book. But these are written so that you may come to believe that Jesus is the Messiah, the Son of God, and that through believing you may have life in his name" (Jn 20:30-31).

Two major differences between the first-century culture and that of the twenty-first century seem to affect the general approach to miraculous events. One is world view, and the other is the development of accessible and effective medical care. Generally speaking, we "moderns" have learned that things happen in the world as a result of interactions, of causes and effects that can be or will be able to be analyzed scientifically, and that most diseases are caused by viruses or bacteria.

First-century people, on the other hand, believed that things happened as a result of the interactions of divine and demonic powers or spirits and that

66

diseases as well as disasters were due to the activities of these superhuman spirits. When people suffered serious diseases or faced crises, they prayed for divine intervention to save them from the demonic powers. In this sense a "miracle" was a sign of divine intervention. It is noteworthy that the word "heal" was often used interchangeably with the word "save" (Mk 4:23, 28).

In the first century physical suffering was everywhere, and people thought of it as an unavoidable consequence of being human. While there were doctors and effective medicines, most ordinary people could not afford to pay for them. Furthermore, hunger and malnutrition, together with undesirable sanitary conditions, made people susceptible to disease. In a crisis situation people relied on magic and the miraculous. Probably because of the lack of effective medications, even for the elite and well-educated people, belief in the power of magic and the miraculous appears to have been all-pervasive in the Greco-Roman world, regardless of gender, ethnicity, or class.[3]

One indication of this pervasive belief in magic and the miraculous is the popularity of magical spells. Archeological evidence shows a variety of uses of magical incantations written on papyrus, as people prayed for the miraculous in their daily lives, wishing for love, curses, well-being, success, or vengeance. Usually these papyri called upon divine and angelic powers, sometimes including demonic powers, to work for the fulfillment of their wishes. The use of magical papyri was so widespread that stores existed where ordinary illiterate people could fill in their names on pre-written forms. People believed that spells, written on magical papyri and chanted repeatedly, would in fact affect reality, such as binding lovers with passion or causing enemies to suffer. It can be said that such spells actually did affect reality, partly because the widespread belief in them influenced people's psychological states, which in turn affected their physical states.[4]

### Sign-Working and Missionary Activities

In the first-century world, where belief in signs was all-pervasive, many religious propagandists appealed to their audiences by presenting their gods and leaders as powerful sign-workers. Signs were seen as a vindication of their teaching and their god and thus were an appropriate and customary means for initiating faith. If a god was truly powerful and present, the god should be able to save people's lives by divine intervention.[5]

Among the many deities in the Greco-Roman world, Isis, Asklepios, and the God of Israel were especially recognized as powerful gods who worked signs. Isis was renowned for her sign-working power particularly in regard to childbirth, fertility, and healing. According to the historian Diodorus of Sicily (first century B.C.E.), "She was the discoverer of many health-giving drugs and was greatly versed in the science of healing," and she was even credited with discovering the drug for immortality. Isis raised her son Horus (Apollo) from the dead to immortality and also taught him to become a benefactor of the world. It is said that her healings occurred when known medical methods had failed.[6]

On the other hand, the male god Asklepios was known specifically for his healing power. He was a historical person, a physician in Greece in the fifth century B.C.E. Some stories note that he worked with his daughters Hygieia and Panacea, and that all three were honored as divine healers. In the extant literature of Greco-Roman times, however, only the healing power of Asklepios was emphasized; he was known as the healing god and the patron of physicians. Temples were built in his name throughout the Greco-Roman world, including Jerusalem and other places in Palestine, and medical schools were named after him.[7]

Powerful healers were deified or recognized as divine by their followers. When a miraculous healing was performed, its miraculous elements were emphasized or enhanced gradually through subsequent storytelling. In the context of competing religious propaganda, sign stories proliferated and grew more noteworthy, and sign-workers were portrayed as more and more worthy of designation as divine persons or gods.[8]

As a result, the Greco-Roman world was crowded with divine persons as well as gods of both celestial divine origins and earthly human origins. While people worshiped all these divinities, a distinction was made between the "celestial gods," who had never been human, and the "earthly gods," who had come down from heaven to lead human lives, even if they were born of divine-human unions. Although no one would argue about the eternal divinity of the celestial gods, people's recognition of the earthly gods or divine persons varied. In competing religious propaganda the same persons who were praised as divine persons or gods by their followers and supporters were often discredited and denounced by their opponents as magicians, charlatans, sorcerers, or demon-possessed.[9]

### *Jewish and Christian Participation*

Jewish people were quite successful in appealing to Greco-Roman audiences by presenting as powerful sign-workers both the God of Israel and their great religious leaders such as Moses, Elijah, and Elisha. Among the Jewish figures who were contemporaries of Jesus of Nazareth, both Honi the Circle-Drawer and Hannina ben Dosa were well-known for their charismatic sign-working.[10]

Members of the earliest Christian movements aggressively joined in the religious competition of sign performances, attempting to present their leader Jesus as an even greater sign-worker than anyone before. In the early stages of Christianity chanting of Jesus' name, as well as the names of Yahweh and Moses, was included in "the repertoires of the professional magicians." In the gospels, when John the Baptizer sent his messengers to Jesus to inquire about his identity, Jesus identified himself as a healing messiah (the anointed king), echoing Isaiah's prophecy (Isa 35:5-6) that "the blind receive their sight, the lame walk, the lepers are cleansed, the deaf hear, the dead are raised, and the poor have good news brought to them" (Mt 11:5; Lk 7:22).[11]

Throughout the gospels Jesus' healing signs are numerous, including some "raising" signs when Jesus resuscitates the dead, including Jairus's daughter (Mk 5:35-43; Mt 9:18, 23-26; Lk 8:49-56), a widow's son (Lk 7:11-17), and Lazarus (Jn 11:1-44). The signs were presented as more powerful and instantaneous than those of Elijah (1 Kgs 17:17-24) or Elisha (2 Kgs 4:18-37), which required physical effort.

The gospels also proclaim that Jesus was an even greater sign-worker than Moses, the great Jewish hero. In the Greco-Roman period various Jewish traditions believed that Moses had a unique status and function as the prophet/agent of God, the king messiah, and the human vice-regent of Yahweh. These traditions were grounded in the Hebrew Bible; for example, "I have made you God (Elohim) to Pharaoh" (Ex 7:1), "Moses, the man of God/Elohim" (Deut 33:1), and so on.[12]

Moses performed the great sea sign at the beginning of the Exodus by stretching out his hand and dividing the sea (Ex 14:15-31) and the feeding sign in the wilderness to ensure the survival of the people (Ex 16:1-36). Echoing these two signs of Moses the gospels present two signs of Jesus. The gospels proclaim that Jesus performed his sea signs (stilling the water and walking on the water) perfectly and effortlessly by using mere words (Mk 4:35-41; Mt 8:23-27; Lk 8:22-25 and Mk 6:45-52; Mt 14:22-23; Jn 6:15-21). Similarly, the feeding signs (feeding of the five thousand and feeding of the four thousand) of Jesus satisfied the whole crowd, with abundant leftovers (Mk 6:30-44; Mt 14:13-21; Lk 9:10-17; Jn 6:1-14 and Mk 8:1-10; Mt 15:32-39).

The Christian Testament reports that the disciples also performed signs (Mk 9:18, 28), and it was taken for granted that the apostles would also present "signs and wonders," as a means of vindicating their teaching and their God (Acts 2:43; 5:12; 14:3). Paul mentions that "signs and wonders and mighty works" are "the signs of a true apostle" (2 Cor 12:12; cf. Rom 15:19). Early Christian propaganda thus portrayed Jesus as an ever greater sign-worker, whose model was followed by the disciples, apostles, and other Christian missionaries. On the other hand, the historical Jesus himself seems to have engaged particularly in a healing ministry as a prophet healer or folk healer.[13]

## Human Ailments and Healing

An understanding of the nature of human ailments and healing during this time is essential to understanding the significance of healing activities in the reign-of-God movement and the earliest Christian communities. As noted above, we "modern" people tend to approach human ailments in terms of physical function or non-function. For people in the Greco-Roman world, however, health was more a state of well-being than the mere ability to function.[14]

Modern medical anthropology differentiates three terms, allowing us to see three distinct but overlapping aspects of human ailment or disorder: disease, illness, and sickness. The term "disease" refers to an individual's bodily malfunction. Illness refers to a culturally devalued state of being, including the disease. Thus, the reality and experience of illness depend on the cultural evaluation of certain states. Greco-Roman people seem to have been more concerned about this aspect. The term "sickness," on the other hand, refers to the understanding of a disease in relation to macro-social forces, such as economic, political, and/or institutional power dynamics.[15]

As we understand these different aspects of human ailments—personal disease, cultural illness, and social sickness—it becomes clear that we moderns tend to focus on the disease. Although we sometimes become aware of the sickness, most often we neglect the illness, a primary concern of the Greco-Roman people. Even today, though, illness is not unknown to our societies. For example, many women suffer psychosomatic or neurological problems because they are forced to accept certain sociocultural norms of femininity or motherhood. Many people with physical disabilities suffer more severely from social bias and discrimination than from physical pain or inconvenience. These days, people with AIDS who are rejected by their families and society in general have similar experiences. Suffering from illnesses can be as real and as serious as from diseases. At the same time most illnesses, as cultural realities, can be greatly remedied or healed by means of providing alternative religious and cultural support, even if these may not be "cures" in the technical medical sense.

### Healing and Curing

It seems that both the reign-of-God movement and the earliest Christian communities approached human ailments from all three aspects: disease, illness, and sickness. In terms of sickness their politically critical prophecies directly challenged the social forces that were causing and exacerbating various diseases among the poor people, especially economic exploitation. Meanwhile, their practice of open table fellowship or communal eating must have been one of the most effective ways of challenging this sickness from the bottom, particularly as it was practiced among impoverished people who suffered from perennial malnutrition.

Similarly, their prophecies and formation of communities must have proven effective ways of healing the illness, because they provided alternative religious views, solidarity from the roots, and new hope for the poor and the despised. As the people gained new visions and self-identities, they could also work as healers, thus creating communities of healed healers.[16]

And what about curing the disease? The healing of illness can greatly affect or remedy the process of a disease and sometimes even cure it. While it is undoubtedly true that the healing stories became more and more extraordinary sign stories, given the competing religious propaganda, it seems possible that the miraculous curing of diseases did happen more often than is commonly supposed. Recently medical studies have begun to acknowledge certain therapeutic powers whose existence modern science recognizes but has not yet been able to analyze. For example, even today, strong religious faith and love can sometimes cure a fatal disease. Many traditional African and Asian herbal medicines are often found to be more effective than modern chemical medicines. It is now also recognized that certain hypnotherapies, acupuncture, and chi-therapy, among others, often dramatically decrease not only pain and stress but also the need for medications. Even simple laughter has a marvelous curative power unrecognized until quite recently.

It is certainly possible that some ancient healers were more deeply aware of such therapeutic powers than modern doctors and that their mastery of such therapeutic powers, performed in believing environments, cured diseases much more often than we would expect today. This is not to suggest that ancient healers cured diseases more effectively than modern doctors; instead, it suggests that ancient healers may well have cured many diseases in the course of their healing activities despite their underdeveloped use of scientific medicine.

### Physicians and Folk-Healers

The Greco-Roman health-care system included two types of practitioners: the physician and the folk-healer. A physician was a professionally trained and accredited person who practiced methods of diagnosis of and prescription for human ailments based on observations of the body. A folk-healer was a person whose practice was "real and effective" but not accepted by everyone as legitimate.[17]

Three schools of physicians formed the core of the professional sector in Greco-Roman society: the schools of Asklepios (since the fifth century B.C.E.), Hippocrates (initiated in the fifth to fourth century B.C.E.), and Soranus (late first century C.E.). The school of Asklepios aimed at assisting the curative forces of the body itself, mainly through diet, baths, and exercise. The school of Hippocrates searched for general knowledge of the major organs and bones and practiced some surgical procedures. Hippocratic practices also included diet regulation and remedies based on astronomical observations or theories, in order to assist the natural curative forces of the body itself.

It seems that the authenticity of the various practices depended on people's interpretations of what kind of powers were at work behind each practitioner. For example, for Celsus, an intelligent opponent of Christians in the second century C.E., "Asklepios is a true manifestation of the Divine in human form, while Jesus is an impostor." Celsus based this conclusion on the fact that Jesus was from a low class and attracted low-class followers. In the gospels, Jesus of Nazareth was never called a physician but is depicted as a folk-healer or prophet healer. The practices of professional physicians were considered medicine, while folk-healers were (and are) often degraded as magic or sorcery. On the other hand, when people interpreted an instance of healing as the result of divine intervention, it was generally acknowledged as a sign or a miracle. The practices or treatments of professional physicians and folk healers were not always distinguishable, and in our eyes they both involved the elements of medicine, natural remedies, and superstition.[18]

### The Health-care System and Women

Let us now examine how women fit into the Greco-Roman health-care system as healers and patients. In the extant literature, the product of elite males, while women are visible as patients, they are almost invisible as healers. Some archeological evidence, however, indicates a somewhat different picture. In the accounts of Asklepios's miraculous healings, written or edited by priests, stories of male healings are valorized while those of women patients occupy less than one-third the space. However, archeological discoveries at two shrines of Asklepios indicate that women dedicated more than 50 percent of the healing inscriptions. This discrepancy suggests that while women might have constituted more than half of the patients, male writers recorded less than one-third. This would indicate that male literature of the time tended to trivialize women and make them less visible, even as patients.

How about women healers? The extant literature contains only occasional references to women professionals. The Hippocratic tradition mentions "female healers who attend births," and the "female who is doctoring," who was instructed on the removal of a dead fetus. The late first-century physician Soranus wrote that those women who became midwives should indeed be literate "in order to be able to comprehend the art through theory too."[19]

There are limited references to women healers or, more specifically, to midwives. Within Jewish literature, Exodus, which is the telling of Israel's foundational story, mentions the midwives Shiphrah and Puah. This suggests a long history of women in this profession. According to Tal Ilan, the profession of midwife must have been limited to women in Palestine in the Greco-Roman period, because only feminine forms of related words are used in rabbinical literature.[20]

There are also public inscriptions that commemorate professional women practitioners, both as midwives and as physicians, in the Greco-Roman period. For example, some of the inscriptions commemorate women physicians, such as Antiochis, Primilla, Terentia Prima, Julia Pye, Minucia Asste, Venuleia Sosis, and Melitine, mostly from first-century Rome. In her research about women in the Greco-Roman health-care system, Elaine Wainwright notes that "from behind the written text there emerges an image of a significant body of well-trained female medical professionals whose knowledge and skill were central to the entire health care system especially as related to women."[21]

If women healers operated even in the male-dominated professional sector in the Greco-Roman health-care system, it seems safe to assume that women must have been much more active as folk-healers than we might otherwise think and played a larger role in the sign stories or miracle stories of the time.[22]

## Sign Stories and Women

### In Greco-Roman Literature

Antoinette Wire undertook a cross-cultural examination of sign and miracle stories in Greco-Roman literature. She discovered that many miracle stories involving women took place at certain times of crisis in a woman's life: betrothal, conception, bodily disability, or the death of a son. These were the times when a woman's role and survival as a daughter, wife, and mother were at stake. Other times of crisis were occasions of false accusations or imprisonment.

Wire also observed that while there are a few stories in which women exhibited miraculous powers, in many of these cases women's sign-working powers were labeled as sorcery or as the work of an evil spirit. She also noted that, remarkably, childbirth, statistically the time with the most frequent fatalities for women, was not featured as a sign event, at least in the extant literature.[23]

What do these observations indicate? First, extraordinary healings seem to predominate in Greco-Roman sign stories about women, perhaps indicating the great need for healing. Second, many of the healing stories in extant texts described the restoration of a woman's ability to serve and survive in the patriarchal household. In these stories women were typically passive recipients of healings performed by powerful male figures.

While there should have been powerful healing activities at the time of childbirth—the occasion of most women's fatalities—stories about such an occasion were lost. It seems likely that healings at childbirth would have been performed almost exclusively by midwives or women, and precisely because of this their stories did not survive. This may be further evidence that women's healing and sign-working powers were trivialized and even ignored in the literature written by elite males. In any case, it should not be assumed that any lack of stories of healings and miracles performed by women reflects a lack of signs performed by women. Rather, caution should be shown in acknowledging stories in the extant texts as fair representations of the Greco-Roman sign stories that circulated among ordinary people, especially among women.

### In the Christian Testament

Given the context of the Greco-Roman world, it is interesting to look at sign stories involving women in the Christian Testament. There seem to be many sign stories in which women must have been involved but are invisible. For example, women, who are generally invisible in most biblical texts, were undoubtedly included among the "crowd(s)" (see, for example, Mk 6:34; Mt 14:14; Lk 9:11; Jn 6:2).

Thirteen sign stories contain specific mention of individual women. Two are the unexpected conceptions by Elizabeth, the mother of John the Baptizer (Lk 1:5-25), and by Mary, the mother of Jesus (Mt 1:18-25; Lk 1:26-38). Another is the account in which Jesus' mother is the mediator of Jesus' wine sign at a wedding in Cana (Jn 2:1-11). Two other stories tell of signs related to Jesus' resurrection—the empty tomb of Jesus found first by Mary Magdalene (Jn 20:1-10; Mk 16:1-6; Mt 28:1-10; Lk 24:1-12) and the appearance of the risen Jesus to Mary Magdalene (Jn 20:11-18; Mk 16:9-11).[24]
The other nine stories tell of healings:

1. *Peter's mother-in-law:* Jesus' performance, with the mediation of disciples, to heal Peter's mother-in-law (Mk 1:29-31; Mt 8:14-16; Lk 4:38-39);

2. *Jairus's daughter:* Jesus' performance, with the mediation of her father, to heal his daughter (Mk 5:21-24, 35-43; Mt 9:18-19, 23-25; Lk 8:40-42a, 49-56);

3. *A woman with a hemorrhage:* Jesus' performance, at the woman's own mediation (by reaching out and touching), to heal her (Mk 5:25-34; Mt 9:20-22; Lk 8:42b-48);

4. *Syrophoenician (or Canaanite) woman's daughter:* Jesus' performance, with the mediation of her mother, to heal her daughter (Mk 7:24-30; Mt 15:21-28);

5. *The raising of a widow's son:* Jesus' performance, without being asked, to restore the son's life (Lk 7:11-17);

6. *A woman with a spirit of infirmity:* Jesus' performance, without being asked, to heal her (Lk 13:10-17);

7. *The raising of Lazarus, the brother of Martha and Mary:* Jesus' performance, with the mediation of the sisters of Lazarus, to restore their brother's life (Jn 11:1-44);

8. *The raising of Tabitha, a disciple:* Peter's performance, with the mediation of the disciples, to restore her life (Acts 9:36-43);

9. *A slave girl with a Pythian spirit:* Paul's performance, without being asked, to heal or exorcise her (Acts 16:16-18).

We should note that, as was the case in Greco-Roman stories in general, healing stories predominate. However, these stories do not follow the same pattern. Stories in the Christian Testament do not feature the occasions of a woman's betrothal, conception, or disability in order to safeguard her place and role in the patriarchal household. Although two stories do relate to conception, they do not serve to reinforce the patriarchal households. Rather, they function to undermine patriarchal households. In Elizabeth's story, her husband is powerless (Lk 1:19, 59-63). Similarly, Mary appears as an unwed mother (Mk 1:18-25; Lk 1:26-38), and the women are allowed to stay together on their own (Lk 1:39-44, 56).

Indeed, healing stories in the Christian Testament affirm the affectionate concern of supplicants for their family members, but they do not serve to reinforce either stereotypical women's roles or the patriarchal household. A father can become a supplicant, and not for a son, but for a daughter. A mother appears as a supplicant for a daughter and actually argues against Jesus, a teacher, and Jesus accepts her argument; both of them ignore the patriarchal social codes of gender and social status. In another story a man becomes a supplicant not for his own mother, but for his mother-in-law. This tendency to depart from traditional roles may reflect the earliest Christian ethos that did not share in the patriarchal ethos of Greco-Roman households but that instead strongly affirmed familial relationships.[25]

In the entire Christian Testament, however, there are no accounts of sign-working specifically attributed to women—not even to Mary Magdalene. Does this mean that there were no women sign-workers either in the reign-of-God movement or in the earliest Christian movements? This does not seem logical.

As noted above, religious leaders in the Greco-Roman world were expected to perform signs and wonders, and the Christian Testament texts tell us that both the disciples and the apostles actually performed signs as a legitimate means for vindication of their God and their teachings. Since there is firm evidence of women's leadership and their presence as "prominent among the apostles" (Rom 16:7), it is reasonable to assume that these women were also expected to perform signs and actually did.[26]

How then should we interpret this absence of women's sign-working stories? Two major explanations seem possible. First, the general tendency of male-centered material selection was to filter out stories of women, including those telling of women's sign-workings. Second, competing religious propaganda, which presented leaders as powerful divine sign-workers, promoted a kyriocentric (hero-centered) message. Stories of the miraculous and powerful were appropriated from various sources and attributed to leaders, enhancing the leaders at the expense of other active participants in the movements. As a result, the gospels portrayed only Jesus as the ever greater sign-worker, and the Acts recounted the stories of signs worked by Peter (for example, Acts 3:1-10; 9:32-35; 9:36-42) and Paul (Acts 14:8-10; 16:16-18; 20:7-12). Other male participants were rendered as shadowy figures or otherwise marginalized, and women as leaders and sign-workers disappeared from the canonical texts.

### *In the* Apocryphal Acts of the Apostles

Some extant Christian literature outside of the canon hints about the ways in which women's working of the miraculous was degraded and made invisible, not only by hero-making propaganda, but also by later misogynist interpretations. This literature, referred to as the *Apocryphal Acts of the Apostles (AAA)*, includes Christian documents of apostles that are not included in the Christian Testament. Written in the second to third centuries C.E., these stories, or earlier versions of them, probably circulated orally long before they were collected and written down. Some of these accounts depict women performing signs or miracles. According to Virginia Burrus, stories in the *AAA* are not fictional novels but legends. That is, the women protagonists in these stories are presented as historical figures.[27]

The *Acts of Thomas* includes the story of Tertia, Mygdonia, and Marcia. These three women visit a prison that is firmly locked and guarded by the command of a king. They enter the prison miraculously and free the apostle Thomas and all of the Christians imprisoned there. The text presents this story somewhat differently than other sign stories. The women are not depicted as performing a sign per se; rather, the text downplays what the women did by saying that when they went to the prison door, the king's son opened it for them without knowing what he was doing, and that all the guards fell asleep at the time of rescue.

The *Acts of John* presents a story in which a woman, Drusiana, raises a dead man. Raising the dead would certainly have been the most powerful form of healing. Surprisingly, however, there are as many as seventeen raising sign stories in the five extant *Apocryphal Acts of the Apostles*. This large number of powerful sign stories may be the result of the competing religious propaganda of the Greco-Roman world. In comparison, the entire Hebrew Bible—which covers the period of thousands of years—has only two raising sign stories: one by Elijah (1 Kgs 17:17-24) and the other by Elisha (2 Kgs 4:18-37). The Christian Testament includes five raising sign stories, in addition to the story of Jesus' resurrection: three by Jesus (of Jairus's daughter: Mk 5:35-43; Mt 9:18, 23-26; Lk 8:49-56; of a widow's son: Lk 7:11-17; of Lazarus: Jn 11:1-44), one by Peter (of Tabitha in Acts 9:36-43), and one by Paul (of Eutychus in Acts 20:7-12). We notice that no raising sign story was attributed even to Moses, the great hero of ancient days. In contrast, in Greco-Roman times even disciples were said to have performed raising signs.

Of the seventeen raising stories in the *Apochryphal Acts of the Apostles*, most are performed by apostles, but six raisings are performed by others. These signs are performed following step-by-step instruction of the apostles, except for the raising sign performed by Drusiana, who does not receive any instruction. Her manner of raising the dead is precisely the same as that of all the other apostles depicted in the *AAA*. This suggests that Drusiana, or a historical woman and a legendary figure, was an apostle or equal in stature to those males called apostles in the *AAA*. In the *Acts of John*, however, Drusiana appears only as a prominent follower of the apostle John, and her sign is narrated in a manner that dilutes its power: the raised man is not led to faith but soon dies again.

A probable conclusion may be that Drusiana was an apostle, or of equal standing with the apostles, in earlier oral versions of the story. Drusiana's sign-working power was perhaps firmly grounded in an earlier version. There were probably more stories of Drusiana and women like her, whose powerful sign stories were either appropriated by male apostles or lost through patriarchal redaction.

### Sign Stories in the Johannine Gospel

The author/s of the Johannine gospel clearly state the importance of signs as a medium for faith (Jn 20:30-31). The gospel includes twelve different sign stories:[28]

1. *The wine sign at a wedding:* Jesus' performance, with the mediation of his mother, to provide wine (Jn 2:1-11);

2. *A royal official's son:* Jesus' performance, with the mediation of the father, to heal his son (Jn 4:46-54; Mt 8:5-13; Lk 7:1-10);

3. *A man ill at a pool:* Jesus' performance, without mediation, to heal the man (Jn 5:1-9);

4. *Feeding of the five thousand:* Jesus' performance, without mediation, to feed the crowd (Jn 6:16-21; Mk 6:30-44; Mt 14:13-21; Lk 9:10-17);

5. *Walking on the sea:* Jesus' performance, without mediation, of walking on the sea (Jn 6:16-21; Mk 6:45-52; Mt 14:22-27);

6. *A man born blind:* Jesus' performance, without mediation, to heal him (Jn 9:1-12);

7. *Raising of Lazarus, the brother of Martha and Mary:* Jesus' performance, with the mediation of the sisters, to restore their brother's life (Jn 11:1-44);

8. *Empty tomb or raising of Jesus:* God's performance, at God's own initiative, found first by Mary Magdalene (Jn 20:1-10; Mk 16:1-6; Mt 28:1-10; Lk 24:1-12);

9. *Resurrection appearance of Jesus to Mary Magdalene:* risen Jesus' performance, without mediation, to show his resurrection (Jn 20:11-18; Mk 16:9-11);

10. *Resurrection appearance of Jesus to disciples:* risen Jesus' performance, without mediation, to show his resurrection (Jn 20:19-23; Mk 16:14-18; Mt 28:16-20; Lk 24:36-49);

11. *Resurrection appearance of Jesus to disciples, including Thomas:* risen Jesus' performance, without mediation, to show his resurrection (Jn 20:24-29);

12. *Resurrection appearance of Jesus to disciples:* risen Jesus' performance, without mediation, to show his resurrection (Jn 21:1-14).

How would the presentation of these sign stories in the Johannine gospel be understood in the Greco-Roman world? First, all of the signs are attributed to Jesus, earthly or risen, except for Jesus being raised up by God. Thus, this gospel shows a strong tendency toward kyriocentric (hero-centered) attribution of everything powerful and attractive to Jesus. By adopting this approach, the Johannine gospel shares in the tendency of Greco-Roman literature, written by male elites, to present a male image of divine miraculous power. Given that of the twelve stories, women are visibly involved in only four stories, it appears that this gospel shares the tendency of Greco-Roman literature to diminish the involvement of women.

However, some reversals of gender are apparent. In this gospel women are *not* passive recipients or patients of powerful male healers. Rather, it is males who are passive recipients of the healing signs: a man ill at a pool was healed, a man born blind was healed, Lazarus was raised, and Jesus was raised. Women are not passive recipients of healing but instead are active agents or mediators for signs. The mother of Jesus acts as the agent for the wine sign, and the sisters Martha and Mary act as agents to save their brother Lazarus. This presentation of active women and passive men is worth noting. Does this show a resistance to the elite male tendency that makes women passive recipients of male power? This presentation might also imply that there were powerful women leaders, healers, and sign-workers in the Johannine communities.

A closer look at the two sign stories that specifically involved women suggests that perhaps women might have been active storytellers who enhanced Jesus' sign stories, or earlier versions of them, in the midst of the competitive Greco-Roman missionary context.

In the story of the wine sign at a wedding in Cana, Jesus turns the water in six stone jars into good wine (2:1-11). The story, told only in this gospel, is the first sign performed by Jesus at the beginning of his public ministry. That Jesus turned Jewish purification water into festive wine implies that a new age has come with the ministry of Jesus: the time of sin and repentance has become the time of grace and joy. This is a reminder as well of Wisdom/Sophia, who invites all her children to her festive table of abundant food and wine (Prv 9:5-6). These implications might have been both challenging and attractive to the Jewish people, inviting them to believe in Jesus.

However, this story also shows literary affinities with a wine sign, or miracle story, of Dionysus, in which three bottles of water are changed into wine. Dionysus, the famous wine god, turns three bottles of water into wine, but Jesus, the prophet of Sophia, turns six big jars of water into good wine. This suggests that the Johannine storytellers are saying, "Jesus is a true messenger of Sophia, or even Sophia incarnate, and his/her wine sign is much greater than that of Dionysus. Why not come and join us?"[29]

The story of Lazarus's raising sign (11:1-44) might suggest another appropriation, this from Asklepios. An archeological discovery made in the twentieth century indicated a connection between the raising of Lazarus and Asklepios. Excavation of a site located four hundred meters from the "tomb" of Lazarus in Bethany, named Lazarium, revealed a subterranean sanctuary of Asklepios's healing rituals. There, a piece of graffiti was found that reads, "Lord God who raised Lazarus from the dead, remember your servant Asklepios and Chionioy, your female servant." Other evidence suggests that Christian churches gradually replaced many former healing centers of Asklepios. It is possible that the Lazarus raising story was originally an Asklepios healing story. Because it is impossible to date the graffiti, it is impossible to determine if the appropriation of this Lazarus story was made from Asklepios to the

Johannine gospel, or vice versa. It is also possible that both parties appropriated the story from elsewhere.[30]

Since women work as active agents in both of the stories in the gospel, it is intriguing to imagine that it was perhaps Johannine women or pre-Johannine women who composed, appropriated, or revised these stories. If so, did they attribute the signs to Jesus? Or to the women characters who are now recast as agents? As is true of most oral cultures, there was likely more than one version of each sign story—perhaps even many—and the versions written down by the authors were not necessarily more popular than other oral versions.

# 6

## Storytelling and Tradition-Making

### The Jewish Heritage of Women's Storytelling

In most church settings, stories in the Bible have been told in such a way as to foster respect for the men in the stories but rarely for the women. It has often been easier, even for women, to identify with the men. We feel sympathy for them—in their failures and repentance, in their struggles, sorrows, and joys—rather than for the women, who often seem to be undeveloped, one-dimensional characters. This perspective comes about not only from the biblical texts themselves, which most often feature patriarchs and patriarchal images, but also from various patriarchal interpretations of them. However, readers who pay careful attention to the biblical texts may become aware of many more elements that are positive for women. This is not to deny, however, that the overall thrust of the biblical stories is male-centered and unflattering to women.

Some stories in the Hebrew Bible, such as those of ancient matriarchs and the women in Exodus, do present women positively. Nevertheless, even the texts of the law (*Torah*, the first section of the Hebrew Bible), which are highly justice-oriented, and those of the prophets (*Nevi'im*, the second section of the Hebrew Bible), that show solidarity with the poor and the oppressed, still present a negative treatment of women. It is painful to read some texts of the prophets that present clear images of woman as adulterous wives who deserve punishment from their husbands or God, including violence and humiliation that border on the pornographic. Such images of women have been used to justify the status of women as dependent on and inferior to men. Hebrew law basically does not even address women, instead instructing men how to protect and punish women in order to keep them under patriarchal control.[1]

Biblical law gives women status and honor in the role of mother, yet, even in the role of mother, the Hebrew Bible does not offer "a full-fledged human role model." In most biblical texts, a woman's serious concern is to give birth to her son(s). She interferes actively on behalf of her son(s) but not on behalf of her daughter(s)—even on occasions of rape or life-sacrifice (for example, in the stories of Dinah, Tamar, the Levite's wife, and Jephtha's daughter). While the motif of female rivalry appears time and again, it is rare to find positive mother-daughter relationships. As Esther Fuchs says, biblical texts seem to imply that "sisterhood is a precarious alternative to the patriarchal system." What mothers would wholeheartedly hope that their daughters would seriously follow most women models in the Bible in the ways they are presented in these texts? If ancient Jewish women had resembled these biblical figures, would their voices have been heard or appreciated? However, throughout the Hebrew Bible, there are some fragmented or broken pieces that do present women differently.[2]

In the Hebrew Bible, according to Carol Meyers, both the term *bet ab* (father's house) and its variants and the term *bet em* (mother's house or household) function as technical terms for specific units of the community of Israel. The "mother's house" is the household where the life activities of all Israelite women (and most men) take place (Gen 24:28; 28:67; Ruth 1:8; Songs 3:4; 8:2; Prv 1:8; 4:1-3; 6:20, 23; 10:1; 15:20; 23:22-25). This household of the "mother's teaching" is not limited to individual households. The communities of a region serve as the household for the "wise woman" (see, for example, 2 Sam 14; 20:16-20; Jer 9:16), and the entire community of Israel paid heed to Deborah, the "mother in Israel" (Judg 5:7).[3]

Other forms of wife images echo the concept of "mother's house" and differ from the negative images in the prophets. As Claudia V. Camp notes, "There are two images of wife that recur regularly throughout the biblical literature: the wife as manager of the household and the wife as counselor to her husband." A good wife is a capable woman whose actions are independent and who makes decisions. She is not merely an obedient subject to her husband (see 1 Sam 25; 2 Kgs 4:8-10; Prv 31:14, 16, 24).[4]

> A capable wife who can find? . . .
> She seeks wool and flax,
>     and works with willing hands. . . .
> She rises while it is still night
>     and provides food for her household
>     and tasks for her servant-girls.
> She considers a field and buys it;
>     with the fruit of her hands she plants a vineyard. . . .
> She opens her hand to the poor. . . .
> Strength and dignity are her clothing. . . .
> She opens her mouth with wisdom . . .
>     her husband . . . praises her:
> "Many women have done excellently,
>     but you surpass them all." (Prv 31:10-29)

It appears that a wife was also expected to be a counselor to her husband when he made decisions of significance (Judg 13:22-23; 1 Kgs 1:17-21; 21:7; Est 5:14; 6:13; Dan 5:10-12; Job 2:9; Prv 31:26). Camp maintains, "In virtually no case, whether for better or for worse, do their husbands question their advice"; she suggests that the range of dates of these writings and the variations in the function of the images make it likely that the motif of the wise wife reflected a commonplace reality in ancient Jewish culture.[5]

If ancient Jewish women's talk was heeded by both women and men, it is understandable that young Jewish men were supposed to have been tutored by Wisdom/Sophia, the Jewish female divine figure. Many proverbial sayings in the wisdom literature in the Writings (*kethuvim*, the third section of the Hebrew Bible) contain contextual and practical wisdom. They may reflect the experiential wisdom and resourceful instructions for daily life of both ancient Jewish women and men (see, for instance, Psalms 127, 128).[6]

To be sure, wisdom literature in the Hebrew Bible was primarily written for and used to educate elite males, and its texts present patriarchal and anti-women world views and teachings. It is certainly probable that among the vast majority of poor peasants many proverbial, and possibly subversive, wisdom sayings existed that were never recorded but were handed down orally for generations. Where can such voices, especially those of women, be found?

### Women as Creators of Biblical Genres

Solomon D. Goitein suggests that women actually created some biblical genres; that is, the Hebrew Bible contains songs, speeches, and stories that originated from women and were transmitted by women but were later edited and recorded by men. Using Goitein's study as a guide, Athalya Brenner and Fokkelein van Dijk-Hemmes collaborated to identify "female voices in the male texts." These women's genres include the "birth song" and "naming speech," the "vow" and "prayer," the "wisdom speech" and "warning speech," the "victory song," "mockery song," and the "lament."[7]

Among women's genres, victory songs and laments seem to have been particularly important. Women had a long history of expressing their political evaluation and criticism powerfully and persuasively through singing these songs. In the act of composing and singing, women (not exclusive of men) participated in community tradition-making, shaping how historical and political events would be remembered by the whole community.

Victory songs were sung communally in an antiphonal style, in which each woman in turn would lead the song while other women followed with a refrain while dancing with timbrels in their hands. Most songs were short, with a phrase repeated over and over. In longer victory songs women leaders praised God, described the political situation, depicted how victory was won, mocked the opponents, and ended with praise to God.

Textual evidence of these victory songs is present in the songs of Miriam (Ex 15:20-21), Deborah (Judg 5), Jephthah's daughter (Judg 11:34), the women of "all the towns of Israel"(1 Sam 18:6-7), and Judith (Jdt 16). The effect of these songs would have been powerful if, for example, the women of "all the towns of Israel" would have sung "Saul has killed his thousands, and David his ten thousands" again and again while dancing through the towns. Indeed, the biblical text tells that this song was partly responsible for Saul's tragic decision to kill David (1 Sam 18:7-9; 19:1).

Similarly, laments were also sung in communal settings, often in an antiphonal style. They addressed God, complained about a situation to God, commemorated the dead, sympathized with the pain of the dead, mocked the enemy, denounced the men who did not help, and prayed to God for the bereaved (see, for example, Jer 31:15). A typical example was the lament of Hannah (1 Sam 1:1-19). Jewish literature of the first century retells many old biblical stories, including the "Lament for Deborah" and "Seila's Lament."[8]

The singing of laments was essential to funerals and memorial services, and laments were sung by women relatives of the deceased and by professional keening women. It is interesting to note that the lament performances of keening women were sometimes connected to necromancy (the evoking of the spirit of the dead) and were likened to the power of raising the dead. Moreover, it is believed that these women's powerful lament songs sometimes actually did raise the dead.[9]

### Suppression of Women's Voices

From the seventh to the third century B.C.E. various forms of legislation dealing with funerals were issued and revised in different districts of Greece. These legislations varied according to different regional customs, but there were remarkable similarities. Although they state their aim as the restriction of extravagant mourning, a closer look at them indicates that they were particularly aimed at restricting women's lament singing. They severely restricted the number and identities of women participants in funeral mourning, while no such restrictions were aimed at males. The legislations generally said that the dead should not be lamented but be praised, and that the laments (sung by women) at private memorial services should be replaced by a eulogy (spoken by men) at public memorial services, in which soldiers who bravely died in the war and women who died in childbirth should be especially praised. Furthermore, it was recommended that the bereaved, especially widows, live in total silence and public oblivion.[10]

In classical literature we can see a changing ethos for death and laments. There was a progression from "For no good comes of cold laments" (Homer, written in eighth century B.C.E.) to "death is not a terrible thing" (Plato in the fourth century B.C.E.) to "Mourning is something feminine, weak, ignoble" (Plutarch in the first century C.E.). Women's lament singing continued regardless. Goitein describes how powerful political criticism and communal mocking of these women's laments could be, even in the early seventh century C.E. When the Arabian leader Mohammed conquered his native city, he was careful not to spill the blood of his own tribespeople, but he excepted from his amnesty two women prophets who had wounded him more than anyone else with their lament songs of mockery.[11]

Within Jewish communities, a similar tendency started in the first century C.E. that limited women's rituals of mourning as well as women's practices of visiting tombs and burial grounds. However, ancient Jewish mourning tractates that included different or contradictory regulations and comments of rabbis still affirmed weeping and verbal expressions of grief. This observation suggests that Jewish communities were actually supportive of women's lament singing against the wider Greco-Roman ethos; that Jewish funeral customs varied by region and were fluid even at the time of codification in the third century C.E.; and that editors did not yet intend a single ruling for all the Jewish people.[12]

As women's powerful lament singing was broadly and severely attacked, women's daily storytelling activities were also harshly denounced by male writers. There are many extant pejorative comments on women's storytelling, dating from Plato in classical Greek times to Christian Testament times, such as:

> Then we must first of all, it seems, control the storytellers. Whatever noble story they compose we shall select, but a bad one we must reject. Then we shall persuade nurses and mothers to tell their children these we have selected. . . . The majority of the stories they now tell must be thrown out. (Plato in the fourth century B.C.E.)

> For in dealing with a crowd of women . . . a philosopher cannot influence them . . . , and this is not possible without mythic tales and miracles. (Strabo in the first century B.C.E.)

> Have nothing to do with profane myths and old wives' tales. (1 Tm 4:7, in the early second century C.E.)[13]

While ordinary poor children grew up listening to the pedagogical and amusing storytelling of their mothers and neighboring women, upper-class children listened to stories told by nurses who were usually slave women. Indeed, ancient women used story-weaving and storytelling for raising and educating children and for their own amusement while engaged in time-consuming tasks with other women, such as spinning. The continuing denunciation of women's storytelling by various elite males implies that the storytelling activities of ordinary women, including Jewish women, were influential and powerful.[14]

## Biblical Stories in Greco-Roman Times

Scholars consider that while a form of canonization of the Hebrew Bible had started as early as the sixth century B.C.E., the actual stabilization of certain texts took place during the first centuries B.C.E. and C.E. During this same period the Jewish people began rewriting major portions of the Hebrew Bible. The term "rewritten Bible," coined by Geza Vermes, was described by Daniel Harrington as "those products of Palestinian Judaism" at the turn of the era "that take as their literary framework the flow of the biblical text itself" but "freely omit words and whole incidents and add material without any foundation in the text." Portions of the "rewritten Bible" were written at different periods by different authors and made use of different types of Hebrew texts. "What holds all of them together is the effort to actualize a religious tradition and make it meaningful within new situations."[15]

This process of re-visioning and retelling the past by reinterpreting and transforming traditions was already part of the Jewish community. The placement of the book of Deuteronomy (the second telling of the law) immediately after the five books of the law is a good example of this process. Changing the emphasis on different aspects of divine metaphors in the Hebrew Bible may be another example. As the historical context changed and the metaphor of the warrior and the punishing God no longer appealed to people's present experience, more attention was given to the divine metaphors of the lamenting mother, the compassionate woman, and the language of the divine figure Wisdom/Sophia. Such changes or shifts of focus did not negate the old ones but rather added different images. By rewriting the Hebrew Bible, the Jewish people were developing a historical heritage of re-visioning and creative "traditioning" appropriate for their own contexts.[16]

Three characteristics of the religious education and storytelling activities of the first-century Jewish people were noteworthy. First, they did not have an authorized or standard version of the biblical texts, so people used various forms. Second, in adapting to a new situation, they did not negate or discard old traditions but felt free to modify them radically by rewriting, omitting, or adding new material. Finally, they had a variety of different versions of biblical stories, both old and new, in their storytelling repertoire.

As we know, stories do affect people's understanding of who they are. Who tells what kind of stories, and how, matters. Different versions of biblical stories in the first century illustrate this point. They also surface Jewish women's visions and experiences of the time in the midst of interlocking layers of patriarchal power.[17]

### Seila's Lament

In the Hebrew Bible, when Jephthah "returns victorious," his daughter comes out and sings a victory song, but her life is then sacrificed because of her father's earlier vow that "whoever comes out of the doors of my house to meet me" is to be offered "as a burned offering." When Jephthah saw his daughter "coming out," Jephthah rebuked her, saying, "Alas, my daughter! You have brought me very low." However, as noted above, it was customary that women received the victors upon their return, singing songs "with timbrels and with dancing." This means that Jephthah could anticipate that his wife or daughter would be the first to receive him. By blaming his daughter for coming out to meet him, Jephthah doubled his violence against his daughter (Judg 11:34-39).[18]

*The Biblical Antiquities of Philo*, one of the books of the "rewritten Bible," tells a different version of this story. While the authorship of this book is unknown, the author is called Pseudo-Philo, because it was found attached to the end of a book by Philo. *Biblical Antiquities* has a tendency to tell stories of women more positively than other sources. It seems to have been popular and was used for religious education at Palestinian synagogues.

In this book Jephthah's daughter is remembered by the name Seila, and her lament song stands out as the book's only "full-blown lyrical composition." Seila's lament combines elements of both lament and eulogy. In the first half Seila claims honor for herself, not for her father, in her determination to make her sacrifice in faith. In the second half she speaks of "her mother," who is totally absent in the Hebrew Bible, and explicitly states a woman's point of view and experience. As a whole the song criticizes the way male honor is maintained at the cost of women's lives and praises the connectedness of women, between a mother and a daughter and between a girl and her companions. Perhaps Seila's lament was independently circulated among women and incorporated into the narrative of the *Biblical Antiquities*.[19]

On the other hand, according to Cheryl Exum, a critical reading of the Hebrew biblical text itself hints at a different voice in the story. In the Hebrew Bible (Judg 11:34-40) Jephthah's daughter is presented as performing a daughter's duty without resistance, thus supporting patriarchal ideology. The text, however, still shows that in her speech she journeys from the domain of the father to that of the female companions. This may be an indication that from the beginning there have been other versions of her story in which she was not a silent victim. If the first-century women circulated Seila's lament, they might have had other versions of her story also kept alive in their storytelling repertoire.[20]

### Miriam, Co-Leader of the Exodus

Would there have been any "women-friendly" versions of the Exodus, the foundational story of Israel, in the "rewritten Bible"? Unfortunately, in the "rewritten Bible" women do not feature in the retelling of the Exodus. This might result from the first-century tendency to compete in making heroes, which could have greatly enhanced the figure of Moses to set him against Greek heroes. Moreover, not only in Josephus's *Jewish Antiquities* but also in Pseudo-Philo's *Biblical Antiquities* Moses' father, Amram, is given a much more developed role than in the Hebrew Bible. This might also reflect the ancient hero stories in which the son is identified by his father. Even in the *Biblical Antiquities* Moses' mother, Jochebed, and his "sister," Miriam, are not given developed roles.[21]

On the other hand, fragments of the Hebrew Bible do indicate traces of "female voices in the male texts." Moses owes his own life to twelve women. The wise and courageous midwives Shiphrah and Puah thwarted Pharaoh's decree to kill Jewish babies and saved them at the risk of their own lives. Moses' mother, Jochebed, made the decision to raise him and then to hide him in a basket against Pharaoh's decree. Moses' sister made sure that the baby Moses would be rescued and made arrangements for Moses' real mother to become the child's wet-nurse. Pharaoh's daughter thwarted her own father's decree by saving and raising Moses. Later, when Moses fled from Pharaoh, his life was actually saved by meeting the seven daughters of Reuel, a Midian priest who invited Moses to stay in his house. Then, Moses' wife, Zipporah, saved his life when Yahweh "sought to kill him" (Ex 4:24).[22]

Furthermore, Phyllis Trible's feminist critical reading of the Hebrew Bible reveals Miriam as a co-leader of the Exodus and the first prophet in the Hebrew Bible (Ex 15:20). It also highlights that the story of the actual Exodus from Egypt concludes with Miriam's victory song at the Red Sea (Ex 15:21-22). This victory song, the oldest recorded in the Hebrew Bible, forms the basis for the longer version composed and put in the mouth of Moses (Ex 15:1-20). Although marginalized in the present text of the Hebrew Bible, Miriam's song at the sea became the prototype of Jewish traditional victory songs.

After Miriam and Aaron had a conflict with Moses regarding leadership, according to the Hebrew Bible, only Miriam was punished by God. When, however, she was secluded for seven days because of "leprosy," the people of Israel did not abandon her. They refused to proceed on their journey without her (Num 12:15), and when she died, not only "the whole congregation" but also nature mourned and the people suffered because there was no water in the desert (Num 20:1-2). Later, the prophet Micah (eighth century B.C.E.) provides us with a divine reference to the co-leadership of the Exodus: Yahweh says, "I brought you up from the land of Egypt, and redeemed you from the house of slavery; and I sent before you Moses, Aaron, and Miriam" (Mi 6:4).[23]

Were different versions of these women's stories still circulated among women in the first century? There is no extant textual evidence to answer this question. However, *Biblical Antiquities*, which highlighted the actions of Moses and his father but marginalized Miriam, nonetheless applied the language of prophecy to Miriam and referred to the triad co-leadership of the Exodus: "These are the three things that God gave to his people on account of three persons; that is, the well of Marah for Miriam, the pillar of cloud for Aaron, and the manna for Moses" (20:8). This may indicate that the memory of Miriam as a prophet and co-leader of the Exodus was still alive in the first century, probably but not exclusively in women's storytelling.

The contemplative community of the Therapeutrides and the Therapeutae in first-century Egypt sang hymns in chorus, as if the men were being led by Moses and the women by Miriam. This may be additional evidence that Miriam's memory remained strong there as the co-leader of the Exodus and the initiator of liturgical victory songs. May we also speculate that other oral versions also survived in which various women of the Exodus story were not relegated to the margins?[24]

### Judith's Victory

The Book of Judith, one of the Hebrew Bible apocryphal books (biblical, but not included in the canon) written in the first century B.C.E., includes a story of a Jewish woman who rescued the entire Jewish community at the risk of her own life. In the story of Judith, the conqueror Nebuchadnezzar demanded that the conquered Jewish people assist him in engaging his enemy. When the conquered citizens rejected his demand, he mounted a campaign against them. The people of Israel cried for God's help. In this crisis Judith summoned the elders of the town, rebuked their faithlessness, and saved all the people of Israel with her faith, wisdom, and brave action.[25]

This story, along with others, is also characterized by the female "double voice." She is a beautiful, rich, and pious "heroine," "ideal" in men's eyes. Judith is, however, not simply "feminine." She summons and rebukes the elders; she chooses to be an autonomous widow rather than to remarry; and she has a capable and trustworthy woman servant to whom she entrusts the administration of her entire estate. Moreover, in the midst of Greco-Roman male heroism, she mocks male military power and leads "a new exodus of Israel." Elisabeth Schüssler Fiorenza notes that anyone who heard this story in the first century C.E. would see a mirror image of the situation under Roman occupation. "In such a hopeless situation, the image of a wise and strong woman could incite Israel's imagination and engender hope and endurance in the religious-national struggle."[26]

### Daughters of Job

The Testament of Job, another apocryphal book written in the first century B.C.E. or C.E., narrates a story of the daughters of Job. This story seems to reflect a woman's point of view and counters a patriarchal mind-set or practice. As Job is about to die, he distributes his estate to his seven sons. While it was taken for granted that the sons would receive their inheritance, Job's daughters ask for theirs. In response Job gives a "better" inheritance: a "protective amulet." As a result, Job finds that each of his daughters now possesses a spiritual gift of prophecy and each daughter's prophetic hymns are said to have been recorded.[27]

According to Ilana Pardes, a critical reading of Job in the Hebrew Bible itself reveals a "counter tradition" that is fragmented and distorted but nonetheless contained in the biblical story. When Job has suffered for a long time, losing his wealth, sons, daughters, and friends, and suffering bodily afflictions, Job's wife challenges his obsession with the ideal of pious submission to God and urges him to confront God (2:9). Although Job rejects his wife's word at the time, he later follows her advice and in the end obtains God's full blessing; he then finds himself emancipated from his former obsession with piety. In the patriarchal narrative of the Hebrew Bible, Pardes maintains, because Job's wife's challenge to his obsession with piety was so strong, she was not allowed to appear in Job's happy ending. The stories of Job's daughters in the apocrypha may suggest, however, that first-century women may have had different versions of Job's wife's story as well.[28]

## Birth of Popular Literature

First-century women and men, including those in Jewish communities, did not grow up listening only to biblical stories. They had a variety of opportunities to hear other stories and to be influenced by them.

### *Hellenistic Education*

The Greco-Roman world had a universal Hellenistic education system that consisted of three stages: primary, secondary, and advanced. Children of the aristocratic families had tutors at home, but children of the lower classes could barely or rarely attend even primary schools. While it is not clear what percentage of boys and girls attended school, those who could began schooling at the age of seven.[29]

After learning the alphabet, students hand copied, memorized, and recited classical literature, such as Homer and Euripides. In secondary schools students learned writing mostly by imitating classical literature, and Homer was most important. Only very privileged students proceeded to advanced schools, where they studied rhetoric, law, medicine, or military training.

Not all learning, however, took place in schools. Poor Jewish children, for example, who could not attend schools, still studied biblical teachings at home and at synagogues. People also had many occasions to listen to wandering philosophers, preachers, and storytellers on the street.

Greek classical literature undoubtedly occupied the major part of Greco-Roman school education, and even poorer people became familiar with some representative stories, especially those of Homer, through hearing them recited on various occasions. On the other hand, the Greco-Roman world also gave birth to "popular literature," expanding the variety of ordinary people's storytelling repertoire.

In ancient times, even though mass production by the printing press was not yet possible and the literacy rate remained around 3 percent, "popular" literature still existed. Mary Ann Tolbert suggests that "popular literature" be defined as literature written to be read aloud, "composed in such a way as to be accessible to a wide spectrum of society, both literate and illiterate." It is distinguishable both from the elite literature composed "by the canons of and for the approval of the artistic establishment" and from folklore that was "mostly local and tribal in compass."[30]

Differing from classic Greek literature, in which protagonists are usually heroic males, the protagonists in Greco-Roman popular literature were often young couples. This popular literature had conventional plots with elements of verisimilitude. A typical Greco-Roman novel told of the adventurous travels of young and beautiful male and female protagonists, with elements of love, separation, violence, and a happy ending, complete with the disclosure of the true identities of the protagonists and their marriage. There was a general tendency to portray female protagonists as more admirable and faithful than male protagonists, serving perhaps to educate women and to encourage men to do better. Some scholars suspect that women formed a major part of the audience.[31]

Stories of popular literature were usually read aloud, heard, and retold. Stories were often performed in a theatrical manner, not only at theaters and elite male symposia but also on the street, at public baths, and at religious gatherings. Synagogue services were no exception. Biblical stories and other missionary stories were enacted in a theatrical manner outside the synagogue to draw the attention of passersby.[32]

According to Tolbert, the Christian gospels exhibit some of the common features of Greco-Roman popular literature; they were written in unadorned common Greek, in a simple style with unpolished rhetorical development, no philosophical pretensions, and conventional narration. They required a relatively low level of language competence and used the codex form, which was less expensive and easier to carry than scrolls.[33]

At the same time, the gospels also show a resemblance to Greek classical hero stories. As classical Greek literature was used at school—and even primary schoolchildren memorized and recited at least Homer—the pattern of these hero stories was appropriated by Greco-Roman religious leaders as part of their religious propaganda. The gospel presentations of Jesus also fit well with the Greek hero pattern and show a tendency to enhance the figure of Jesus as the greatest hero.

Lord Raglan analyzed Greek classical hero stories and identified twenty-two typical elements. Alan Dundes claims that stories of Jesus in the gospels include seventeen of these twenty-two points, placing Jesus on the same level as ideal heroes such as Asklepios, Apollo, and Zeus. Dundes includes the following elements or patterns in the gospels: a virgin mother, unusual conception, hero reputed to be son of God, attempts to kill hero, hero spirited away (flight into Egypt), reared by foster parents (Joseph), no details of childhood, goes to future kingdom, becomes "king" (the mock title), "reigns" for a time, prescribes laws, loses favor with some of his "subjects" (Judas), driven from throne and city, meets with mysterious death, at the top of a hill, his body is not buried (empty tomb), and he has a holy sepulcher. Missing are traces of a victory over a king (or father or beast) and marriage. Instead, the gospels portray the hero Jesus as obeying the Father/God to the end, with no marriage. In the gospels women "pursue" (follow) him, but Jesus does not pursue women. Based upon this observation, Dundes concludes that the gospels present "a male-oriented worldview which denied power to the female."[34]

There is, however, another aspect to consider. The Jesus of the gospels differs from the hero pattern in that he invites women not to marriage but to participation, equally with men, in his ministry. He is not succeeded by his children, as in the hero pattern; instead, all the gospels present women as the followers who "succeed him." As a whole, it seems that the gospels interweave a classical Greek heritage with the new form of Greco-Roman popular literature, perhaps in order to appeal to a wide range of Greco-Roman audiences.

### Women's Lament Singing and the Passion Narrative

As noted above, it seems plausible that many women (and men) participated in storytelling about Jesus' life and death, trying to understand or make sense of it. In particular, it's likely that many women composed and sang laments for the crucified Jesus. To be sure, Roman law prohibited the use of laments for those executed for political crimes against the state, and any public lament sung for the death of Jesus could have resulted in the death penalty for the singer. Therefore, women likely would have composed and sung their laments for Jesus secretly in their gathering places.[35]

In their lament singing they would have lamented bitterly for Jesus, who was crucified because of his life-giving ministry as Sophia's prophet. They would have portrayed Jesus in the best possible way to commemorate their teacher, the great folk-healer and sign-worker who was faithful to God to the end. They would have mocked the enemies who killed Jesus, but their most severe accusations or denunciations would have been directed, as was the custom of the lament, against their own men who did nothing. In this case they would have denounced the men in the reign-of-God movement, as well as their fellow Jews and the Jewish authorities.

The passion narratives in the gospels are texts written by male editors. However, given a historical imagination expanded by considering ancient women's lament-singing traditions, it is possible that the passion narratives of the gospels originated from the lament singing of women.[36]

The gospels show no specific use of the lament singing of women. This was probably done because of Roman prohibitions against women's laments, but also, and more importantly, because the community wished to avoid making any link between women's lament singing, with its power to evoke the spirits of the dead, and the resurrection of Jesus. The resurrection of Jesus was not to be seen as due to the mourning or keening of women evoking the spirit of the dead but was rightly recognized as God's raising of Jesus and as the divine vindication of Jesus' ministry. The writers of the gospels wanted to present Jesus' death not as divine punishment, nor as divine will, but as a means to see that in his ministry the crucified one was vindicated and to believe that Jesus was still with them.[37]

### Christian Legends of Celibate Women

In looking at women's story-weaving and storytelling activities and to their stories in the earliest and early Christian movements, it is important not to neglect the stories in the *Apocryphal Acts of the Apostles (AAA)*, written in the second to third centuries C.E. It is intriguing to speculate that some of these *AAA* legends derived from the stories of historical women in the first century.[38]

In the *AAA* women protagonists generally rejected conventional female roles in patriarchal households; instead, they chose a celibate lifestyle, were denounced by their lovers and families, were persecuted because of their Christian faith, and in the end triumphed over all hardship. Seven stories of women who chose celibate lifestyles appear in the five earliest *AAA* that are extant: Agrippina, Nicaria, Euphemia, Doris, and Xanthippe (in *Acts of Peter*); Maximilla (*Acts of Andrew*); Drusiana (*Acts of John*); Thecla (*Acts of Paul and Thecla*); Artemilla and Eubula (*Acts of Paul*); the "princess bride," and Mygdonia and Tertia (*Acts of Thomas*). In these stories "confident and defiant, the women are moved neither by threats of physical punishment nor by pleadings of love. And they triumph." In contrast to novels and fairy tales (and some folklore) in which women are invited to conform to patriarchal roles and lifestyles, these stories support women who reject such roles and lifestyles.[39]

Virginia Burrus suggests that while Greco-Roman romantic novels were written by men to educate women to conform to patriarchal households, the women-related stories in the *AAA* were originally composed and told by women as legends to encourage and support Christian women who challenged patriarchal lifestyles. The story of Thecla seems to have been especially popular. Appointed to be an apostle by Paul, she experienced fierce persecution, almost became an exemplary martyr but was miraculously saved, and devoted herself to apostleship. According to Dennis MacDonald, this story possibly goes back to the time of Paul, about the middle of the first century. He suspects that the authors of the Christian pastoral epistles (1 and 2 Timothy and Titus, probably written in the early second century) knew that these women's legends were popular among women in many Christian communities. Therefore, the authors of the pastoral epistles knew that "there was no more effective way of silencing them (women) than writing in Paul's own name."[40]

Seen in this context it seems likely that story-making activities were popular among women as well as men in the Greco-Roman world and that there were various stories told both by men and women that proposed very different religious and political views and even commended old or new lifestyles for women. The earliest Christian women seem to have been active participants in this new story-making movement.

## From Storytelling to Written Texts

According to James Scott, there are two major types of traditions, the "great tradition" and the "little tradition." The "great tradition" or "public transcript" is found in the dominant written literature, and the "little tradition" or "hidden transcript" is most often found in oral versions of stories that are generally critical of those in power. In the ancient oral world the great traditions of elite males were not necessarily the widely known traditions. Rather, even children of elite families were exposed to the little, or hidden, traditions through the storytelling repertoires of the slave women who cared for them. Ordinary people, both women and men, had free access to oral story "authorship," with versions of various stories as their storytelling repertoire. [41]

The Christian movement took place in this oral setting. As Joanna Dewey notes, "Early Christianity was an oral phenomenon in a predominantly oral culture." In the time of Christian origins there was no Christian canon. Instead, there were numerous versions of biblical stories, told and retold by both men and women in their communities. Since they were a tiny minority group in the Greco-Roman world, all the Christian stories were part of the little or hidden traditions of the time.[42]

However, when certain versions of the Christian stories were written down and attributed to some emerging leading figures, then read aloud as the authentic voices of such figures and hand copied to be circulated, the situation changed, probably slowly but steadily from the second century onward. Only the written versions became "fixed," carrying with them some authority, and the division between the great/public traditions and the little/hidden traditions became gradually defined within the Christian communities. Access to authorship was now limited to the small, elite, mostly male class. Their versions and voices became the communal authority, and other versions and voices were gradually marginalized.

What changes might reasonably result from a shift from oral stories to written texts? Some noteworthy studies have been made on the transformation of European folk tales from earlier oral editions to later written editions. First, there is a substantial decrease in the number of stories in which women or girls are active protagonists. Second, there is a change in the roles of women and girls from being active autonomous agents to being passive recipients of male violence and protection.

One good example, according to Joanna Dewey, is the transformation of "Little Red Riding Hood." In its oral versions it was told by women to young girls. In these versions, when the girl found herself in a crisis situation, she used her own wits to escape the "wolf" and successfully achieved her own rescue. In its later written versions the girl got in trouble for playing on the way and was either left dead or was rescued by a man.

This seems to be a fundamental distortion of the message that women told to young girls. The message was no longer "be resourceful and confident in your actions, and become an independent woman"; it was now "be obedient to your parents (or authority), faithfully perform your task but do nothing on your own, since you are helpless without male protection." Once printed and fixed, with the eventual loss of oral versions in later generations, mothers knew (and know today) only these male versions and read them aloud to their daughters.[43]

Dennis MacDonald's study on the transformation of miracle stories, stories closer to the earliest Christian movements, is illuminating. A good example is the story of Thecla in the *Acts of Paul and Thecla*. In the oral story of the first century, Thecla was led to a conversion to Christianity by Paul. She hoped to be baptized and become a missionary, "teaching the word of God." She became a celibate Christian woman and was persecuted because of this. Unfortunately, Paul failed to baptize her or to protect her from her persecutors. On the other hand, various women (including female animals) helped Thecla, who miraculously survived. She then sought to be ordained by Paul to "teach the word of God" and later established her own successful ministry in Seleucia, Isauria. This story tells of "the pervasiveness of female solidarity and the unfavorable depictions of male characters, including Paul."[44]

In the second century the story was written down and placed in the series of Pauline adventures as the *Acts of Paul and Thecla*. Within this setting the protagonist Paul is redeemed from his original unfavorable depiction in Thecla's story. The authorship replicates Thecla's struggles as Paul's, and thus Paul overshadows Thecla.

In the third century Thecla's story was detached from the *Acts of Paul*, and Thecla became the protagonist in the *Acts of Paul and Thecla*. In this account, however, Thecla was praised as a prototype of a martyr, even though she successfully survived persecution in the oral story. The story of Thecla the martyr was read aloud at the shrine of Thecla in Seleucia and attracted pilgrims to it. In the fifth century the *Acts of Paul and Thecla* was rewritten as the *Acts and Miracles of St. Thecla*, in which she became a holy woman of miracles and healing. Moreover, Thecla, the celibate woman, now became the guarantor of fertility for women pilgrims to Seleucia, making the town famous and prosperous. Next, her story was reappropriated as a story about Andrew in the *Acts of Andrew*, and the book was used as an example of male celibacy and divine power. Further reappropriations took place, emphasizing themes of monasticism and popular pilgrimage. In these stories every trace of the first-century Thecla is gone.

MacDonald suspects that similar transformations occurred during the process of selecting, writing, and editing the stories that now constitute the Christian Testament. Take, for example, the story of the Syrophoenician woman who bests Jesus in argument (Mk 7:24-30). This story might have had quite a different function or message before it was placed in the Markan narrative. As was the case of Paul in Thecla's story, "Jesus does not look good here," but "within the larger context of the gospel, Jesus' reputation is quickly restored."

MacDonald asks, "Do we have here another case of a male narrator domesticating a woman's story?"[45]

It becomes clear that the shift from oral storytelling to reading the written text resulted in more than a change from the spoken to the written word. Even when women's stories survived in the elite male texts, the characters and the messages often changed, largely reflecting the interests and biases of privileged males. Furthermore, another significant shift in the Christian communities, the change of the location of the gathering, also contributed to diminishing women's voices.[46]

In the first century the earliest Christians gathered in one another's houses. Most houses were very small and humble, affording space for only ten to twenty people. Because the setting was the home, the leadership of women probably seemed natural. In such house-gatherings, the early Christians prayed together and shared communal meals. Some were empowered for healing, some were inspired to prophesy, and still others were excellent storytellers.

As the Christian communities grew, these house churches were often modified to permit larger gatherings. Some of them ceased to be private/domestic houses and became independent places for church gatherings. Such a church, externally the same as ordinary houses but with internal ecclesial (church) features, was called a *domus ecclesiae*. This form became most common in the third century and continued to be used in the fourth and later centuries.

In the third century some of the growing Christian communities acquired larger buildings. Such a building or hall that no longer looked like an ordinary house was called an *aula ecclesiae*. At first, most were relatively simple, but soon they created raised daises and pulpits that served to separate the ordained few from the nonordained majority. This trend continued, with a gradual patriarchalization and imperialization occurring among leading churches. The change from the private space of the *domus* to the public space of the *aula* made it easy for the increasingly patriarchalized church to exclude women from participation in leadership.

In the fourth century the Roman emperor Constantine approved Christianity as the state religion. Or, more precisely, he approved one form of Christianity, while rejecting the other forms that represented the majority of Christians. Constantine's direct involvement promoted the church's imperialization as well as fierce persecution, involving the military, of the majority of dissenting churches. The imperialized churches now obtained large ecclesial buildings with elaborate structures and ornamentation. This type of church building, whose form originated from Roman public courts and audience halls, was called a *basilica*. By this time every trace of the first-century house church had disappeared.

These two significant shifts—the move from oral storytelling to reading aloud written texts, and the move from the simple structure of the house church, the *domus ecclesiae*, to the more public and hierarchical structure of the *aula ecclesiae* and the *basilica*—radically changed the Christian communities and contributed to the silencing of women's voices. Pauline Allsop notes, "Just as the new liturgical space (the hall or *basilica*) was discontinuous from the old (the house-church), so the new imperial character of Christianity was discontinuous from the discipleship of equals begun by Jesus."[47]

This continuing process of silencing or diminishing women's voices, however, does not disqualify the earlier voices of women. Rather, it indicates that the lack of women's stories does not necessarily reflect the historical situation in the earliest Christian movements, and that a search for women's voices is indispensable for a more comprehensive understanding of the reign-of-God movement and Christian origins.

# 7

## Persecution and Patriarchalization

### Roman Political and Religious Oppression

The oppressive political power of Rome was a fundamental part of the landscape of Roman colonial towns and villages in the first century C.E. For the Jewish people, and later for the Christians, however, Roman imperial worship was one of the most serious political and religious pressures. As noted above, in the first century all the Roman emperors were adored as "sons of god," and after death they were deified and worshiped. Even though most emperors were not deified until after their death, they were still hailed and addressed as "son of god," "savior," "lord," and "father."

To be sure, the attitude of the various emperors regarding imperial worship differed considerably, but no emperor denied the practice of imperial worship itself. The actual practice varied regionally, as most Roman emperors avoided limiting the freedom of action of their governors. Given the innumerable local ethnic laws and customs, and the difficulties of communication with the capital city of Rome, the empire would have broken down if the local governors' decision-making powers had been strictly limited. Thus, it was up to the local governors to make decisions about the practice of imperial worship in their provinces and the treatment of those who did not participate.

Nevertheless, it is understandable that many local governors were more than willing to demonstrate their loyalty by increasing their provinces' devotion to the imperial worship. Not only did Roman coins picture Roman emperors to celebrate their immortality, but temples for imperial worship were built, and statues of Roman emperors for obeisance were erected throughout the cities of the Roman Empire.[1]

In 40 C.E. Jewish people were granted special privileges regarding religious and political matters. Chief among these privileges was exemption from participating in Roman imperial worship. In *The Jewish War* the Jewish historian Josephus wrote about the incident that led to this privilege: The emperor Gaius (Josephus wrote "Caius Caesar") took "himself to be a god," and "sent

Petronius with an army to Jerusalem, to place his statues in the temple, and commanded him that, in case the Jews (Judeans) would not admit of them, he should slay those that opposed it, and carry all the rest of the nation into captivity." When the army arrived at a city in Galilee, "the Jews got together in great numbers, with their wives and children," and made supplication to Petronius. Of course he would not compromise easily, because his life itself would be in jeopardy if he disobeyed the emperor's command. Finally, "the Jews said, 'We offer sacrifices twice every day for Caesar, and for the Roman people'; but that if he would place the images among them, he must first sacrifice the whole Jewish nation; and that they were ready to expose themselves, together with their children and wives, to be slain." At this, Petronius retreated to persuade the emperor to "countermand his former injunction . . . unless he had a mind to lose both the country and the men in it." Fortunately, Gaius died soon, before his unfavorable response reached Petronius.[2]

Thus, Jewish people obtained their privilege not to participate in Roman imperial worship by risking the slaughter of the entire community. The account of Josephus may well have been idealized from his perspective. Nonetheless, this incident testifies to the determination of the Jewish people, regardless of their diverse theological opinions and practices, not to deify and worship a human being equally with God.

This privilege, however, was always a cause of potential hatred and suspicion by neighboring peoples, most of whom were also colonized under Roman political and economic oppression. Jewish people usually managed to maintain good relationships with their neighbors, but in precarious situations they could easily become scapegoats and targets of their neighbors' hatred. Under such circumstances Jewish communities were forced to be very careful not to offend the Roman power in any way in order to maintain their privilege.[3]

In the middle of the first century C.E. the Jewish people had already experienced hardship because of internal conflicts. In 49 C.E. Emperor Claudius (41-54 C.E.) expelled all Jewish people from Rome because of disturbances within synagogues. The details are not known, but it is probable that they arose from disputes between Christians and other Jewish groups. This exile ended after five years, but it caused the Jewish people to become more cautious. Nevertheless, the situation grew worse. In 64 C.E. Emperor Nero blamed Christians for causing a large fire in Rome. Then a Jewish revolt began in 66 C.E. that ended in 70 C.E. with the destruction of Jerusalem, including the temple.[4]

Later, Emperor Domitian (81-96 C.E.) deified himself and demanded that he be worshiped by all the populace under his rule. Many Jewish people perceived that the maintenance of the Jewish religious privilege was a critical issue for all the Jewish communities in order safely to avoid participating in the Roman imperial worship. It is quite likely that this constant fear and anxiety brought about division within the communities and that some Jewish people or synagogues were inclined to dissociate themselves from "troublemakers."[5]

### Conflicts and Dissociation between "Jews" and "Christians"

In the Johannine gospel the term "put out of the synagogue" appears three times: "The Judeans had already agreed that anyone who confessed Jesus to be the messiah would be put out of the synagogue" (9:22); "But because of the Pharisees they did not confess it, for fear that they would be put out of the synagogue" (12:42); and "They will put you out of the synagogues" (16:2). Many scholars have interpreted these texts as indicating that the Birkat ha-Minim (blessing against the heretics) caused a "formal ban" against Christians. However, such an interpretation seems inadequate.[6]

A Jewish conference held in Yavne in 90 C.E. decided to include the Birkat ha-Minim in the daily Jewish prayer. The prayer lists "outsiders," "heretics," and "the arrogant of the nations" to be excluded from the blessings of God. However, the term "Nazaraei" *(Notzrim)* that may specifically mean Christians was not mentioned at the time; it was added sometime toward the end of the second century or later. Therefore, while the Jewish Christians could be counted among all the various "heretics," they were not particularly referred to in the prayer, at least during the first century C.E.[7]

Moreover, the Jewish people did not have a widespread network of authority that could enforce such a practice as a "formal ban" in the first century. Instead, each local synagogue had relatively autonomous power and varied responsibilities under regional Roman governance, and there was no single criterion of authentic or deviant Jewish beliefs and practices that was shared by all the Jewish people of the time.[8]

As noted above, there was a variety of movements, theological opinions, and religious practices among Jewish people, women as well as men, in the first century. Given the diversity that Jewish people apparently accepted among their communities, it seems that it was up to a group of leaders in each local synagogue to decide which practices were heretical and who were "trouble-makers," using their own criteria, and to enforce "punishment" in their regional situation.

### At the Time of the Reign-of-God Movement

It is now widely accepted that the reign-of-God movement was firmly rooted in Jewish communities, and that the members of the movement regarded themselves as faithful Israel, the people of God. There was no such thing as conflict between "Jews" and "Christians" at the time of the movement, especially because the name or even the concept of "Christians" did not exist.

The enmity and conflict between "Jews" and "Christians" depicted in the Christian Testament gospels reflect conflicts that were being experienced by the authors/editors in their own communal contexts at later periods. These conflicts were then retrojected into their narratives. Such rhetorical devices stem from the later context of competitive theological opinions and conflicts and were not actual historical reports of the reign-of-God movement.[9]

### At the Time of the Earliest Christians

The earliest Christian communities, or at least part of them, experienced some forms of enmity and conflict with some other Jewish people. Claudia Setzer has analyzed Christian writings that mention Jewish reactions to Christians of the time, and her observations are supported by other scholars' studies. She noted three major trends: tolerance, verbal attacks, and physical attacks. Reports of examples of fair-mindedness and tolerance were few in number. She questions, however, if these instances were not under-represented. Sensible and tolerant responses do not make for dramatic reading and would not have served the needs of Christian writers in the midst of competitive theological opinions. In her study the greatest number of examples fall under the heading of verbal attacks. Harsh rhetoric would undoubtedly have been magnified when groups were under extremely oppressive and stressful circumstances.[10]

Some examples refer to physical attacks. Typical among them was judicial flogging. Flogging was a common means of disciplining students, and it was also used in some Jewish communities as a means of educational restraint and punishment for some leaders. The fact that Paul received such judicial floggings indicates that he was regarded as a Jewish leader, although Paul seems to have interpreted them as persecution (2 Cor 11:24). Spontaneous violence against "Christians" might have come from neighboring people, since Jewish people were no strangers to mob violence in civil unrest, and other people usually would not have distinguished "Christians" from other Jewish people.[11]

Probably the most serious punishment for some Christians was public dissociation by the local synagogue. As already noted, under a very oppressive political situation it is possible that some Jewish people or communities were ready to dissociate themselves publicly from some Christians for the sake of communal survival. However, that put some Christians in a vulnerable situation. Those who were publicly separated from their local synagogues automatically lost their Jewish privilege and were therefore exposed to Roman persecution for not participating in imperial worship. In certain regions any action of personal "informing" to the Roman authorities, or even a failure to offer the protection of the Jewish community, may have been perceived as a death threat. Furthermore, as some Roman officials began to have the idea that "Christians" were not "Judeans," the perceived threat gradually spread to all Christians.[12]

## Roman Persecution and Women

The fear of possible persecution felt by all Christians in the second half of the first century escalated during the time of Domitian (81-96 C.E.). In 93 C.E. Domitian's policy brought a charge of *atheotes* (godless people) to those who did not worship Roman emperors as gods. At this time Christians were sometimes brought to local governors and tested for their loyalty by requiring them to make offerings before the statues of Roman emperors.[13]

The earliest literary evidence for this practice comes from the early second century. Around 110 C.E. Pliny, the governor of Bithynia in Northern Asia Minor, sent a letter to the Roman emperor Trajan inquiring about the punishment of Christians. According to the letter, people accused of being Christians were tried and asked whether or not they would confess their Christian faith; if they did, they were threatened with capital punishment. However, if they declared that they were no longer Christians and that they would worship the emperors' images as well as statues of various deities, and cursed Christ, they were freed.

Pliny also mentions that he tortured two women slaves who were ministers in order to "find out the truth about Christians." In response to this letter, Trajan says that Christians are not to be sought out but should be put on trial only when informed against. He does not say anything, however, to stop torture or capital punishment. Pliny's letter shows that slave women could and still did work as ministers at the beginning of the second century. This letter may also indicate that among many prisoners, women slaves, rather than men, were chosen as the objects of torture.[14]

Unfortunately, not much information about early persecution of women is available. Yet at least three extant writings vividly describe women's struggles and persecutions: The *Acts of Paul and Thecla* and the *Martyrs of Lyons* from the second century, and the *Martyrdom of Saint Perpetua* from the early third century, periods when Christians were periodically persecuted. The *Acts of Paul and Thecla* also contains some material from the first century.

The *Acts of Paul and Thecla* consists of a legend of Thecla as well as that of Paul. The earlier versions of the legend of Thecla were circulated orally, probably from the middle of the first century, although the extant text is written and edited from a male perspective in the second century C.E. It still provides information regarding Christian women under Roman persecution.[15]

In the story Thecla is led to Christian faith by Paul. However, because of her Christian faith and choice of celibate lifestyle, Thecla is persecuted not only by her mother and would-be husbands but also by the Roman political power. She is imprisoned, and twice she is almost martyred. One time, when she is about to be burned, she is saved by sudden rain. Another time she is rescued by the collaborative help of females: when she is put in the Colosseum naked, together with beasts, a female lion protects her by fighting with a bear and a lion, after which the animals die together. Then, in order to protect herself from other beasts, Thecla decides to "baptize" herself and plunges into a pool full of seals, but she is not eaten by them because the seals are killed by lightning. After seeing this, all the women in the Colosseum stand up and throw their perfumes upon the beasts in the Colosseum, so that all the beasts fall asleep. Then Thecla is tied between two bulls, and, seeing this, Queen Tryphaena faints. Observing this, the governor, who fears punishment by Caesar, releases Thecla. Queen Tryphaena becomes Thecla's protector as her mother in faith. Thecla seeks out Paul, is ordained to become an apostle, and continues her work as a missionary.

The *Martyrs of Lyons* tells of Blandina, a servant/slave woman who clearly inspired and led all those who were martyred with her, including her "earthly mistress." The text is of a letter from "the servants of Christ who dwell in Vienne and Lyons in Gaul, to our brothers in Asia and Phrygia who have the same faith and hope in the redemption." The letter tells of the martyrdom of several in Lyons, including Blandina, "through whom Christ proved that the things that men think cheap, ugly, and contemptuous are deemed worthy of glory before God." Blandina was hung on a post in the form of a cross, and the other martyrs saw Christ in the person of their sister. On the last day of the gladiatorial games, her courage again inspired all the others, who died one by one. "The blessed Blandina was last of all: like a noble mother encouraging her children, she sent them before her in triumph to the King, and then, after duplicating in her own body all her children's sufferings, she hastened to rejoin them, rejoicing and glorying in her death. . . . The pagans themselves admitted that no woman had ever suffered so much in their experience."[16]

The *Martyrdom of Saint Perpetua* is a woman's diary written in a prison in the early third century C.E. Her writing is another precious testimony to women's martyrdom, although the extant text has also gone through male redaction. Perpetua and her slave Felicitas were imprisoned because of their Christian faith. Both were mothers of newborn babies at the time of their martyrdom. Perpetua's diary vividly describes how her father begs her to conform and live for the sake of himself and her baby. Perpetua, her slave Felicitas, and other prisoners, however, are determined to keep their faith and are martyred in the Colosseum. Scholars assume that Perpetua and Felicitas probably belonged to the New Prophecy movement, and that the movement originated from Johannine communities. More about this later. [17]

Together with Pliny's letter to Trajan, these stories tell us that there were many women who were tortured or martyred. They were virgins and mothers and free and slave women. We can assume that in the first century when the gospels were written the earliest Christian groups did not suffer such terrible persecution because they were small groups of people, still firmly part of Jewish communities and protected by the privilege given to Jewish people. Paul's letters, however, still talk about imprisonment and persecution borne by him and other Christians, both women and men.

Luise Schottroff argues that "women were among the persecuted by Rome just as often as men, if not even more often, and that their tortures and punishments were frequently more brutal than those of men." Unfortunately, the androcentric selection of extant texts makes these women's sufferings and struggles obscure or nearly invisible. However, it would be unjust to discuss the history of the earliest and early Christian movements without restoring and remembering the suffering of these Christian women.[18]

## Christian Patriarchalization and Women

From the second to third centuries the Christians and other Jewish groups gradually separated themselves. Due to this separation the Christian groups lost their parent body's privilege and were directly exposed to Roman political and religious oppression. This coincides with the time when some Christian movements changed their relatively egalitarian ethos and practice to become increasingly and drastically patriarchal. This patriarchalization, however, was not an inevitable move, because there were some churches and communities that resisted it for centuries. Moreover, while some churches chose to make adaptations to Roman patriarchy as part of their survival strategy, some churches went much beyond what would seem to have been necessary for survival. Such actions appear to have been due to some leaders' desire for power and authority within the broader context of the Hellenistic philosophical and social backlash.[19]

### *Contradictory Messages in the Christian Testament*

Some texts in the Christian Testament indicate the egalitarian ethos and practices in early Christian origins. The Markan gospel notes, for example, that some of the male disciples "argued with one another who was the greatest." Then Jesus says, "Whoever wants to be first must be last of all and servant of all" (Mk 9:34-35). Jesus also says, "You know that among the Gentiles those whom they recognize as their rulers lord it over them, and their great ones are tyrants over them. But it is not so among you," and he repeats the above cited message (Mk 10:42-44). The Matthean gospel also cites a similar teaching of Jesus, "The greatest among you will be your servant" (Mt 23:11). In the same way, the Johannine Jesus says, after he washes his disciples' feet, "You call me Teacher and Lord. . . . So if I, your Lord and Teacher, have washed your feet, you also ought to wash one another's feet" (Jn 13:13-14). This text provides an example of the relationship that should exist among Christians, demonstrated in a social context where washing someone's feet was a task normally performed by slaves and lower-class women.

Some texts specifically allude to women, such as the story in which Jesus clearly stated that women's blessings depend on their faith, not on their motherhood. When a woman says to Jesus, "Blessed is the womb that bore you and the breasts that nursed you!" Jesus says, "Blessed rather are those who hear the word of God and obey it!" (Lk 11:27-28). Thus, all the gospels in the Christian Testament include stories that command egalitarian practices in one way or another. Another example is Paul's letter to the Galatians, which quotes a baptismal formula describing the egalitarian ethos of the earliest Christian communities: "There is no longer Jew or Greek, there is no longer slave or free, there is no longer male and female; for all of you are one in Christ Jesus" (Gal 3:28).[20]

Contrary to these messages the Christian Testament also has patriarchal commands that come not from Jesus' stories but from church leaders during the latter half of the first century and the beginning of the second century. The letter to the Colossians, written in Paul's name by someone else after Paul's death, records one of the Christian household codes that is only slightly modified from the Roman household codes. It commands, "Wives, be subject to your husbands," as well as, "Slaves, obey your earthly masters in everything . . . wholeheartedly" (Col 3:18, 22).

In a letter to Timothy, also written in Paul's name by someone after Paul's death, a church leader commands, "Let a woman learn in silence with full submission. I permit no woman to teach or to have authority over a man. . . . Yet she will be saved through childbearing" (1 Tm 2:11-15). These texts indicate that some churches started obvious patriachalizing movements even before the time of severe Roman persecution.

The treatment of Mary Magdalene seems a particular instance of how prominent women were gradually downgraded and marginalized. The three synoptic gospels agree that Mary Magdalene and some other women were in the reign-of-God movement from the beginning (Mk 15:40-41; Mt 27:55-56; Lk 8:1-3). These gospels also agree that Mary Magdalene, together with some other women, played a key role in the continuation of the movement after the death of Jesus (Mk 16:1-8, 9-10; Mt 28:1-8; Lk 24:1-9). While the other women's names differ in the gospels, Mary Magdalene is mentioned by all and usually is the first name given, indicating wide recognition of her special importance. The Johannine gospel goes even further, specifically highlighting her role as the first witness of the resurrection of Jesus and as the first apostle sent by the risen Jesus to announce his resurrection to other members of the reign-of-God movement (Jn 20:11-18).

A section of the *Gospel of Mary,* a non-canonical text, seems to reflect a conflict between the authority of Simon Peter and that of Mary Magdalene. This gospel was written in the second century, although the story probably circulated orally long before it was written down. In the story, when the disciples feared that they might suffer the same fate as their Lord and "were grieved and wept sore," Mary Magdalene exhorts them to proclaim the gospel despite fear, because the savior will be with them. After this, Peter asks Mary to share the revelation that she has received from the savior. When she tells them about a vision she has received, however, Peter and Andrew react with disbelief. Peter says, "Did he then speak privily with a woman rather than with us, and not openly? Shall we turn about and all hearken unto her? Has he preferred her over against us?" Then Mary wept and asked Peter whether he believed that she had imagined that herself in her heart, or that she would have lied about the savior. Levi answered and said to Peter, "Peter, thou hast ever been of a hasty temper. Now I see how thou dost exercise thyself against the woman like the adversaries. But if the Savior *[soter]* hast made her worthy, who then art thou, that thou reject her? Certainly the Savior knows her surely enough. Let us rather be ashamed, put on the perfect Man, as he has charged us, and proclaim the Gospel *[euaggelion]*."[21]

In the later history of the church Peter was exalted as one of the most prominent saints. In contrast, the historical memory of Mary Magdalene was distorted and lost. That is, her image, that of an outstanding woman leader who ensured the continuation of the reign-of-God movement after Jesus' death, was almost utterly destroyed, and it was replaced with the image of a repentant prostitute, although such an image is without biblical or historical foundation.

### Women in the Didactic Writings

A stark difference between two Christian didactic (teaching) writings, one written in the first century and the other in the third century, demonstrates quite clearly the early transformation of the Christian ethos. The late first-century writing is the *Didache: The Teaching of the Twelve Apostles*. In this *Didache* the teachings, aimed at achieving true life, draw a line between the believing and the non-believing. Although it is written in androcentric language, "sons and daughters" are considered equally deserving of education and there is no gender-differentiated teaching. Since it is faith that leads a person to true life, parents should instruct their children, both sons and daughters, to live in faith. Its first chapter begins: "There are two ways, one of life and one of death; and there is much difference between the two ways. Now the way of life is this: First, love God that made you; secondly, love your neighbor as yourself." Passages related to sexuality read: "Abstain from fleshly and bodily lusts," "do not commit adultery, do not corrupt youths, do not commit fornication." Orders related to family life include: "Do not take away your hand from your son or from your daughter, but from youth up teach them the fear of God."[22]

On the other hand, the *Didascalia Apostolorum*, written at the end of the third century, is written in androcentric language *and* filled with gender-differentiated misogynistic teachings. Here the teachings seem to be aimed at adapting to patriarchal lifestyles and draw a line between men and women, instead of between believing and non-believing. Men and women are to behave according to patriarchal Greco-Roman social norms. Women are admonished to stay at home and be humble and silent, possibly to keep them from talking about or preaching gospels that varied from the author/s' standards.[23]

The following examples show the author/s' patriarchal interests and also inform us about what ordinary women were actually doing: "Modest and reverent, [they] sit at home and work at wool"; "For those who are gadabouts and without shame cannot be still even in their houses"; "And because they are gossipers and chatterers and murmurers, they stir up quarrels; and they are bold and shameless"; "A woman void of understanding and boastful

. . . , and knoweth no shame"; "You then who are such ought to be ashamed; for you wish to be wiser and to know better, not only than the men, but even than the presbyters and bishops"; "But if there is no women's bath, and thou art constrained to bathe in a bath of men and women, . . . bathe with modesty and shame, and with bashfulness and moderation; . . . and not at midday."

Actually, such commands restricting and denouncing women's activities, including preaching, are already found in the early second-century writings in the Christian Testament, in the so-called pastoral epistles: "Women should dress themselves modestly and decently in suitable clothing, not with hair braided, or with gold, pearls, or expensive clothes" (1 Tim 2:9). "Have nothing to do with profane myths and old wives' tales" (1 Tim 4:7), and "Avoid them! For among them are those who make their way into households and captivate silly women" (2 Tim 3:5-6).[24]

The difference between commands in the pastoral epistles, written in the early second century, and those in the *Didascalia*, written at the end of the third century, is that the word "shame" is not used in the former, while it abounds in the latter. This difference might imply that the gender-specific concept of shame for such activities was introduced or established in the elite-male written text at the end of the third century, while such a concept of shame was not embraced in the early second century. It might also imply that regardless of such denunciation by male writers, women's activities were not easily controlled. That such writing exists testifies to the strong possibility in the late third century that women were actually doing these things. Nevertheless, the gap between the first-century *Didache* and the third-century *Didascalia* is huge. How different it may have been for a woman to be a Christian in the fourth century compared with what it would have been like in the first century![25]

### Women's Leadership as Heretical

In *In Memory of Her* Elisabeth Schüssler Fiorenza has illustrated how the Christian movements, in which a discipleship of equals in the power of the Holy Spirit was practiced, were gradually transformed into a patriarchal institution. During the first few centuries various communities wrote gospels and tractates to gain support for their theologies. Most of the writings and Christian communities that were supportive and more open to women's leadership were labeled heretical by other more powerful communities. The writings labeled heretical were then altered or destroyed. Information about communities with non-patriarchal orientations is passed on only through altered or fragmented materials or pejorative references in the polemical writings of their opponents. Critical reading of these materials, however, still yields precious information about the women who lived in the midst of the increasing patriarchalization of the church.[26]

According to Jerome, a church father of the late fourth century, alongside every heretical man was an heretical woman. Or, in other words, all the men and the communities that supported women's leadership were labeled heretical. He comments:

> It was with the help of the harlot Helena that Simon Magus founded his sect. Bands of women accompanied Nicolas of Antioch that deviser of all uncleanness. Marcion sent a woman before him to Rome to prepare men's minds to fall into his snares. Apelles possessed in Philumena an associate in his false doctrines. Montanus, that mouthpiece of an unclean spirit, used two rich and highborn ladies Prisca and Maximilla first to bribe and then to pervert many churches. Leaving ancient history, I will pass to times nearer to our own. Arius . . . began by misleading the Emperor's sister. . . . Lucilla helped Donatus. . . . The blind woman Agape led the blind man Elpidius. . . . He was followed by Priscillian . . . and a magician. . . . Galla seconded his efforts and left a gadabout sister to perpetuate a second heresy.[27]

### The New Prophecy Movement

As one of the above denounced "heretical" groups, the New Prophecy movement seems worth a closer look.

The New Prophecy movement emerged in Asia Minor in the second century C.E. Two women, Maximilla and Priscilla, initiated this movement, which was called the New Prophecy movement by its supporters. Soon they formed a co-leadership of three prophets: Maximilla, Priscilla, and Montanus. Its opponents called the group Montanist, identifying the two women co-leaders as the followers of the male co-leader Montanus.[28]

While the writings of Maximilla and Priscilla did not survive, many denunciations of them appear in extant texts of various church fathers. None of the church fathers' comments, however, contains real theological criticism. Rather, the women were denounced for engaging in revelation, prophecy, healing, writing books, and so forth. Some of these writings shed some light on who these women were and what they were doing.

When Tertullian was a member of the movement in the late second century, he wrote:

> We have now amongst us a sister whose lot it has been to be favored with gifts of revelation. . . . She converses with angels, and sometimes even with the Lord; she both sees and hears mysterious communications; . . . and she obtains directions for healing for such as need them. Whether it be in the reading of the Scriptures, or in the chanting of psalms, or in the preaching of sermons, or in the offering up of prayers, in all these religious services matter and opportunity are afforded her of seeing visions. . . . After the people are dismissed at the conclusion of the sacred services, she is in the regular habit of reporting to us whatever things she may have seen in vision; for all her communications are

examined with the most scrupulous care, in order that their truth may be probed.[29]

Their revelations were so highly valued in their communities that they were recorded, collected into books, and circulated widely. Tertullian's statements are the only ones that were written by an insider and not destroyed, possibly because he ceased to be a member of the movement and later achieved fame and status as a church father.

All the other comments came from opponents. Hippolytus stated in the early third century:

> But there are others who themselves are even more heretical in nature. . . . These have been rendered victims of error from being previously captivated by [two] wretched women . . . whom they supposed [to be] prophetesses. And they assert that into these the Paraclete Spirit had departed. . . . Being in possession of an infinite number of their books . . . they allege that they have learned something more through these wretched women above the Apostles and every gift of Grace, so that some of them presume to assert that there is in them a something superior to Christ.[30]

In the early third century Origen wrote, "Even if she says admirable things, or even saintly things, that is of little consequence, since they come from the mouth of a woman." Further, these women were denounced because of their daring to compose books under women's names. According to Eusebius (fourth century), a bishop Sotas tried to "drive the demon out of Priscilla," although unsuccessfully. Epiphanius (fourth century) writes that not only did they "revere Priscilla and Quintilla as prophets and founders of the movement, but women among them continued to prophesy and served as bishops, presbyters, and so forth."[31]

Since "an infinite number of their books" were utterly destroyed, and the only sources are scattered fragments found mostly in their adversaries' writings, it is difficult to reconstruct their messages correctly or comprehensively. The fragments do show, however, that they claimed that they were "compelled . . . to learn the knowledge of God" by the power of the Spirit, and that the power of the Spirit is given to every believer. One such fragment tells us about the Christ's appearance in the form of a female figure.

The movement encouraged and supported celibacy and chastity, and both Maximilla and Priscilla seem to have been celibate women. On the other hand, inscriptional evidence suggests that marriage and childbearing were common among the women of the movement. This indicates that the movement consisted mostly of families with children, but they advocated celibacy, probably to support especially those women who desired to have such a lifestyle in the midst of the patriarchal expectation for all women to marry.[32]

In the fourth century, when Christianity became the Roman state religion and those who held power in the patriarchal church obtained Roman political and military support, persecution against the New Prophecy movement became deadly. Under the first Christian Roman emperor, Constantine, "their churches were confiscated, their writings destroyed. . . . Their nearest Catholic relative could confiscate their estates and seize all their possessions." The New Prophecy movement managed to survive this severe persecution as well as other forms of persecution.

However, the persecution by the emperor Justinian in the sixth century seems to have been fatal. He began "by confiscating the properties of these sanctuaries, thus stripping them suddenly of all their wealth." They still persevered in the midst of such severe persecution. But finally, it is written that they shut "themselves up in their own sanctuaries . . . [and] set their churches on fire, so that they were destroyed." This report, however, should be read critically and with a certain amount of suspicion as to how they were actually "destroyed" in the end. Nevertheless, it is amazing that they survived even until the sixth century under such horrifying persecution.[33]

This brief glance at the New Prophecy movement gives much information about Christian women in the second and third century. Their struggle was the struggle against the patriarchal power that defined women's leadership as heresy and silenced women into patriarchal submission. Jerome's "summary" tells us that despite all the patriarchal male attempts and violence, women were not so easily controlled or restricted. There is no doubt that they suffered, but they really strove well in spite of great hardship. The constant denunciation and violence used to suppress women's leadership and to silence women are strong indicators of how prevalent women's leadership was and how influential their messages, prophecies, storytelling performances, and communal practices were in the earliest centuries.

PART TWO

# Hearing the Story of Martha and Mary with New Ears

# 8

## The Story and Its Characters

A feminist reading of the text of Martha and Mary (Jn 11:1—12:8) from the Johannine gospel brings into relief many of the characteristics of women's lives and roles in the early Christian communities. In itself, the text is very significant. It is located toward the end of the public ministry of Jesus and has at its center the last and the greatest sign of Jesus in his ministry. This culminating sign, the raising of Lazarus, is sandwiched between two strong faith confessions, both made by women. The first, Martha's christological confession that Jesus is the messiah, the son of God, can be viewed as a personal confession but also as the faith expression of the community. The second confession is made through the action of Mary's anointing of Jesus. This, again, can be viewed as a sign of personal devotion but also a communal model of discipleship.[1]

While the importance of a feminist rereading of this text seems obvious, little study of this text has been undertaken from critical feminist perspectives. Many scholars have examined this text, but their focus has been almost exclusively on the raising of Lazarus by Jesus, with two males as the focus and the two women left vaguely in the background. Consequently, Martha and Mary are known almost exclusively from the Lukan text (Lk 10:38-42), with the Johannine version of Martha and Mary's story receiving little critical attention. It would seem, though, that the Johannine text of Martha and Mary is a fertile ground for a critical feminist reading, particularly given our expanded historical imagination of women's lives during this period of time.[2]

To be sure, the Martha and Mary of the text were not members of actual Johannine communities. Instead, as characters in the story, Martha and Mary are contemporaries of Jesus and participants in the reign-of-God movement in the beginning of the first century. They are residents of Bethany, a village located on the east slope of the Mount of Olives in Judea, not quite two miles east of Jerusalem. As long as the text preserved certain elements of earlier oral traditions, these characters reflected some aspects of the historical Martha and Mary, or women like them, in the reign-of-God movement.

However, it was customary at that time for author/s to edit freely and recast earlier traditions in order to address their current audience. In this case, the audience was likely the Johannine communities of the last quarter of the first century. We should assume that the characters of Martha and Mary in the text do reflect aspects of people, especially women, in the Johannine communities. Thus, any re-visioning of Martha and Mary is also a re-visioning of the women and men in the Johannine communities.

## The Story

There is a general consensus among scholars that the core of the Johannine text 11:1—12:8 is a raising sign or miracle story into which other traditions have been interwoven. In first-century storytelling the customary components of a miracle story were a problem, a miracle, and the reaction to the miracle. In this case, the core tells of (1) a man who was sick and died, (2) Jesus' raising of the dead man, and (3) people who thus believed in Jesus.[3]

The text is structured in a chiastic form, or a cross-parallel (A-B-C-D-C'-B'-A') form. This is a common form for stories in oral/aural cultures and was used to focus the basic message of the story and to aid in memorization. Scholars differ somewhat in their division of the verses, because most ancient oral stories do not have a simple linear plot development but rather are like an "interwoven tapestry," with foreshadowing and echoing motifs, as well as overlapping structures. The form of Dorothy A. Lee's basic structure division, with modified titles based on this particular reading of the text, may be laid out as follows:[4]

> **A**. Lazarus under death threat
>    **B**. Martha's faith confession
>       **C**. Jesus' sharing in tears with Judean neighbors
>          **D**. Jesus' life-giving sign in the raising of Lazarus
>       **C'**. Judean authorities' plot to kill Jesus
>    **B'**. Mary's anointing service
> **A'**. Lazarus and Jesus under death threats

Thus, the story is constructed around the protagonist Jesus. Jesus and his believers live in a hostile world under death threats (A, A') because of his life-giving ministry (D). Two Judean groups, one of sympathetic neighbors and the second of hostile authorities, are presented in contrast (C, C'). Two models of discipleship, Martha's faith confession and Mary's anointing service, are presented in echoing contrast (B, B').[5]

In the text of the story of Mary and Martha, as well as in the entire Johannine gospel, the protagonist is the male character of Jesus. The character Jesus, a literary construct of the author/s, does not necessarily reflect the historical person of Jesus of Nazareth who lived in Palestine in the early first century, yet each story in the gospel reveals something of the author/s' understanding of him. Minor characters are presented as illustrative figures, representing different groups of people in the community, and they also illuminate Jesus.[6]

A careful analysis of how the character of Jesus is presented, along with an examination of the historical background, should yield a better understanding of who Jesus was in the eyes of the author/s and of what messages and visions the author/s wanted to convey through the story. Such an analysis may also indicate information the author/s chose to exclude or suppress.

Such a "resistant" reading—that is, a reading that goes against the grain— that critically reflects on how the characters are presented and that pays attention to gaps and contradictions in the text can help re-vision the Johannine women and their messages in their historical context.

## The Characters

### *Jesus—A Messiah Designated as Such by Women*

In this text it is the women who identify Jesus as the messiah. This is highly unusual. In the history of Israel, kings were designated by ritual anointing on the head by a prophet. The Hebrew word *messiah* (in Greek, *christos;* in English, christ) means "the anointed one." In this text (Jn 11:1—12:10), Jesus is mentioned first in reference to his having been anointed by a woman (11:2). In the middle of the story another woman verbally names him as messiah (11:27), and, then, toward the end of the story, he is presented again as the recipient of a woman's anointing (12:3). So Jesus, the protagonist, is first and foremost a messiah, the anointed one, and this designation has been made by both the words and action of women.

The act of anointing Jesus in the text has both conventional and unconventional aspects. The conventional image would call for a male prophet to anoint a king, but here the act is performed by a woman. The way in which the author/s introduce the character of Mary (11:2) indicates that this story of a woman anointing Jesus must have been well-known to the audience. In addition to this unusual anointing by a woman, the author/s make a peculiar shift in the story. It is Jesus' feet rather than his head that are anointed. This shift from head to feet may imply an attempt to downgrade the prophetic aspect of the Mary's action, but may also suggest a different conclusion. Later in his ministry (Jn 13) this messiah follows the woman's action by anointing/washing the feet for his own disciples. What the woman does for Jesus at the Bethany dinner, Jesus does for the disciples at the Last Supper as an example of model discipleship. By accepting his title from a woman and by following a woman's action, Jesus appears as a non-patriarchal and unconventional messiah.

## Jesus—An Elusive Prophet

As the story unfolds, when Jesus receives the message of Lazarus's sickness, he reveals his prophetic knowledge of the event. He knew that "this sickness is not unto death" (11:4), but that although "Lazarus is dead" (11:14), he is going to "awaken" Lazarus so that "you may believe" (11:15). The passage reads, "Then Jesus told them plainly, 'Lazarus is dead.'" To tell or speak plainly (or boldly; *parresia* in Greek) is a characteristic term for prophetic speech. In this gospel this term appears several times in reference to the speech of Jesus as a prophet (7:26; 10:24; 11:14; 16:25, 29; 18:20). However, given Jesus' prophetic knowledge and his "plain" speech, his disciples and the crowd find his behavior strange and incomprehensible. Jesus loves his friends in Bethany (11:5), but his delay makes him seem irresponsible or uncaring (11:6). In the end he decides to go there only after his friend is already dead (11:7-8), risking exposure to the hostile Judeans, who already have attempted to stone him.[7]

The audience may suspect that Jesus was inviting his own death and that of his friend Lazarus. However, the narrator has already repeatedly told the audience that Jesus can escape from any kind of violent circumstances, because it is not the power of the hostile Judeans but the "hour" the Father has set that will determine Jesus' life and death (2:4; 7:6; 10:18; 16:25, 32; 17:1). This Jesus cannot be grasped by mental comprehension or physical control. This elusiveness conforms to conventional Jewish and Greco-Roman understandings of inspired prophets, whose actions and speeches depend completely and only on the will of the divine and are often incomprehensible to ordinary people.[8]

Thus, the character Jesus plays the role of a divinely inspired and protected prophet whose actions and speeches derive from God. The people are to trust Jesus—even if his actions and speech are incomprehensible—because he does and will act according to God's will.

## Jesus—A Teacher of Ambiguities

When Jesus delivers a discourse on light to the disciples, none of them understands what he means (11:9-16). His teaching style appears intentionally ambiguous and open to misunderstanding.[9]

People of the Greco-Roman age appreciated certain elements of ambiguity. It was said that if the style of speech was too clear, people assumed that they had nothing new to learn and therefore were no longer interested in listening. To clothe a teaching with obscurity, sublimity, and solemnity was a storytelling technique to impress upon the audience that there was yet more to learn and comprehend. Furthermore, presenting characters as misunderstanding or not comprehending the teaching was a didactic or educational device used to create more occasions for the teacher to teach and to entertain the audience, giving the people the impression that they were making progress. It appears that the Johannine gospel may be utilizing these Greco-Roman rhetorical devices in its presentation of Jesus' teaching.[10]

At the same time, the ambiguity of Jesus' teaching comes mainly from his use of conventional Jewish terms but with unexpected meanings. For example, when Jesus meets Martha, she expresses her regret and grief. Jesus responds, "Your brother will be resurrected" (11:23). These are conventional Jewish words of condolence, yet Jesus meant more than this. Such use of ambiguity seems to suggest three things: (1) it appreciates the Jewish traditional heritage and claims that Jesus' teaching is rooted in this heritage; (2) it revises this heritage in its own context; and (3) it avoids immediate rejection or clashing confrontation, and invites the audience to different levels of "(mis)understanding." Thus, the character Jesus plays the role of a teacher who invites everybody to be interested in listening more and understanding more. While his teaching is rooted in its Jewish heritage, at the same time there is something new to be learned.

### Jesus—A Friend Responding in Love

When Jesus comes toward the village and meets Martha, she expresses her regret and grief and also articulates her trust in Jesus. Jesus responds immediately with the conventional Jewish words of condolence, "Your brother will be resurrected" (11:23). When he meets Mary, she also expresses her regret and weeps before Jesus (11:33). Jesus responds by expressing his own grief. Seeing Mary and the consoling neighbors weeping, Jesus "groaned *(embrimaomai)* in the spirit and troubled himself" (11:33). Then "Jesus shed tears" (11:35) and groaned again in front of the tomb (11:38). In the Greco-Roman world the term "groaned" was often used to express a miracle-worker's highly charged emotional condition as a preparation for the performance of a powerful miracle. It is possible that the use of the expression actually evoked this image to the Greco-Roman audience. If so, the gospel modifies its meaning to reflect Jesus' emotional involvement as "in the spirit."[11]

Jesus is presented as displaying very human emotion. Until this point the gospel has described Jesus as being without emotion. In commenting on the text 11:33-35, Sandra Schneiders says, "Jesus, in his most human moment in the Johannine gospel, legitimates human agony in the face of death." Jesus is a responsive friend who acts on behalf of the ones whom he loves (11:5), even at the risk of his own life.[12]

At the same time, the text affirms concern for the bodily life as well as the eternal life. In the synoptic gospels it is the temple incident that triggers the arrest of Jesus (Mk 11:15-19; Mt 21:12-17; Lk 19:45-48 versus Jn 2:13-22); in the Johannine gospel this raising sign is the decisive trigger for the plot to kill Jesus (Jn 12:9-12). The message is that the Johannine Jesus dies for the love for his friends (15:13) and that, while the character Jesus tells them that they will live even if they die (11:25), he does not dismiss the importance of bodily life. In the end Jesus risks his own life to raise Lazarus from bodily death.

It should also be noted that Jesus' friendship with two women, Mary and Martha, is mutual. Jesus receives his friends' designation as messiah, verbally by Martha and figuratively in the act of anointing by Mary. He is also a guest at a dinner presided over by Martha. The text presents these aspects of Jesus quite simply, without any polemical tone.

### Jesus—The Son of the Father

Before calling Lazarus to come out of the tomb, Jesus prays in thanksgiving, saying "Father, I thank you that you heard me" (11:42). Although Martha said, "Whatever you ask God, God will give you" (11:22), Jesus does not need to ask; he thanks the Father for having already heard him even before he asks. This thanksgiving indicates that Jesus' relationship with God is portrayed as something beyond even Martha's trust, and that it is not Jesus but God who raises Lazarus.

Jesus' relationship to God is much closer than Martha thought, and it is expressed using the father-son metaphor. As noted before, use of the father-son metaphor in the ancient culture of corporate personality presents Jesus as the most authentic and trustworthy agent of God. This allows him to say that he and the Father are one and that, at the same time, the Father is greater than the son.

Jesus makes it clear publicly that it is God, not he, who has raised Lazarus. Thus, precisely speaking, the text does not ascribe the divine power of raising the dead to Jesus. It is important to note that in the seven raising-sign stories in the Hebrew Bible and the Christian Testament, all miracle-workers pray to God before performing a raising sign, except Jesus. Only in the Johannine gospel does Jesus also pray to God.[13]

Before calling Lazarus to come out of the tomb, Jesus "lifted his eyes upward" (11:41). This expression probably sounded familiar to the Greco-Roman audience as part of a miracle-working performance. Yet in the present text this action leads Jesus to a thanksgiving prayer. He does not ask for the power to perform a sign or the miraculous. Rather, he acknowledges that it is God who has already given the sign. The humble Johannine Jesus does not equate himself with his contemporary Greco-Roman miracle-workers. While they work miracles by their own power, Jesus does not; it is God who performs the miraculous.[14]

### Jesus—The Leader of the New Exodus

When Jesus goes to Bethany, he does not immediately enter the village. Martha leaves her house and walks out to meet him. After talking with him, she then returns home and calls Mary, who, followed by consolers, also leaves the house and village to see Jesus. Strangely, Jesus is still there, outside the village, making both women go out.

At the tomb Jesus calls Lazarus to come out using colloquial language, something like "Lazarus, out here, out!" After Lazarus appears, Jesus' last word is "Let him go" (11:44), a rather strange remark in the presence of Mary and Martha, who would have been expected to take him home with them. Jesus is thus portrayed as calling everyone out. This use of language makes sense if exodus is a major underlying theme of the gospel.[15]

Three of the canonical gospels include the two signs in Galilee—a feeding of the multitude and the stilling of the storm at sea (Jn 6:1-21; Mk 6:30-52; Mt 14:13-27). Luke presents only the feeding sign (Lk 9:10-17). It is widely acknowledged that these stories evoke the signs of manna and the crossing of the sea in the Exodus, the foundational story of Israel. The intent seems to be to show that Jesus' feeding is more abundant than that of Moses and that Jesus' control over the sea is more perfect than that of Moses.[16]

In the Johannine gospel these two signs (Jn 6) are followed by the discourses at the Feast of Tabernacles, the feast that commemorates God's grace in the Exodus (Jn 7—8). Jesus presents himself as a greater leader than Moses (7:38; 8:12). These chapters are followed by Jesus' healing of the man born blind and the ensuing discourses on spiritual blindness and the lost sheep (Jn 9—10). On the surface these do not immediately connect with the theme of exodus, but, indeed, the theme continues in these chapters. The narration does not evoke the Israelite Exodus but rather the exodus story of Homer's Odysseus from a cave of death to life.

Oona Ajzenstat has identified seventeen motifs that appear in almost the same sequence in these chapters of the Johannine gospel and in chapter 9 of Homer's *Odyssey*, one of the most popular stories of the Greco-Roman period. In the story Odysseus and his men became captives of a monstrous man and are locked in a dark cave closed by a stone door. In the end Odysseus leads a successful exodus to life by making their captor blind.[17]

Parallel motifs include blindness, a good shepherd, a stranger, a thief, a cave door blocked by a stone, escape, and so on. It is interesting to observe that the sequence of Jesus' references to "father" exactly corresponds to those in the *Odyssey* (10:25-30/475-79, 10:32/502-5, 10:34-38/523-25) and that Jesus' saying, "No one takes it [my life] from me" (10:18), corresponds to the saying "No one is killing me" (408) in the *Odyssey*. Again, Jesus is presented as an even greater leader than Odysseus. When one of Odysseus's men dies and falls into hell, Odysseus visits him but cannot bring him back. Jesus, however, was able to bring his dead friend back to life. This somewhat broader look at chapters 6 to 10 of the Johannine gospel includes images of the exodus for life from both Jewish and Greek traditions. Chapter 11, when Jesus makes everyone "go out" toward him, presents Jesus as the great leader of the new exodus for new life, not only for Jewish people but for all the children of God.

### Martha—A Trusting Disciple and Friend

The character Martha, is, along with Mary, first identified as a friend of Jesus, one whom Jesus loves (11:5). The sisters are disciples. The Johannine gospel identifies the teacher-disciple relationship using two terms for Jesus, "teacher" and "lord" (13:13). Martha and Mary both call Jesus "teacher" (11:28) and "lord" (11:21, 32), using the same form of address as the male disciples (11:8, 12). Thus, Jesus, their friend, is also presented as a teacher for Martha and Mary, and they are presented as his disciples.[18]

In the midst of hardship and grieving for her brother, Lazarus, Martha asks Jesus for help. Even after the disappointing absence of Jesus at her brother's death, she states both her regret and her trust in him: "But even now I know that whatever you ask God, God will give you" (11:21-22). Martha's statement contains the first two elements of the traditional Jewish lament, the address and the complaint. Martha is petitioning God through Jesus and, at the same time, acknowledging God as the source of Jesus' power.[19]

In response Jesus engages Martha in a brief theological dialogue and pronounces his seventh and last "I am" revelation: "I am the resurrection and the life" (11:25). Martha responds with a confession of her faith. At first Martha says "I know" without realizing her partial knowledge; however, upon receiving Jesus' "I am" revelation, Martha says, "I have believed," using the perfect tense in Greek (11:27). The growth of her faith is shown in the movement from "I know" (11:22, 24) to "I have come to believe" or "I continue to believe" (11:27)—even before seeing the sign Jesus will perform.[20]

### Martha—A Representative Spokesperson of the Community

Martha's faith confession, "You are the Christ, the son of God, the one who is to come into the world" (11:27), echoes the author/s' motivation in writing this gospel: "and these things are written so that you may believe that Jesus is the Christ, the son of God, and that believing you may have life in his name" (20:31). Martha thus takes on the role of the spokesperson who attests for the faith of this community. This is noteworthy because this role is played by Peter in the other three gospels (Mt 16:16; Mk 8:29; Lk 9:20).[21]

Martha's hesitation at the removal of the stone (11:39) has puzzled many scholars. However, if the exodus story of Odysseus is a subtext, as noted above, the hesitation or questioning of Martha becomes significant and understandable. In the story of Odysseus's exodus, the removal of the stone door is a crucial symbol for the exodus from the cave of death to life. If the audience of the time had this imagery in mind, then Martha's hesitation and her implied assent to remove the stone has a symbolic importance. Martha appears as a representative spokesperson and leader whose trust and assent are sought by Jesus at the last moment in his sign inviting an exodus to new life. At the same time, I would suggest that through the description of Martha's hesitation we may hear whispers of dissenting voices within the Johannine communities regarding the kind of new exodus they seek.[22]

### Martha—A Leader in Ministry

Martha serves by ministering (serving) not only by word (11:27) but also at a communal table at which Jesus is a guest (12:2). The significance of Martha's serving is apparent in the specific use of certain words in this gospel.

1. The word "dinner" *(deipnon)* is used only twice: for this dinner in Bethany, and for the Last Supper in Jerusalem (12:2; 13:2, 4; 21:20).

2. The word "serve" *(diakoneo)* is used only twice: for Martha's serving (12:2), and in Jesus' discourse on true discipleship (12:26).

3. The noun form of "serve," namely "servant" *(diakonos)*, appears only twice: in Jesus' discourse on true discipleship (12:26), and in Jesus' first miracle in Cana, where Jesus' mother tells the servants *(diakonos)* to do whatever Jesus tells them (2:5).[23]

The limited use of these words for dinner, serve, and servant implies that Martha's service here is a ministerial service. She is a representative disciple who engages both in service of the word (to proclaim communal faith) and in service at the table (to preside at the communal table/the eucharist).

The same term for serve is also used in the Lukan gospel (Lk 10:40). This may reflect an early or different version in which Martha served as a minister. The Lukan text also addresses Martha by calling her name twice: "Martha, Martha . . . " (10:41). This usage has biblical parallels of others being called to ministry, for example, Jacob (Gen 46:2), Moses (Ex 3:4), Samuel (1 Sam 3:4), and Paul (Acts 9:4). It is conceivable that Luke's passage ("Martha, Martha, only one thing is necessary") is reminiscent of a tradition in which Jesus called Martha for ministry. Perhaps the story of Martha's ministry was widely known, since it was used in both the Lukan and the Johannine gospels. It is regrettable that this image of Martha as a minister is not clearly developed in either text.[24]

At the same time, there is a significant and clear difference between the Lukan text and the Johannine text. The Lukan gospel pits Martha against Mary. As a result, both her ministry and personality are severely downgraded. In this instance the Lukan text trivializes women and portrays them as quarrelsome and helpless, relying on male authority. By contrast, in the Johannine gospel the two sisters collaborate, each engaging in service. While the Johannine gospel maintains the significance of Martha's ministry through the use of specific terms for her service, the reference to her service is described in a short, unstressed phrase that may have considerably downplayed her role. This somewhat contradictory presentation may indicate some editorial manipulation that has obscured the reality of women's ministry.[25]

### Mary—A Well-known Disciple and Friend

The beginning of the text identifies Bethany as Mary's village (11:1), Lazarus as her brother (11:2), and it refers to her act of anointing Jesus. Mary's name must have been well-known to readers or listeners, and it must have been recognized that she was important not only for the Johannine communities but for other Christian communities as well.

The character Mary is also a trusting disciple and friend of Jesus. Like Martha, Mary leaves her house and village to meet Jesus, and she expresses her grief in tears in front of him. The Judean neighbors who follow her also weep, as does Jesus, and together they go to the tomb. In the text Mary appears as a well-known disciple and friend of Jesus who is firmly grounded and supported in the Judean community. There is no hint of conflict with "the Judeans."[26]

### Mary—A Leader with Judean Followers

In the text Mary is repeatedly described in connection with Judeans: they "had come to her" (11:19), were "being with her" (11:31), "followed her" (11:31), "came with her" (11:32), and "had come to Mary" (11:45). Elisabeth Schüssler Fiorenza suspects that in an earlier tradition Mary may have had some followers around her who were led to believe in Jesus (11:45). So Mary appears as a friend and disciple of Jesus and is a leader of Judean followers. These aspects are present in the text, but they are not rhetorically stressed or, rather, they are ambiguous. This may be another example of the editorial suppression of women's leadership.[27]

### Mary—A Model for Jesus

When Mary witnesses Jesus' raising miracle, she perceives the loving action of Jesus that is carried out at the risk of his own life. She responds by anointing his feet with costly oil and wiping off the oil with her hair. Soon after this incident Jesus himself performs footwashing at the Last Supper. It could be said that Mary is assigned the role of modeling discipleship, a model followed even by Jesus. The two scenes have several parallels:

1. Both occur within the context of Passover.
2. As noted above, the word "dinner" *(deipnon)* is used only twice: here in Bethany, and elsewhere for the Last Supper.
3. At both dinners Jesus is with those whom he loved.
4. In both scenes a beloved friend (Lazarus/the Beloved Disciple) is described as "reclining" with Jesus.[28]
5. In both scenes Judas's negative presence is mentioned, identifying him as treasurer and referring to his betrayal and the money box.
6. In both scenes the acts of foot anointing/washing are mentioned with the description of wiping off *(ekmasso)*, using a Greek term that appears only in these scenes.[29]
7. Both acts occur rather awkwardly in the middle of the dinner, not before dinner, which was common practice.[30]
8. Both acts are presented as loving service.
9. Both scenes are linked to Jesus' farewell or death.

These numerous parallels strongly suggest intention on the part of the author/s. It seems possible that there might have been different versions of the story of the Last Supper, and that the account of Mary and Martha in the Johannine gospel was used to counter-balance the invisibility of women in the scene of the Last Supper in Jerusalem.[31]

On the other hand, women's anointing stories are presented in all four canonical gospels (Mk 14:3-9; Mt 26:6-13; Jn 12:1-8; Lk 7:36-50). Each one is slightly different, but all four versions have certain elements in common: a woman's anointing of Jesus at a meal, a male objection, and Jesus' support for the woman's action. The male objection to the woman's action may indicate that some tension existed between men and women within the reign-of-God movement from a very early time.

### Mary—Prophet or Devoted Disciple?

An earlier version of this story from Mark tells of a woman anointing Jesus on his head rather than his feet (Mk 14:3; Mt 26:7), an action with certain implications. Anointing a head was associated with the political act of a prophet designating a king. It was also a sign of honor, well-being, prosperity, peace, gladness, abundance, hospitality, comfort, and service, and was used for cosmetic, hygienic, and medical purposes.[32]

Anointing feet with oil was associated with preparation for burial, generally by a close female relative, or it represented extraordinary luxury. Footwashing was also used for rituals, hygiene, hospitality, and service, with the strongest image being the service of a slave. Anointing or washing was usually performed before a meal or some other occasion.[33]

The image of preparation for burial indicates that Jesus acknowledges Mary to be one of the persons closest to him. In the text, however, the shift from anointing head to anointing feet is combined with the mention of Mary's wiping Jesus' feet with her hair and drastically shifts the imagery into a humble, loving act of devotion (feet anointing).[34]

But how and why is the motif of hair introduced? According to Marianne Sawicki, the verb *katacheo* (to pour down) means "to let down (hair)" in the middle voice. In the course of the retelling processes, a woman's anointing story seems to have been transformed dramatically. Thus, in one version of the story a woman pours oil on Jesus' head (Mk 14:3; Mt 26:7), and in another she lets her hair flow down (Jn 12:3; Lk 7:38). This flowing down of hair seems to have fascinated some male fantasy. The woman's political and prophetic daring action was diverted, and the woman's position "from above" to Jesus' head was shifted to "from below" to Jesus' feet with the woman's hair being applied to his feet.

Still, the story, in its different versions, is told at the opening of the passion narrative in the Markan and Matthean gospels as well as in the Johannine gospel. Even in the quite different version in Luke, the story was "too important to leave out of the text" or "had to be dealt with, one way or another."

Thus, in the Johannine text, while Mary's anointing seems to be intentionally presented as an especially significant performance of model discipleship, we cannot overlook the possible suppression or omission of political and prophetic aspect of her action.[35]

In the story there is a phrase that makes it plausible that the anointing story goes back to women's memories of the historical Jesus. That is the phrase "Let her be" (Jn 12:7; Mk 14:6). In a group-oriented society, to which the ancient Jewish society seems to have belonged (and I believe that today's Japan still belongs), it is often particularly difficult for a woman to do something that might invite displeasure or cause trouble in the group. In order to dare to undertake such an action, a woman has to be very determined about what she is going to do and about whatever denunciation and difficulty she might face. "Let her be" is the strongest liberating support a woman could wish to receive in such a milieu. If the historical Jesus spoke such words to support a certain daring action of a woman in the face of male opposition, surely women would not let them be forgotten but would hold on to the words for encouragement and support.[36]

### Lazarus

At the beginning of the text, Lazarus is introduced as a person from Bethany, the village of Martha and Mary (11:1). In the Greco-Roman world it was common for a person to be introduced by his or her place of origin or residence, but it was not common at all for a man to be introduced by women's names. The story, however, introduces the character Lazarus as a "brother" of Mary as well as a friend and a disciple of Jesus (11:3, 5; 12:2). In all of these roles Lazarus is a passive recipient of help and love, which was the usual role of female characters.[37]

At the end of the text he is again put under death threat, this time not by illness but by the Judean authorities (12:10). Most biblical scholars understand this to mean that Lazarus represents the Johannine Christians, who were facing the suffering and death of community members. If so, Lazarus's passive role enhances the trusting and active roles the sisters Martha and Mary play in the face of communal suffering and death. This may also suggests that Johannine women were actually practicing leadership roles in their communities.[38]

### Thomas

The figure of Thomas appears briefly, just before Jesus leaves to go to Bethany. When Jesus says, "Let us go into Judea again," the disciples object, "Just lately the Judeans sought to stone you" (11:8). Jesus replies with a discourse on light, and then Thomas bravely suggests to his co-disciples that they accompany him, even if this may end in their deaths as well: "Let us also go, so that we would die with him" (11:16). The term "co-disciples" appears only this one time in the entire Christian Testament. It may reflect Thomas's orientation toward equal discipleship. To die for the sake of a friend is exactly what Jesus later commends to his disciples as the greatest love (15:13), and this is what Jesus is going to do. Thomas is portrayed here as trying to be such a model disciple.

However, when this passage is compared with texts in the *Gospel of Thomas,* different insights emerge. In the *Gospel of Thomas* revelation enlightens everyone who accepts the revelation, and it brings forth a community of revealed revealers. By believing, people obtain light within and become co-disciples—not co-disciples of Jesus, but co-disciples *with* Jesus of God. The words of Jesus in the Johannine text, "he stumbles, because the light is not in him" (11:9), speak a warning directly to Thomas (11:16): although Thomas's determined discipleship is commendable, he does not have the light in him.[39]

In the *Gospel of Thomas,* Jesus says, "I am not your lord," denying his superiority to Thomas, but in the Johannine gospel, Thomas makes a faith confession in the end, "My Lord, my God" (20:29). Thomas, the advocate of equal discipleship with Jesus, and the disciple who reveals this good news of Jesus in the *Gospel of Thomas,* is ironically presented in the Johannine text as a committed disciple but one who must be led to confess Jesus' superiority after seeing the risen Jesus. Moreover, Thomas, the male disciple who believes after seeing, is contrasted with Martha, the female disciple who believes without seeing.[40]

This seems quite a manipulative presentation and causes an alert reader to wonder whether or not other characters might also be manipulated to speak and act in ways that conform to authorial interpretations of who Jesus was. Perhaps some members of the Johannine community were committed to co-discipleship with Jesus, and the author/s were intent on subordinating everyone to Jesus in the way that the author/s believed right.

### *Judas*

In other versions of the anointing story some people or disciples object to Mary's anointing action (Mk 14:4; Mt 26:8), but in the Johannine text it is Judas Iscariot who objects, saying, "Why is this perfumed oil not sold . . . and the money given to the poor?" (12:5). Mary uses the costly perfumed oil not on Jesus' head but on his feet. To a first-century mind such an action would have been a wasteful display of luxury. Judas's objection makes sense, but it is refuted by Jesus. Why was Judas chosen to make the objection?

In all the canonical gospels Judas is the betrayer. In the Johannine gospel, however, whenever Judas appears on the scene, he is referred to as a betrayer. After Peter's confession Jesus foretells Judas's betrayal (6:71). At the dinner in Bethany (12:4) and at the Last Supper (13:2, 21) Judas is also mentioned as a betrayer, with a reference also to the "money box" (12:6; 13:2, 26, 29). Finally, at the arrest scene of Jesus, Judas is portrayed as a betrayer, leading and standing with the Roman soldiers (18:2, 5).

Since the word "betrayer" is repeatedly attached to Judas' name, the labeling seems intentional. What Judas actually does in the entire gospel consists of only two things: he objects to Mary's action in Bethany, and he helps the Roman authorities arrest Jesus. In the gospel Judas's objection to Mary's action is not simply a male objection. It is identified clearly as the objection of Judas the betrayer. Therefore, anyone who objects to a woman's commitment to Jesus would have had to consider the risk of being linked to Judas, the betrayer of Jesus. This can be seen as extraordinarily strong support for women's commitment.

It is also helpful to consider the specific link between Judas the betrayer and the "money box." As noted above, anointing feet with costly oil evoked an image of extravagant luxury. It would make sense for someone in charge of the group's finances to object to such extravagance. Although Jesus' repudiation of such an objection could be used to silence or trivialize financial concerns for the poor, the text is careful about this danger. Immediately after Judas's objection the narrator of the gospel adds that "he [Judas] said this not because he cared about the poor, but because he was a thief; he kept the common purse and used to steal what was put into it" (12:6). Later in the gospel, when Judas is mentioned again, the narrator says, "Some thought that, because Judas had the common purse, Jesus was telling him, 'Buy what we need for the festival'; or, that he should give something to the poor" (13:29). This shows that, according to the gospel, it was customary for the group to be concerned about and to aid the poor.[41]

This portrayal conveys a criticism of those men who had access to funds and pretended to care for the poor, but who were not really concerned for the poor, the majority of whom were women. As a whole, the negative presentation of Judas seems to offer strong support for Mary's commitment and at the same time validate concerns for the poor.

While this account of Mary and Martha seems somewhat affirming of the role of the women, if the Johannine gospel had indeed presented Mary anointing Jesus on his head and had then presented Judas the betrayer as opposing her, with Jesus defending her daring political and prophetic action, it would surely have offered direct affirmation of the role women played. However, the Johannine text does not tell the story this way. Mary's position above Jesus' head is shifted to below Jesus' feet. This invites the audience to discipleship to Jesus in devotional service while subtly dissuading the audience or the Johannine women and men from thinking of themselves as co-prophets who work as co-disciples with Jesus.

### Judean Neighbors, the Crowd, and Authorities

In the Johannine text the Judean neighbors appear supportive of Martha and Mary in their grief: "And many of the Judeans had come to Martha and Mary to console them" (11:19). When Mary left the village to meet Jesus, they followed her, wept with her, guided Jesus to Lazarus's tomb, witnessed

Jesus' sign, and came to believe in Jesus (11:31, 33, 34, 45). Later in the gospel these supportive Judean neighbors become the core of "the great crowd of the Judeans" who welcomed Jesus into Jerusalem and "bore witness" to him (12:9, 12, 13, 17). In contrast, the Judean authorities played the role of oppressive non-believers who plotted to kill Jesus because of their fear of the Romans (11:48, 53, 57; 12:10, 11). There seems to be a clear distinction between the Judean neighbors and the Judean authorities. This division of people into two camps started at an early stage of Jesus' ministry. What at first was described as "murmuring" among various people (6:41, 61; 7:12, 32) later developed into division (7:43; 9:16; 10:19). Toward the end of Jesus' ministry these divisions are repeatedly presented as being between the non-believing authorities and the believing crowd (11:45, 46, 53, 57; 12:9, 10, 11, 17, 19).

The word "crowd" *(ochlos)* appears twenty times in the gospel. Ten times it is depicted in a positive way, as following or believing (6:2, 5, 22, 24; 7:31, 40; 11:42; 12:9, 12, 17); nine times in a neutral way, as puzzled, murmuring, divided, and denounced by the Judean authorities (5:13; 7:12x2, 32, 43, 49; 12:18, 29, 34); and only once in a negative way (7:20). So, seen as a whole, while the Judean authority figures are presented quite negatively, the "crowd" is portrayed in a favorable light. Not particularly courageous fighters against the authorities, they murmur and stumble, and their believing is neither stable nor satisfactory. Nevertheless, many are gradually led to support or believe in Jesus.[42]

This contrast between the authorities and the crowd is also seen at the time of Jesus' arrest. All the other canonical gospels mention the Judean authorities and the crowd. Only the Johannine gospel clearly points to the primary presence of the Roman power and the complicity of the Judean authorities but not the crowd (18:3, 12). Thus, the Judean authorities are the oppressive hostile leaders of the Jewish people and allies of the oppressive Roman power.[43]

In this gospel the Judean authorities' *gathering* to plot to kill Jesus (11:47, 53) is contrasted with the purpose of Jesus' life and death: "to *gather* into one the scattered children of God" (10:15-16; 12:32). In the present text Jesus' powerful life-giving sign (the raising of Lazarus) leads a great crowd of Judeans to desert their authorities and believe in Jesus; this same action drives the Judean authorities to plot to kill both Jesus and Lazarus (12:9-11). Therefore the gospel seems to be asking readers or hearers to join "the crowd" instead of "the authorities." The Johannine communities seem to have consisted of people who identified or had no difficulty in identifying themselves this way.[44]

As we have seen, the Johannine gospel shows daring political resistance in its clear depiction of the Roman initiative to arrest Jesus, as well as in its appropriation of Roman imperial titles for Jesus. At the same time, the gospel is careful not to offend Rome or to invite Roman retaliation by using the phrase "not of this world" in regard to the concept of Jesus' *basileia* or the reign of God (18:36). Scholars agree that this gospel uses nuanced expressions with double meanings. Such a phrase as "not of this world" enables the communities to survive under Roman imperial rule. On the other hand, the gospel's polemic or criticism against the Judean authorities leaves no room for ambiguity. This reflects the keen insider criticism with which the ancient Jewish people were familiar.[45]

## Summary

The protagonist Jesus plays the roles of messiah, prophet, teacher, friend, son, and new exodus leader. In portraying Jesus in all these roles the audience is being asked to trust and believe in Jesus even in the midst of incomprehensible hardship, since he is a most trustworthy agent and sign-worker of God, a non-patriarchal messiah whose teaching is rooted in the Jewish heritage, and also a responsive friend who will act on behalf of his friends even at the cost of his own life.

Supporting this message, Martha appears as a trusting disciple and friend who engages both in the service of the word (to proclaim the communal faith) and in the service of the table (to preside the communal table at the Bethany dinner). In her actions of service (ministry) she plays the role of community representative. In an echoing and contrasting way to Martha's discipleship, Mary plays the role of trusting disciple and friend with prophetic perception whose performance is later imitated by Jesus as a model of discipleship for the community.

Lazarus is assigned the role of a man who is under death threat both at the beginning and at the end of the story. He is a brother of the sisters Martha and Mary, and a disciple and friend of Jesus. In all of these roles Lazarus is a passive recipient of help and love, the role typically assigned to women characters in Greco-Roman stories.

Some important observations can be made. First, Jesus is presented as the greatest person: a healer/sign-worker and the most trustworthy prophet/revealer of God. At the same time, the gospel is careful to show that all his power is derived from God; Jesus is not made a god. Jesus is also presented as a non-patriarchal messiah/Christ, so designated by women both verbally and figuratively in an unconventional way. The Johannine communities seem to have shown a strongly negative and resistant ethos toward authority figures, both Roman and Judean.

Although women appear as firmly embedded in their Judean neighborhood, there is a strong message for the audience to enact a new exodus from the Judean parent body. There seem to have been different opinions or perhaps internal community conflicts about what kind of new life the communities envision flowing out of the exodus, given their oppressive political and religious situations.

Finally, the gospel presents a contradictory message regarding women. On the one hand, women play leading roles in making faith confessions and in modeling discipleship, roles that are not assigned to any male figures. On the other hand, some aspects of their prophetic and ministerial leadership are considerably downplayed. This may also reflect internal conflicts within the communities about the distinctive leadership practices of women. The author/s and editor/s seem intent at times on obscuring the significance of women's leadership, although not denying their leadership practices. The author/s may also be intent on subordinating them under the lord Jesus, as interpreted by the author/s, while many of the Johannine women had their self-identities as prophets and children of Sophia, viewing themselves in co-ministry with Jesus, their teacher and friend.

# 9

## Ethnicity, Class, and Gender of the Story World

The previous chapter observed that the Johannine gospel presents the character of Jesus as the greatest sign-worker and the most trustworthy prophet or revealer of God, without making him God. It was also noted that there were possible intra-community conflicts and different theological views regarding the future and different understandings of discipleship advocated by community members. An examination of the areas of ethnicity, class (social status), and gender should shed some light on these different views and help better envision Martha and Mary in their historical contexts.[1]

### Ethnicity

It is widely accepted that the historical Jesus and his first followers were ethnic Jews. More specifically, Jesus and most of his first followers were Galileans. It is safe to assume that the first-century Jewish audience "knew" that the characters Jesus and his disciples were Galileans, but how is the ethnicity of the other characters constructed in the text?

Their names are popular Jewish names. Lazarus, a common name at the time, means "God helps" in Hebrew. Mary derives its origin from Miriam, recalling the prophet Miriam, who seems to have been remembered in oral traditions as a co-leader of the Exodus journey of Israel. It was a very popular name. Martha means "matron" or "sovereign lady" in Aramaic but does not necessarily imply wealth. According to Tal Ilan's study, in the first century about half of all Jewish women were called Miriam (Mariamme/Mary) or Salome. Martha was next in popularity. Since all three characters were presented with common Jewish names, it can be assumed that Martha, Mary, and Lazarus were presented as Jewish. More specifically, their residence in Bethany in Judea, close to Jerusalem, strongly suggests that they were Judeans.[2]

It becomes clear in this gospel that Jewish people from different regional backgrounds were all explicitly included among those who believed in Jesus. First, those from Transjordan (east of the Jordan river) came to believe in Jesus (Jn 1:28, 49; 10:40-42), followed by the Samaritans (Jn 4:39-42) and the Galileans (Jn 4:43-54). Then, in chapter 11, after earlier negative descriptions of Judeans, the Judeans are described as supportive neighbors of Martha, Mary, and Lazarus, who were friends of Jesus. This may reflect an authorial intention to invite all Jewish people into this inclusive community.

### Redefinition of "People of God"

The intention to build a new communal identity based not on ethnicity but on faith may be reflected in the author/s' use of the words "people" *(laos)* and "nation" *(ethnos)* (Jn 11:49-52). After Jesus' raising of Lazarus, the Judean authorities gather together and the high priest Caiaphas says, "It is better to have one man die for the people than to have the whole nation destroyed" (11:49-50). In the verses that immediately follow, Caiaphas's prophecy is rephrased by the narrator: "Jesus was about to die for the nation, and not for the nation only, but to gather into one the dispersed children of God" (11:51-52). When Caiaphas's prophecy is referred to a third time, in 18:14, the wording is repeated exactly as the character Caiaphas said it. This repetition of Caiaphas's prophecy in the middle of the passion narrative indicates how important that phrase was for the gospel: Jesus should die for the people.[3]

The replacement of the word "people" *(laos)* with "nation" *(ethnos)* in 11:51-52 seems intentional. Caiaphas prophesies that Jesus should die for the people (the Jewish people as the chosen people of God), so that the entire nation (the Jewish people as the civil organization) will not perish. In the rephrasing of Caiaphas's words by the narrator, Jesus is going to die for the nation (the Jewish people), but also for all the children of God (all people) so that all people might be gathered into one (become "people of God"). By attaching the word "all" to the "children of God," the narrator emphasizes inclusivity: both Jewish people and gentiles. And, in the narrative, the definition of the new and truly chosen people of God derives from their faith, not their birth. When Caiaphas's prophecy is repeated a third time (18:14), it is presented as Jesus' dying for those who are "people" of God, referring again to their belief rather than their birth. These people include not only the Judean crowd but also "Greeks" who come to see Jesus at the end of his ministry (12:20). Thus, while all the characters in the text are Jewish, the author/s seem intent on blurring or crossing ethnic boundaries.[4]

### The Ambiguous Use of "Judeans"

This ethnically inclusive vision of a new identity seems to come not simply from innocent open-mindedness, but more from an authorial intent to encourage a new exodus from the hostile Jewish parent body. The Judean neighbors were not hostile but supportive, and the crowd, as a whole, is depicted positively rather than negatively, in contrast to the Judean authorities. Needless to say, the crowd is the majority and the authorities are the minority of the Judeans. However, it has been pointed out by most scholars that the gospel still gives the impression that the Judeans were quite hostile to Jesus.

In the first century the term "Judeans" was used loosely to refer to the entire Jewish people as well as to those of Judean residence. The word appears in this gospel as many as seventy times, both specifically and broadly, as if the author/s are intentionally making use of the ambiguity. The gospel never articulates that "good" characters such as Jesus and the first followers were among the "Judeans" in a broader sense of the term (meaning Jewish persons). Rather, the gospel uses a different word, "Israel," in positive references to Jewish people (1:31, 47, 49; 3:10; 12:13). The result is a negative impression of Judeans as a whole.[5]

Scholars assume that this may reflect the Johannine communities' conflicts with some local synagogues. It may also indicate internal criticism of the Jewish authorities' response or lack of response to the extremely oppressive and life-threatening circumstances that existed under Roman imperial rule. The Johannine author/s might have been encouraging Johannine communities to enact a new exodus from their Judean parent body. At the same time, it is worth noting that women-related texts in the gospel do not show any sign of conflict; rather, the women characters are firmly embedded in and supported by their Judean neighbors.

## Class

Most scholars assume that Martha and Mary were wealthy sisters who lived without too many worldly or economic concerns. This would have placed them among the privileged few, as most of the people in colonized lands were poor. Unless there is firm evidence to the contrary, it should not be simply assumed that they belonged to the elite over against the majority of the poor.

As indications of their wealth, some scholars point out that Martha's name means "matron" or "sovereign lady"; that the presence of "many hired mourners" testifies to their wealth; that Lazarus was buried in a tomb, indicating their comfortable economic situation; and that Mary used costly oil for anointing Jesus' feet. Scholars also note that Martha has a house where she offers a dinner to Jesus and the disciples and that their reclining to eat indicates a large house.[6]

However, these may not serve as adequate proof. As mentioned already, the name Martha was a very common name and did not necessarily signify wealth. The text does not specify that the many weeping Judean people around Martha and Mary were "hired mourners." The text says only, "Many of the Judeans had come to Martha and Mary to console them" (11:19). These Judean neighbors are never referred to as mourners or (professional) keening women but described as Judeans who came to console the sisters. The word "console" *(paramutheomai)*, used twice in the text to describe them (11:19, 31), is not a typical word for mourning or keening, as were "lament," "cry," or "beat [one's] breasts" *(threneo, klaio,* or *kopto)*. On the other hand, the wording and descriptions in the text—that they came to console the sisters and that they followed Mary and wept with her in front of Jesus (11:31)—indicate that the many Judeans were sympathetic friends rather than hired mourners.[7]

Similarly, the burial of Lazarus in a tomb does not necessarily indicate wealth. The text refers to Lazarus' tomb as a cave (11:38). The use of cave tombs seems to have been common and does not itself indicate wealth. In the first century cave graves were accessible to common people, even the poor. It is possible that the deceased destitute were buried in cave graves or field graves by charitable Judean groups in the neighborhood as a sign of reverence for the deceased. Such charitable or mutual-help systems existed among many ethnic, religious, and collegial groups. The sisters' simple use of a cave grave, not a large tomb of complex interlocking chambers, can indicate their "ordinary" status.[8]

Mary's use of costly oil for Jesus can indicate wealth. It is also possible that, even though poor, she might have had such an item at her disposal. In such a case, if she was poor, she would have saved it for a very special occasion. For Mary, this dinner might have been such an occasion, and Jesus' words "she has kept it" (Jn 12:7) seem to imply such a situation, rather than that Mary bought it specifically for this use.[9]

The narrative does not describe Martha's house or the dinner she offered. The house did not have to be large or the dinner elaborate for Martha to extend the invitation. She may not have been destitute, yet a poor woman still could have owned or rented a humble house and offered a humble dinner to her friends. As discussed above, it appears that most of the earliest house churches were quite humble.

One phrase in the text requires caution. Lazarus is depicted as "one of those who were reclining with him [Jesus]" (Jn 12:2). It was customary at elite male public meals to recline on couches in the dining room. For guests to recline on couches required a spacious dining room, and thus, the above phrase seems to imply a sizable house, not a small *insula* (apartment) or tenement house. Should we, then, assume that Martha owns a sizable house and is not among the ordinary poor?

Here I wonder whether the expression "reclining" for eating in a house always meant "reclining on a couch," thus implying a spacious and luxurious dining room. Even if it was the stereotypical picture we get from the ancient elite male literature, is it not possible that the majority of the poor people had differing images? For example, is it not conceivable that some people pictured Martha as a woman like someone in their neighborhood who happened to own an old, sizable house and lived very humbly with her sisters and/or children? Or, is it not plausible that ordinary poor people also occasionally reclined to eat, not on couches but on the floor in a small house?

In the texts of Jesus' feeding of the multitude, all four gospels tell us that people reclined to eat on the ground (*analkinomai*: Mk 6:39; Mt 14:19; Lk 9:14, 15; *anapisto*: Jn 6:10). If they reclined on the ground, should we not imagine that in smaller houses poor people sometimes reclined on the floor, especially on special occasions of dinners among close friends? The room must be very crowded, but who among the poor, especially among close friends, would mind being together in a crowded closeness? Is it not likely that ordinary poor people who were gathering at small house churches heard the story with this kind of imagination, rather than the stereotypical image of elite males? If the answer is yes, then, we may imagine that Martha's house was not necessarily presented in the text as a spacious, luxurious one.

In parallel texts of the anointing story, Jesus reclined in the house of Simon the leper (Mk 14:3; Mt 26:6-7) and in a Pharisee's house (Lk 7:37). This may imply that the setting of the story in some traditions was a spacious house of wealthy men, and that the Johannine text preserved the word "reclining" to maintain the special parallels between this dinner in Bethany and the Last Supper in Jerusalem.

Another possible sign of the status of the family is the material used for Lazarus's burial cloth. As Lazarus comes out of the tomb, he is described as having his feet and hands "bound with strips of cloth *(keiriais)*" instead of "wrapped with the burial cloth" (11:44). Scholars agree that this story comes from a very early tradition, and that the gospel tends to keep the wording of earlier traditions. Scholars also agree that the Johannine gospel's language is often both symbolic and practical. What, then, does this word for burial cloth possibly indicate?[10]

In the gospel stories it is mentioned that Jesus' body was wrapped in a linen cloth. The Greek term for linen cloth is *sindon*, which refers to "fine cloth," usually linen. In Mark 15:46, the Greek text reads "wrapped it [Jesus' body] in the linen cloth *(sindon)*"; in Luke 23:53, Jesus is "wrapped in a linen cloth *(sindon)*"; and in Matthew 27:59, he is "wrapped in the clean linen cloth *(sindon)*." Each author shows a concern for a proper burial for Jesus.

In the Johannine gospel we find different terms. Jesus' body is "bound . . . in linen cloths *(othonion)*" (19:40), a Greek term for cloths of lesser quality. In Lazarus's case the verb "bind" is the same as is used for Jesus, but the term for Lazarus's burial cloth is strips of cloth *(keiriais)* (11:44), not fine cloth or linen cloths. They would not have been large enough for wrapping a body or chosen for decent burials. This seems one more indication that the Johannine gospel presents Mary and Martha as ordinary poor women.[11]

In general, the text seems to take for granted the ordinary "class" situation of the characters and the audience. This interpretation seems to be supported by the way the gospel as a whole depicts the Judean crowd against the Judean authorities. While the authorities play the role of villains, the crowd (made up of ordinary poor people) plays a role with which the audience is invited to identify. The majority of the Johannine communities seem to have consisted of ordinary poor people who had no difficulty identifying themselves with the crowd.

One additional phrase in the Johannine gospel seems to reflect a concern for the ordinary poor. In the story of Jesus' feeding miracle in all the canonical gospels, the phrase "so that nothing may be lost" appears only in the Johannine gospel. Other gospels, which note that "they took up the broken pieces left over" (Mk 8:8; similarly Mt 14:20; Lk 9:17), emphasize the abundance of the feeding. Only in the Johannine gospel does Jesus say, "Gather up the fragments left over, so that nothing may be lost" (6:12).

Again, it is probable that the phrase was either retained from or added to an earlier tradition to convey a symbolic meaning of Jesus' concern for the lost. Yet, keeping such words may also reflect the daily concern of the poor people not to lose or ruin any leftover food, even when they are satisfied. This reflects a major concern of many poor women, rather than men, who experience the worrying struggle to sustain their family members' lives. The accumulation of these minor aspects seems to suggest that the Johannine communities consisted of women and men familiar with poverty.

It should also be noted that the Johannine text does not present women in a way that divides them along lines of class (social status). In patriarchal societies, using class to divide women between legal wives and prostitutes or between "respectable women" and "disreputable women" has been a common strategy to "divide and control." Contrary to such a tendency, this text obscures or at least ignores the lines between classes of women. Martha and Mary have a male in their household, not the typical father or husband but a sick (or dying) brother. This weakens stereotypical class divisions between women who were protected by males in the patriarchal household and those who were not. Thus, although the text is obviously hostile to both Judean and Roman power holders, it does seem intent on building an egalitarian communal identity.[12]

## Gender

The characters' gender is generally in accord with conventional "kyriarchal" (master-centered) usage. The protagonist, who is the messiah, prophet, teacher, as well as leader for the true life, is male. God, the super-protagonist, so to speak, is also male, presented as father to the son. Thus, the spiritual world in the text, at least on the surface, is kyriarchal.

Males like Lazarus and Judas represent certain groups of people, both male and female. To give males the roles of disciples who don't understand was a common rhetorical device in Greco-Roman times. This gave the protagonist more occasions to teach; to entertain the audience by letting it feel superior to the male characters; and to enable the audience to reach a better understanding of the protagonist. To cast females as more positive figures was also a common rhetorical device, both to entertain and to educate women (and men) so that women would be motivated to conform happily to those desirable characteristics. Thus, on the surface, the basic characterization of gender seems conventional.[13]

### Breaking Stereotypical Roles

A close look at the actual roles that these gendered characters play, however, exhibits a more nuanced use of gender. In many ways the text breaks or simply ignores the social codes typical in elite male literature. The social code of honor/shame appears to be maintained in the relationship between the male teacher Jesus and disciples. Later, however, this code is subverted by the action of the male teacher Jesus, who follows a female disciple's example in his act of footwashing.

Neither the honor/shame code nor the public/private code seems to affect Martha and Mary. According to these codes it would have been shameful behavior for a woman to go out to a public (male) sphere without being accompanied by some male member of the family or to associate publicly with a male outside of her family. The text does not present Martha and Mary as shameful women, but the story is told as a matter of course that a woman, presumably not in a marriage relation, went out to meet a man who was not related to her through family ties. This is true of both Martha and Mary. The public/private code was also broken by the dinner at Bethany, where women and men ate together in a non-family setting.[14]

The social code applying to patrons, agents, and clients would require that a male work as agent to the patron for the sake of clients. A brother would be expected to help his sister. However, the text presents the sisters as agents working for the sake of their brother, pleading his case to the patron Jesus. This presentation subverts further social codes that expected males to be active and vocal and females to be passive and silent.

In this text and in the entire Johannine gospel the recipients of Jesus' healings are men, while women act as mediators on their behalf: Jesus' mother acts for a bridegroom in Cana, and the sisters in Bethany act for their brother. These women play active and vocal roles, and they do not serve patriarchal households. It is also worth noting that this rejection of typical gender roles does not lead to the destruction of mutually supportive relationships between women and men; rather, it simply presents them in a familial setting. Later in the story the sisters work as patrons for their client Jesus. Martha hosts a dinner at which Jesus is a guest, and Mary anoints Jesus; both of these activities make him the recipient of their benevolence.[15]

### Non-Patriarchal Familial Relationships

In this regard it is interesting to look at the household setting of Martha and Mary. In the text the sisters of Lazarus send a message to Jesus, asking for help. This implies that Lazarus lives with his sisters and not with his parents or brothers or with a wife, who would then have been the message sender. Perhaps Lazarus's parents are deceased and he does not have a brother or a wife. The gospel is not interested in these details, but it does tell us that Martha, Mary, and Lazarus live in the household in a sister-brother relationship, not the typical one of a father and his family.

Later in the gospel a mother-son relationship is established between Jesus' mother and the beloved disciple at the foot of the cross (19:26, 27). While the gospel speaks of Jesus in terms of a father-son relationship, the father refers always and exclusively to God. By this use of language the gospel seems to ignore patriarchal relationships on earth and to invite the audience into affectionate familial relationships that are non-patriarchal and not kinship based.[16]

### Crucial Roles of Women

It has been noted that both Martha and Mary play significant roles in the text. Remarkably, such significant roles for women are not limited to this text. It is commonly acknowledged by scholars that at critical points throughout the Johannine gospel women play crucial leadership roles, and neither the roles nor the significance of these women derives from their relationships with men. Women act on their own. They do not act against other women, nor do they serve patriarchal interests. Even if it was a common Greco-Roman device to present women in a more admirable way than men, this presentation of women is remarkable.[17]

Furthermore, the crucial roles women play are not merely episodic. While, on the surface each woman appears episodically, their roles are echoed in various ways throughout the gospel. The limited use of the word for service and servant, for example, connects Martha to Mary, the mother of Jesus. She is the mediator of Jesus' first miracle, performed at the beginning of his public ministry, while Martha's action mediates Jesus' last miracle, the raising of Lazarus, and her service is performed at the end of his public ministry.[18]

Martha's faith confession, on the other hand, connects her to Photini, the Samaritan woman. Responding to Jesus' first "I am" revelation, Photini makes the first faith confession in this gospel. Both of these testimonies connect Martha and Photini to Mary Magdalene, who gives testimony to the resurrection. At the same time, Jesus' sharing tears with Mary connects her to Photini, to whom Jesus showed his sympathetic understanding of the hardship she experienced. While Mary is followed by Judeans, Photini is followed by Samaritans.

In addition, Mary's anointing of Jesus' feet connects her to Jesus' mother. Anointing of Jesus' feet before burial would normally have been the task of the closest female relative. Here, Mary does what Jesus' mother could not do. Later, the mother of Jesus is found at the feet of Jesus on the cross, and Jesus offers her life within a familial community based on faith rather than kinship.

Mary's closeness to the body of Jesus also connects her to Mary Magdalene. Mary anoints Jesus' feet, prophesying figuratively his imminent death, and later Mary Magdalene is found at the tomb, close to the body of the risen Jesus, who makes his first resurrection appearance to her.

These overlapping echoes link individual women throughout the gospel. They create a gentle chorus that starts quietly as a solo, continues subtly, and ends with an undeniable harmony of female voices.

### Obscured Significance of Women

The Johannine text, however, certainly does not emphasize the crucial roles and significance of Martha and Mary. After Martha's faith confession and Jesus' revelation, she hesitates at Jesus' removing the stone from the tomb (Jn 11:39). This scene is ambiguous enough for the reader to question the extent of Martha's trust in Jesus. The text then presents Martha presiding over the dinner in Bethany, a meal that seems comparable to the Last Supper. However, Martha's *diaconia* (service/ministry) is referred to quite briefly in a short sentence (12:2). In the same way Mary's possible leadership among a certain group of Judeans is almost invisible. Similarly, her politically daring and prophetic role in anointing Jesus' feet is considerably downplayed.

This tendency to obscure and downplay women's leadership roles or significance is not limited to the text of Mary and Martha. For example, although Jesus' mother prompts his first miracle, Jesus makes a rather harsh statement to her, "Woman, what concern is that to you and to me?" (2:4). And, while Photini leads the Samaritan villagers to faith, they ungratefully say to her, "It is no longer because of what you said that we believe" (4:42). Although the risen Jesus stands by the distressed Mary Magdalene and calls her by name, he immediately says, "Do not hold on to me" (20:17). To be sure, each of these statements may have a variety of nuances and meanings, including some that are positive and affirming for women, as we carefully explore each text. However, at least on the surface, the present gospel gives the impression that the significance of women is not emphasized but rather obscured. It is difficult to determine to what extent this is due to compromises in the midst of Roman persecution, to the patriarchalization of the church and the wider society in general, to the patriarchal perspectives of the Johannine authors/editors, or to on-going theological debates. Women such as Martha and Mary and their sisters seem to await further critical feminist studies for a more inclusive remembrance of the Johannine communities.[19]

# 10

# Martha, Mary, and Christian Women (and Men) Today

Is it possible to re-vision women such as Martha and Mary, and their sisters? After taking a careful look at their historical situation and their portrayal in the Johannine gospel, they no longer appear to be wealthy or middle-class women who were free from worldly or economic concerns and thus able to devote their time to spiritual pursuits. Rather, most of the Johannine women were probably ordinary poor women, living under the exploitation and oppression of Roman colonial rule. If some women like Martha opened their houses as house churches for their communal gatherings, their houses were not necessarily spacious or luxurious, and most of the Johannine house churches may well have been humble dwellings.

In the midst of Greco-Roman patriarchal society the Johannine communities practiced something that might be called kyriocentric egalitarianism. That is, placing Jesus at the center, they created alternative communities of equals. Or, in a sense, by imaging Jesus as the totally obedient son of the Father in heaven, and thus leaving no room for an earthly father, their communities radically undermined the patriarchy of Greco-Roman society. There were sisters, brothers, and mothers, but no fathers; they also built sibling relationships across the patriarchal boundaries of ethnicity, class, and gender.

It appears that the Johannine communities imaged Jesus not only as the son of the Father but also as Sophia's prophet or messenger; this is reflected both in the prologue and in the "I am" sayings throughout the gospel. Many or most of the Johannine women and men may well have seen themselves also as Sophia's prophets, messengers, or children.

In the textual story of Martha and Mary, Jesus is presented as the non-patriarchal messiah/Christ who is so designated by women. He sits at a table where a woman presides and will later follow a woman's service model of discipleship. Furthermore, this Christ is not only their teacher but also their friend. It can thus be said that the basic kyriocentrism of their communities is also radically subverted in their non-patriarchal, non-authoritarian understanding of who Jesus was for them.

It is noteworthy that, in the text, it is women rather than men who play both of the two representative roles. Moreover, Martha and Mary engage in collaborative co-ministries. Nowhere in the Johannine gospel are there women pitted against each other, competing against each other, or divided by class or ethnic differences. Nor do they serve patriarchal values through acting against their own interests. Furthermore, women are not the passive objects of men's help but are always active and vocal on their own behalf.

It seems plausible that women also took on central leadership roles in their communities and that there was no division of work between the service of the word and the service of the table—or competition between the two. Also, there were probably many women gifted in prophetic perception, some who were blessed with healing powers, and some who performed other signs. Some women seem to have been particularly talented in missionary storytelling, claiming their long-standing religious heritage, integrating daring and savvy political resistance, evoking a variety of cultural images, and showing witty syncretistic applications to attract diverse audiences. Among them were communal story-weavers who skillfully structured their gospel in a woman-affirming way. Some of their stories may have informed the writing of the Johannine gospel.

Under the oppressive and even threatening imperial rule, some of the Johannine communities probably suffered serious conflicts with their fellow Judeans (Jewish people) or local synagogues. As a result of these conflicts some Johannine members concluded that they were hated and exposed (abandoned) by their parent body and envisioned a new exodus from their parent communities. They claimed that they held the true heritage of biblical traditions and redefined who belonged to "the children of God."

On the other hand, it seems that many women (and men) were still firmly grounded in their Judean neighborhoods or friendships and sought an alternative exodus for survival. This exodus would have taken place not from the Judean parent body but from the destructive and dehumanizing patriarchal power, which increased under Roman imperial rule in the latter half of the first century.

These women and men may well have appealed to those who sought to leave their Judean communities to remain united in their communities so that together they could challenge the enormous power of Rome. They may have been struggling as well to maintain inclusive leadership practices, instead of turning to the patriarchal powers that were increasing in the Jewish/Christian communities as a whole, and possibly even within the Johannine communities.

In this attempt to hear the gospel with ears more sensitized to its historical situation, it is noted that the Johannine gospel speaks the language of political resistance throughout, both overtly and covertly. It should be noted as well that the Johannine women and men who challenged the enslaving political and patriarchal power may have risked their comfortable lifestyles and family ties and even put their lives in danger. Women's challenge to patriarchal power is not the invention of modern-day feminists. The happenings within these early Johannine communities, and in the broader Christian communities, are part of our Christian heritage.

We should remember that if Christians today do not read the gospel texts with an expanded and inclusive historical imagination, we will fail to hear the messages of parts of the Johannine communities that were suppressed or manipulated in the gospel texts. This applies as well to other Christian documents and to the earliest Christian women. At the same time, there is no need to idealize the Johannine communities or the messages and practices of women in these communities. It is important to "re-member" them in their diversity, to learn critically from them, and to appreciate the inherited treasure from our spiritual ancestors.

## Making the Best of Jesus

Although there was a mixture of different voices within the Johannine communities, the communal memories of Jesus and of the reign-of-God movement were certainly at the center. Particularly powerful was the remembrance that Jesus was killed on the cross as a criminal by the imperial Roman power. In their story-weaving about Jesus the Johannine women such as Martha and Mary undoubtedly "made the best" of Jesus; that is, they did what they could to tell the story of Jesus so as to reflect their loving memory of him. This expressed their solidarity with their beloved teacher and friend, who, because of his daring life-giving ministry, died a violent and humiliating death.

Their story-weaving also expressed their spirituality of political resistance in that they believed that such death-dealing power should not have the last victory. They believed that the God who sent Jesus is the God of resurrection and life, revealed to them through Jesus' life and death. They preserved the stories of Jesus to keep alive their memories of him. In their communal remembrance of Jesus they perceived the divine within him.

However, it seems likely that the divinity they perceived was not identical to that of later doctrinal statements that claimed for Jesus a divinity equal to God. Nor was Jesus' divinity seen in a modern individualistic and dualistic sense as opposed to or completely alien from the human. In other words, the divine they witnessed in Jesus did not make Jesus identical with or equal to God, nor did it make this person Jesus a deity, nor uniquely different from other human beings.

Their effort not to make Jesus equal to God and not to worship a human being as God was evidenced in their use of father-son language. As noted above, in the first century a son sent by a father was the father's best agent. Although to believe in the son was to believe in the father, the father and the son were definitely not identical and, apart from the father, the son claimed no power. This distinction of the father and son was also evidenced in their storytelling about Jesus as the ever greater sign-worker, the son of God, who was so humbly presented in comparison to Greco-Roman divine humans. In other words, the divine they witnessed in Jesus was God's divinity at work or manifested in the life and death of the person Jesus.

The Johannine women, such as Martha and Mary, would surely have said that their encounter with Jesus was special for them, but that Jesus was a human being just as they were. They understood that they as well as Jesus were Sophia's children, and they were confident of being invited to follow their teacher and friend. Active and vocal, they joined in his life-giving ministries in their own ways as they participated in an inclusive community-making, crossing various social boundaries, in the midst of dehumanizing patriarchal power.

As God was imaged not only as a father but also as Sophia, it may well be that the Johannine communities imaged the Christ not exclusively as male. The Johannine communities could also have imaged Christ as a female figure, as did some Jewish odists as well as the New Prophecy movement. This seems conceivable since the "I am" sayings of the Johannine Jesus reveal not only Yahweh but also Sophia. Furthermore, since women like Martha and Mary related to Jesus, Sophia's prophet, not only as teacher but also as friend, it is plausible that they were shaping their identities as Sophia's children to be co-workers, co-healers, and co-prophets with Jesus.

In their communal stories of the life and death of Jesus their spirituality was inseparable from their political resistance and solidarity. In their visions and practices of the reign of God their spirituality pictured both God and Christ by means of diverse yet rich images. This form of spirituality invited their audience to join in boundary-crossing community-making wherever the gospel was heard.

## Old Stories, Our Stories, and New Identities

Countless times in my youth I sang, "I love to tell the story . . . to tell the old, old story, of Jesus and his love," one of my favorite hymns. Actually, I loved to hear and read many of the old, old stories in the Bible. Now, no longer as a child but as a woman conscious of my ethical responsibility for the communities and the world in which I live, I hope to tell the old, old stories, but with a difference. I hope I have also encouraged many women and men from different backgrounds to tell the old stories in many possible different versions coming from various Christian origins—including stories, visions, and struggles that have long been lost from our communal memories.[1]

And the old stories should be accompanied by new stories too. In retelling old and new stories I hope we emancipate our spirituality from later doctrinal interpretations of the Bible as well as from a modern Western dualistic mind-set that exclusively identifies Western culture with the "pure" Christian tradition.

In 1991, at the Seventh Assembly of the World Council of Churches held in Canberra, the Korean woman theologian Chung Hyun Kyung performed a powerful ritual and told a Korean story of *han*, the spirit of anguish and bitterness stemming from injustice done to the people. As she integrated some elements of Korean shamanism into her presentation, she challenged the church to move toward mindful "syncretism" in drawing from the richness of non-Western spirituality.[2]

It is good to bear in mind that there is no such thing as a "pure" Jewish or Christian tradition. Both Judaism and Christianity were enormously diverse in their early days and, at the same time, actively syncretistic in appealing to a wider audience. They did not hesitate to embrace mutual learning from other spiritualities. Indeed, the success of the earliest Christian movement was probably due, at least partly, to its successful integration of some syncretistic practices. In this way Christianity made itself more accessible and attractive to diverse peoples and also enriched its perception and understanding of God.[3]

Many cultures in the world have long histories of imaging the Divine not only in female and male figures, and beyond, but also within the beauty and power of nature and the universe. Appropriations of this kind, when done critically and creatively, will aid Christians in emancipating themselves from imagining the Divine rigidly or narrowly in a dualistic way of male or female, or as utterly transcendent and therefore alien to the human experience. We should always remember that God is beyond our naming, and that God is better than our best theology. Otherwise, speaking about God or claiming the absolute transcendence of God is, in reality, seeking to contain God within the limitations of our language and world view.

The retelling of old stories and the telling of new stories with various cultural and contextual reflections can assist in re-visioning Christian identities. The process should not abandon our historical heritage but rather build on it, ethically transforming it in our own historical contexts. I hope women and men from diverse backgrounds will collaborate in re-visioning our Christian messages and identities in ways that will be empowering and inspiring for us, without negating other people's spiritual paths.

In this way I hope we may further the wholeness and well-being of women and men of all colors in their global diversity today. Perhaps the time has come when we need to see more consciously, even beyond our globe, to envision the wholeness of the cosmos as the reign of God. This would be especially appropriate for us as we hear the stories of the Johannine gospel, which starts with the cosmic imagination of Sophia's creation, "In the beginning" (Jn 1:1; Gen 1:1).

Allow me to tell a contemporary story from television. In a segment of "Star Trek: The Next Generation," a science-fiction series, a twenty-fourth-century spaceship, the *USS Enterprise*, encounters people from a planet who believe that they are the most superior beings and that they are at the center of the universe. Their science is just beginning to enter into the age of the spaceship. After encountering the people on the *Enterprise*, the chancellor of the planet says something like, "This morning I was the leader of the universe as I knew it. This afternoon I am only a voice in a chorus." Although the chancellor himself thinks that "it was a good day," he concludes that his people are not ready to accept this reality and decides to slow down scientific progress to avoid encountering other beings in this cosmos until the people of the planet become ready to accept the new reality.

While watching this television show, I was thinking about Christians today. In church we still use the language of the absolute uniqueness of the Jesus Christ event, locating it at the center of our history and universe. Are we ready to face "different" realities? Let those of us who believe in the God of all creation not be like the chancellor who prevented new encounters with a broader universe. Let those of us who believe in the God who loves and cares for the whole creation, and who keeps on being present with us throughout history, not be afraid to decentralize our Christian traditions. A decentralization does not in any way decrease the amazing grace we embrace in our traditions and in our communities, but it does increase our perception of the profound wisdom in which we are embraced.

I hope that many Christians will become ready to board our spaceship at the beginning of this twenty-first century. And our collaborative search will be for ever richer encounters with God, for more sensitive perceptions of the diverse manifestation of the divine, and for the well-being of the whole creation.

# Notes

## Introduction

1. See Satoko Yamaguchi, "Original Christian Messages and Our Christian Identities," *In God's Image* 16/4 (1997): 24-31.

2. Regarding the Johannine gospel as a basis for the creed, see James D. G. Dunn, "Let John Be John: A Gospel for Its Time," in *Das Evangelium und die Evangelien: Vortrage vom Tubinger Symposium 1982,* ed. Peter Stuhlmacher (Tubingen: J. C. B. Mohr, 1983), 309-39; John Robinson, *The Priority of John* (London: SCM Press, 1985), 394-95; Robert Kysar, "Coming Hermeneutical Earthquake in Johannine Interpretation," in *"What Is John?"* ed. Fernando Segovia (Atlanta, Ga.: Scholars Press, 1996), 185-89.

3. For the importance of reading this gospel in its first-century context, see Dunn, "Let John Be John"; R. Arlan Culpepper, *Anatomy of the Fourth Gospel: A Study in Literary Design* (Philadelphia: Fortress Press, 1983), 237; Jeffrey Lloyd Staley, *The Print's First Kiss: A Rhetorical Investigation of the Implied Reader in the Fourth Gospel* (Atlanta, Ga.: Scholars Press, 1988), 36-37; Margaret Davies, *Rhetoric and Reference in the Fourth Gospel* (Sheffield, England: Sheffield Academic Press, 1992), 14-16.

4. Robert Kysar, *The Fourth Evangelist and His Gospel: An Examination of Contemporary Scholarship* (Minneapolis, Minn.: Augsburg Press, 1975), 269-76; R. Arlan Culpepper, *John, the Son of Zebedee: The Life of a Legend* (Columbia, S.C.: University of South Carolina Press, 1993). Regarding plural authors, see James. H. Charlesworth, "Reinterpreting John: How the Dead Sea Scrolls Have Revolutionized Our Understanding of the Gospel of John," *Bible Review* 9 (1993): 18-25, 54; Pieter J. J. Botha, "Letter Writing and Oral Communication in Antiquity," *Scriptura* 42 (1992): 17-34. Regarding the possibility of female authorship, see Elisabeth Schüssler Fiorenza, *In Memory of Her: A Feminist Theological Reconstruction of Christian Origins* (New York: Crossroad, 1983), 329-30; Craig A. Evans, *Word and Glory: On the Exegetical and Theological Background of John's Prologue* (Sheffield, England: Sheffield Academic Press, 1993), 192; Sandra M. Schneiders, "'Because of the Woman's Testimony . . . ': Reexamining the Issue of Authorship in the Fourth Gospel," *New Testament Studies* 44/4 (1998): 513-35.

5. Probably there already existed a variety of combined traditions that were circulated mostly orally. Regarding some of the compositional processes, see Robert T. Fortna, *The Fourth Gospel and Its Predecessor: From Narrative Source to Present Gospel* (Philadelphia: Fortress Press, 1988); T. L. Brodie, *The Quest for the Origin of John's Gospel: A Source-Oriented Approach* (New York: Oxford, 1993).

6. See, for example, Robert Kysar, "The Gospel of John," *ABD* 3 (1992): 912-31; Evans, *Word and Glory,* 193.

7. For the existence of plural communities, see Adele Reinhartz, "The Gospel of John," in *Searching the Scriptures,* ed. Elisabeth Schüssler Fiorenza (New York: Crossroad, 1994), 2:561-600.

8. See Kysar, "John," 919.

9. See Daniel J. Harrington, "'The Jews' in John's Gospel," *The Bible Today* 27/4 (1989): 203-09; Reinhartz, "The Gospel of John"; Sharon H. Ringe, *Wisdom's Friends: Community and Christology in the Fourth Gospel* (Louisville, Ky.: Westminster John Knox Press, 1999), 14.

10. For the anti-language, see Bruce J. Malina, *The Gospel of John in Sociolinguistic Perspective* (Berkeley, Calif.: Graduate Theological Union and University of California-Berkeley, 1985), 12-14. Regarding the possibility of the second or immigrant language, see Ringe, *Wisdom's Friends*, 12-13. See also Evans, *Word and Glory*, 193.

11. Regarding the fruitfulness of recognizing women's gender identities as inseparable from their racial and class identities, see Karen Brodkin Sacks, "Toward a Unified Theory of Class, Race, and Gender," *American Ethnologist* 16 (1989): 534-50.

12. See Elisabeth Schüssler Fiorenza, "Text and Reality—Reality as Text: The Problem of a Feminist Historical and Social Reconstruction Based on Texts," *Studia Theologica* 43 (1989): 19-34. The recognition of both kinship and the distinction between history and fiction is important for our understanding of who we are as historical and relational beings. On the one hand, ignoring the kinship between the two in the story and seeing history as an objective description of historical facts may lead us to the uncritical acceptance of dominant ideological historical interpretations of our past. On the other hand, failing to distinguish between the two and seeing history as if it were merely subjective fiction may make both our present self-identity and our future vision irresponsible and rootless. Thus, it is important for us to understand history, or historiography, as the rhetorical construction that narrates events that actually happened in the past. Since our historical knowledge has been constructed almost exclusively from privileged male perspectives and kyriocentric (master-centered) world views, our historical knowledge needs especially to be complemented by various women's perspectives. Without such an inclusive historical knowledge and a relatively adequate understanding of our foresisters, we women will repeat the same mistakes that our foresisters made and will always have to "invent" our strategies all over again, without learning anything from their wisdom and experiences (see Rosemary Radford Ruether, "How Not to Reinvent the Wheel: Feminist Theology in the Academy," *Christianity and Crisis* [1985], 57-62; Schüssler Fiorenza, *Searching the Scriptures*, 1:1).

13. Regarding the importance of tradition as the "the god-term of social remembering," Edward Farley notes, "It means that a people does not have to reinvent all truth, all wisdom, all life solutions every generation" ("Re-thinking the God-terms— Tradition: The God-term of Social Remembering," *Toronto Journal of Theology* 9/1 [1993]: 67-77, quotation at 67).

14. See Elisabeth Schüssler Fiorenza, "Feminist Hermeneutics," *Anchor Bible Dictionary*, vol. 2 (New York: Doubleday, 1992): 783-91; *Rhetoric and Ethic: The Politics of Biblical Studies* (Minneapolis, Minn.: Fortress Press, 1999), ix. Regarding some particularities of Japanese patriarchy, see Hisako Kinukawa, *Women and Jesus in Mark: A Japanese Feminist Perspective* (Maryknoll, N.Y.: Orbis Books, 1994), 9; Satoko Yamaguchi, "The Impact of National Histories on the Politics of Identity: The Second Story," *Journal of Asian and Asian American Theology* 2/1 (1997): 95-107.

15. Schüssler Fiorenza, "Feminist Hermeneutics." Regarding the importance of integration of interior and external liberations, see Virginia Fabella, "A Common Methodology for Diverse Christologies?" in *With Passion and Compassion: Third World Women Doing Theology*, ed. Virginia Fabella and Mercy Amba Oduyoye (Maryknoll, N.Y.: Orbis Books, 1988), 108-17.

16. Mary Rose D'Angelo, "Re-Membering Jesus: Women, Prophecy, and Resistance in the Memory of the Early Churches," *Horizons* 19/2 (1992), 202.

17. For biblical quotations, I use the *New Revised Standard Version* unless otherwise noted. In chapters 4, 8, and 9 I use my own translation. For the Christian Testament, I use the twenty-sixth version of the *Nestle-Arland Greek New Testament*, consulting with the NRSV, RSV, and KJV. For the Hebrew Bible I use the Masoretic text in the *Interlinear Bible: Hebrew-Greek English*, ed. J. P. Green (Peabody, Mass.: Hendrickson Publication, 1986). In my effort to use inclusive language, I also wish to avoid religious ethnocentrism. It is an English custom to capitalize God exclusively for the god of Jewish and Christian traditions. Such a custom, together with the use of the word "pagan" for all the other spiritual traditions, perpetuates the Jewish/Christian-centric mind-set that degrades diverse traditions of other peoples' spirituality. However, this issue requires much more discussion to arrive at a satisfactory solution. So, I follow the English custom of capitalization in this book.

18. Regarding the placement of Christian movements within the diverse streams of Judaism, see Schüssler Fiorenza, *In Memory of Her*, 105-59; Luise Schottroff, *Lydia's Impatient Sisters: A Feminist Social History of Early Christianity* (Louisville, Ky.: Westminster John Knox Press, 1995), 3-16.

19. Norman K. Gottwald, *The Hebrew Bible: A Socio-Literary Introduction* (Philadelphia: Fortress Press, 1985); Anthony R. Ceresko, *Introduction to the Old Testament: A Liberation Perspective*, rev. and exp. ed. (Maryknoll, N.Y.: Orbis Books, 2001).

20. John J. Pilch, *The Cultural Dictionary of the Bible* (Collegeville, Minn.: Liturgical Press, 1999), 100-04; Christopher D. Stanley, "Ethnic Conflict between 'Jews' and 'Greeks' in the Greco-Roman Era" (paper presented at the annual meeting of the Society of Biblical Literature, 1995); Craig Koester, *Symbolism in the Fourth Gospel: Meaning, Mystery, Community* (Minneapolis, Minn.: Fortress Press, 1995), 19. Lawrence M. Wills observes that Greek literature around the time shows an ethnocentric concept of Greeks versus "barbarians" (*The Jewish Novel in the Ancient World* [Ithaca, N.Y.: Cornell University Press, 1995], 29).

21. Regarding Greco-Roman inscriptional evidence, see Ross Shepard Kraemer, "On the Meaning of the Term 'Jew' in Greco-Roman Inscriptions," *Harvard Theological Review* 82/1 (1989): 35-53. See also Louis H. Feldman, *Jew and Gentile in the Ancient World: Attitudes and Interactions from Alexander to Justinian* (Princeton, N.J.: Princeton University Press, 1993), 338-445.

22. For readers who are already familiar with feminist scholarship on the first-century world, I would suggest first reading Part Two, where I present my reading of the text of Martha and Mary. Readers can then return to the sections of interest in Part One that offer social background information by introducing various fruits of feminist scholarship.

PART ONE

### 1   Looking at Christian History in a New Way

1. Elisabeth Schüssler Fiorenza, *In Memory of Her* (New York: Crossroad, 1983), 60-61.

2. Susan Guettel Cole, "Could Greek Women Read and Write?," in *Reflections of Women in Antiquity*, ed. Helene P. Foley (New York: Gordon and Breach Science, 1981), 219-45; William V. Harris, *Ancient Literacy* (Cambridge, Mass.: Harvard University Press, 1989), 194-95, 272, 323-37; Rosalind Thomas, *Literacy and Orality in Ancient Greece* (Cambridge: Cambridge University Press, 1992), 123-27.

3. Kenneth E. Bailey, "Informal Controlled Oral Tradition and the Synoptic Gospels," *Asian Journal of Theology* 5/1 (1991): 34-54.

4. For the importance of using interdisciplinary or multi-disciplinary information, placing "women" at the center, see Bernadette J. Brooten, "Early Christian Women and Their Cultural Contexts," in *Feminist Perspectives on Biblical Scholarship*, ed. A. Yarbro Collins (Atlanta, Ga.: Scholars Press, 1985), 65-92.

5. Bernadette J. Brooten maintains that "evidence for female non-subordination in the first-century Mediterranean world in general or in Judaism in particular undercuts the theory of female subordination as a cultural necessity" ("Jewish Women's History in the Roman Period: A Task for Christian Theology," *Harvard Theological Review* 79 [1986], 22-30).

6. See, for example, Bernadette J. Brooten, *Women Leaders in the Ancient Synagogue: Inscriptional Evidence and Background Issues* (Chico, Calif.: Scholars Press, 1982), 103-38.

## 2    Daily Lives of Jewish Women and Men in the First Century

1. For this section, see, e.g., Amy L. Wordelman, "Everyday Life: Women in the Period of the New Testament," in *The Women's Bible Commentary*, ed. Carol A. Newsom and Sharon H. Ringe (Louisville, Ky.: Westminster John Knox Press, 1992), 390-96; James Malcolm Arlandson, *Women, Class, and Society in Early Christianity: Models from Luke-Acts* (Peabody, Mass.: Hendrickson, 1997), 24-66.

2. For the patron-client and kinship-based economic system, see Douglass E. Oakman, *Jesus and the Economic Questions of His Day* (Lewiston, N.Y.: Edwin Mellen, 1986), 197-216; John H. Elliott, "Patronage and Clientism in Early Christian Society: A Short Reading Guide," *Forum* 3/4 (1987): 39-48; Richard A. Horsley, *Galilee: History, Politics, People* (Valley Forge, Pa.: Trinity Press International, 1995), 216-18.

3. Horsley, *Galilee*, 199, 220-21.

4. Richard L. Rohrbaugh, "Introduction," *The Social Sciences and New Testament Interpretation* (Peabody, Mass.: Hendrickson, 1996), 5; Joseph Zias, "Death and Disease in Ancient Israel," *Biblical Archeology Review* 54/3 (1991): 147-59; Carolyn Osiek, "Forum: Gospel and Enculturation: The Long Road," *Religion and Theology* 6/1 (1999): 83-92; Steve Mueller, "Thoughts on the 'Thirtysomething' Jesus," *The Bible Today* 37/2 (1999): 91-95.

5. "[T]he men of Judah" and "all the elders of Israel" "anointed David king" (2 Sam 2:4; 5:3). However, there were various visions of messiah among various Jewish people; they did not confess a coherent and normative messianology. See Richard A. Horsley, "Messianic Movements in Judaism," *Anchor Bible Dictionary*, vol. 4 (New York: Doubleday, 1992), 791-97. Regarding the "eschaton" as happening now, see Luise Schottroff, "The Sayings Source Q," in *Searching the Scriptures*, ed. Elisabeth Schüssler Fiorenza, vol. 2 (New York: Crossroad, 1994), 510-34.

6. Josephus, *Jewish War*, 2:56, 68-69; *Antiquities* 17: 271, 289; Richard A. Horsley, "Popular Messianic Movements around the Time of Jesus," *Catholic Biblical Quarterly* 46 (1984): 471-95.

7. Josephus, *Jewish War*, 2:308, 7:203; Gerald G. O'Collins, "Crucifixion," *Anchor Bible Dictionary*, 2:1207-1209; Zias, "Death and Disease."

8. Elisabeth Schüssler Fiorenza, *In Memory of Her: A Feminist Theological Reconstruction of Christian Origins* (New York: Crossroad, 1983), 254-56; Carolyn Osiek, "The Family in Early Christianity: 'Family Values' Revisited," *Catholic Biblical Quarterly* 58/1 (1996): 1-24; Jane F. Gardner, *Women in Roman Law and Society* (Bloomington, Ind.: Indiana University Press, 1986), 137-38.

9. See the above note.

10. Gardner, *Women in Roman Law*, 18, 31-44, 82, 138.

11. Schüssler Fiorenza, *In Memory of Her*, 225, 116-18; Gardner, *Women in Roman Law*, 31-116; Sarah B. Pomeroy, *Goddesses, Whores, Wives, and Slaves: Women in Classical Antiquity* (New York: Schocken Books, 1975), 121-48.

12. S. Safrai, "Home and Family," in *The Jewish People in the First Century*, ed. S. Safrai and M. Stern, with D. Flusser and W. C. van Unik (Assen: Van Gorcum, 1976); Stuart L. Love, "The Household: A Major Social Component for Gender Analysis in the Gospel of Matthew," *Biblical Theology Bulletin* 23/1 (1993): 21-31.

13. S. Safrai, "Home and Family"; Luise Schottroff, *Lydia's Impatient Sisters: A Feminist Social History of Early Christianity* (Louisville, Ky.: Westminster John Knox Press, 1995), 80-98.

14. Wordelman, "Everyday Life"; Douglass E. Oakman, "The Archaeology of First-Century Galilee and the Social Interpretation of the Historical Jesus," *Society of Biblical Literature Seminar Papers* (1994), 220-5l.

15. Schottroff, *Lydia's Impatient Sisters*, 84.

16. Ibid.; Gardner, *Women in Roman Law*, 41-44; Amy-Jill Levine, "Second Temple Judaism, Jesus, and Women: Yeast of Eden," *Biblical Interpretation* 2/1 (1994): 8-33; S. Safrai, "Home and Family."

17. See the above note.

18. Osiek, "The Family in Early Christianity"; Douglass E. Oakman, "The Ancient Economy in the Bible," *Biblical Theology Bulletin* 21 (1991): 34-39; Oakman, *Jesus and the Economic Questions*, 206.

19. Unni Wikan, "Shame and Honour: A Contestable Pair," *Man* 19 (1984): 635-52; Schottroff, *Lydia's Impatient Sisters*, 91-100.

20. Ze'ev Safrai, *The Economy of Roman Palestine* (London: Routledge, 1994), 104-7, 131-36; S. Safrai, "Home and Family."

21. K. C. Hanson, and Douglas E. Oakman, *Palestine in the Time of Jesus: Social Structures and Social Conflicts* (Minneapolis, Minn.: Fortress Press, 1998), 109-10; Schottroff, *Lydia's Impatient Sisters*, 243 n. 112; Jerome Murphy-O'Connor, "Fishers of Fish, Fishers of Men," *Bible Review* 15/3 (1999): 22-27, 48-49.

22. Hanson and Oakman, *Palestine in the Time of Jesus*, 106-10; K. C. Hanson, "The Galilean Fishing Economy and the Jesus Tradition," *Biblical Theology Bulletin* 27/3 (1997): 99-111.

23. See the above note.

24. Jerome Murphy-O'Connor, "Prisca and Aquila," *Bible Review* 8/6 (1992): 40-62; James E. Packer, "Housing and Population in Imperial Ostia and Rome," *Journal of Roman Studies* 57 (1967): 80-95; Gillian Clark, *Women in the Ancient World: Greece and Rome* (Oxford: Oxford University Press, 1989): 14; Osiek, "The Family in Early Christianity."

25. Packer, "Housing and Population." Some of the magical spells that include public-bath-related words and images are papyri such as PSI 28.26; PGM 2.1-64; 7.467-77, 480-95; 36.333-41; Jennifer Trimble, "Bathwomen and Other Undervalued Phenomena: A Study of PSI 28, a Love Spell between Women" (presentation at Professor Bernadette Brooten's seminar 1875, Harvard Divinity School, 1992).

26. Pomeroy, *Goddesses, Whores, Wives, and Slaves*, 198-204; Luise Schottroff, *Let the Oppressed Go Free: Feminist Perspectives on the New Testament* (Louisville, Ky.: Westminster John Knox Press, 1993), 88-90; Schottroff, *Lydia's Impatient Sisters*, 80-85; Wordelman, "Everyday Life."

27. Schüssler Fiorenza, *In Memory of Her*, 180-81; James Malcolm Arlandson, *Women, Class, and Society in Early Christianity: Model from Luke-Acts* (Peabody, Mass.: Hendrickson, 1997), 86-91.

28. Schottroff, *Lydia's Impatient Sisters*, 94.

29. Schüssler Fiorenza, *In Memory of Her*, 172; Mary Rose D'Angelo, "Women Partners in the New Testament," *Journal of Feminist Studies in Religion* 6/1 (1990): 65-86. On traveling, see Jerome Murphy-O'Connor, "On the Road and on the Sea with St. Paul: Traveling Conditions in the First Century," *Bible Review* 1/2 (1985): 38-47; Louis H. Feldman, *Jew and Gentile in the Ancient World: Attitudes and Interactions from Alexander to Justinian* (Princeton, N.J.: Princeton University Press, 1993), 335-37.

30. On slaves, see Pomeroy, *Goddesses, Whores, Wives, and Slaves*, 190-204; Wordelman, "Everyday Life"; Schottroff, *Let the Oppressed Go Free*, 89; Carolyn Osiek, "Slavery in the Second Testament World," *Biblical Theology Bulletin* 22/2 (1992): 174-79.

31. Charles Whibley, *Apuleius: The Golden Ass* (New York: Boni and Liveright, 1927), 36-45.

32. Osiek, "Slavery in the Second Testament World."

33. Ross Shepard Kraemer, *Her Share of the Blessings: Women's Religions among Pagans, Jews, and Christians in the Greco-Roman World* (Oxford: Oxford University Press, 1992), 65-66.

34. Mary R. Lefkowitz and Maureen B. Fant, *Women in Greece and Rome* (Toronto: Samuel-Stevens, 1977), 13; Pomeroy, *Goddesses, Whores, Wives, and Slaves*, 147; Wordelman, "Everyday Life"; Clark, *Women in the Ancient World*, 8-9; Schüssler Fiorenza, *In Memory of Her*, 182-83; Arlandson, *Women, Class, and Society*, 24-45; Bernadette J. Brooten, *Women Leaders in the Ancient Synagogue: Inscriptional Evidence and Background Issues* (Chico, Calif.: Scholars Press, 1982); Ross Shepard Kraemer, "Hellenistic Jewish Women: The Epigraphical Evidence," *Society of Biblical Literature Seminar Papers* (1986): 183-200.

35. On *symposion*, see Marianne Sawicki, *Seeing the Lord: Resurrection and Early Christian Practices* (Minneapolis, Minn.: Fortress Press, 1994), 258-60; Kathleen E. Corley, "Were the Women around Jesus Really Prostitutes? Women in the Context of Greco-Roman Meals," *Society of Biblical Literature Seminar Papers* (1989): 487-521; Kathleen E. Corley, *Private Women, Public Meals: Social Conflict and Women in the Synoptic Tradition* (Peabody, Mass.: Hendrickson Publications, 1993), 78-79; Pomeroy, *Goddesses, Whores, Wives, and Slaves*, 147.

36. Philo, *On the Contemplative Life*, 4:34-36; Ross Shepard Kraemer, "Monastic Jewish Women in Greco-Roman Egypt: Philo Judaeus on the Therapeutrides," *Signs* 14/2 (1989): 342-70; Silvia Schroer, "The Book of Sophia," in *Searching the Scriptures*, vol. 2, ed. Elisabeth Schüssler Fiorenza (New York: Crossroad, 1994), 17-38.

37. Schüssler Fiorenza, *In Memory of Her*, 313; D'Angelo, "Women Partners."

38. Douglass E. Oakman, "Was Jesus a Peasant?: Implications for Reading the Samaritan Story (Luke 10:30-35)," *Biblical Theology Bulletin* 22/3 (1992): 117-25; Schüssler Fiorenza, *In Memory of Her*, 320-21; Schottroff, *Lydia's Impatient Sisters*, 243 n. 112.

39. Schüssler Fiorenza, *In Memory of Her*, 122, 127-28; John R. Donahue, "Tax Collector," *Anchor Bible Dictionary*, 6:337-38.

40. Schüssler Fiorenza, *In Memory of Her*, 127-28; Hanson and Oakman, *Palestine in the Time of Jesus*, 113-16; Corley, *Private Women, Public Meals*, 40, 92.

41. Schüssler Fiorenza, *In Memory of Her*, 128-29.

42. Ibid., 128.

43. Corley, *Private Women, Public Meals*, 78-79.

44. Quotation is from Origen, *Against Celsus*, 3.49. See Kraemer, *Her Share of the Blessings*, 128; Schottroff, *Lydia's Impatient Sisters*, 146-69.

45. Ivoni Richte Reimer, *Women in the Acts of the Apostles: A Feminist Liberation Perspective* (Minneapolis, Minn.: Fortress Press, 1995), 31-69; Douglass R. Edwards, "Dress and Ornamentation," *Anchor Bible Dictionary*, 2:232-38.

46. Reimer, *Women in the Acts of the Apostles.*

47. For opinions that Lydia was a wealthy woman, see Ben Witherington, "Lydia," *Anchor Bible Dictionary*, 4:422-23.

48. Schottroff, *Let the Oppressed Go Free*, 135-36; *Lydia's Impatient Sisters*, 88-89, 145; Reimer, *Women in the Acts of the Apostles*, 71-127.

49. Ibid.

50. Jerome Murphy-O'Connor, "Corinth," *Anchor Bible Dictionary*, 1:1134-39; idem, "Prisca and Aquila," 40-62.

51. For the following, Reimer, *Women in the Acts of the Apostles*, 195-215; Murphy-O'Connor, "Prisca and Aquila" and "On the Road and on the Sea with St. Paul."

52. Miriam Therese Winter, *Womanword: A Feminist Lectionary and Psalter: Women of the New Testament* (New York: Crossroad, 1990), 241-42.

53. Robert Jewett, "Tenement Churches and Pauline Love Feasts," *Quarterly Review* 14/1 (1994): 43-58.

54. Ibid.; Murphy-O'Connor, "Prisca and Aquila."

55. Schüssler Fiorenza, *In Memory of Her*, 203-9, 135-36.

56. Luise Schottroff draws a caricature of scholars whose interpretations of biblical texts reflect their privileged life-situation of sitting in a study room, surrounded by well-sorted bookshelves, and always served by their wives or maids. "Discussion of a Feminist Introduction Using the AFECT Project as a Starting Point" (paper presented at the annual meeting of the Society of Biblical Literature, 1993).

57. I am indebted to Elaine Wainwright regarding the importance of recognition of "significant differences within the audience in relation to gender, ethnicity, class, and religious affiliation" (Elaine M. Wainwright, *Shall We Look for Another?: A Feminist Rereading of the Matthean Jesus* [Maryknoll, N.Y.: Orbis Books, 1998], 36).

58. Regarding the conflict between Samaritans and other Jewish people, see Robert T. Anderson, "Samaritans," *Anchor Bible Dictionary*, 5:940-47. Regarding the historical woman figure behind the story, see Schüssler Fiorenza, *In Memory of Her*, 138, 327; Sandra M. Schneiders, *The Revelatory Text: Interpreting the New Testament as Sacred Scripture* (San Francisco: Harper San Francisco, 1991), 179-99.

59. Regarding the name Photini, St. John the Baptist Russian Orthodox Church, among others, identifies her as "Holy Martyr St. Photini," as in the Russian and Greek Orthodox tradition. The Orthodox Community of St. Photini the Samaritan Woman has a Temple in Santa Rosa, California. I owe this information to my friend Barbara Kelum-Scott, who obtained the above information and more through Internet websites.

60. Archeological research has yielded the story of a Jewish woman in the early second century. When her husband died young and she was left with a baby, Babatha remarried, becoming the second wife of an old man who died soon afterward. Her life ended in a cave where she was hiding with other Jewish people near the Samaritan town and where she was found and killed by Roman soldiers. A woman like Babatha might have had to continue remarrying because she did not yet have the required three children, and the Roman law penalized women who did not remarry within a short period of time. Or, perhaps she would have wanted to offer better protection to her children by way of her remarriage. Or, perhaps, it would have been necessary simply to survive. Luise Schottroff, "Important Aspects of the Gospel for the Future," in *"What Is John?"* ed. Fernando Segovia (Atlanta, Ga.: Scholars Press, 1996), 205-10; Anthony J. Saldarini, "Babatha's Story," *Biblical Archeology Review* 24/2 (1998): 28-37, 72-74; Tal Ilan, "How Women Differed," *Biblical Archeology Review* 24/2 (1998): 38-39, 68.

61. Luise Schottroff, "Die Samaritanerin am Brunnen (John 4)," in *Auf Israel hören: Sozialgeschichtliche Bibelauslegung*, ed. Renate Jost, Rainer Kessler, and Christoph M. Raisig (Lucerne, 1992), 115-32.

## 3   Deities and Religious Leadership

1. See M. E. Boring, "Introduction to the English Edition," in *Hellenistic Commentary to the Christian Testament*, ed. Eugene Boring, Klaus Berger, and Carsten Colpe (Nashville, Tenn.: Abingdon Press, 1995), 11-12.

2. John J. Pilch, *The Cultural Dictionary of the Bible* (Collegeville, Minn.: Liturgical Press, 1999), 147-52.

3. Quotation is from Ross Shepard Kraemer, *Her Share of Blessings: Women's Religions among Pagans, Jews, and Christians in the Greco-Roman World* (Oxford: Oxford University Press, 1992), 3. See also Pilch, *The Cultural Dictionary of the Bible*, 81.

4. Rosemary Radford Ruether, "The Female Nature of God: A Problem in Contemporary Religious Life," in *God As Father?*, ed. Johannes-Baptist Metz and Edward Schillebeeckx (Edinburgh: T & T Clark, 1981), 61-66; Peggy L. Day, "Why Is Anat a Warrior and Hunter?" in *The Bible and the Politics of Exegesis*, ed. David Jobling, Peggy L. Day, and Gerald T. Sheppard (Cleveland, Ohio: Pilgrim Press, 1991), 141-46. The word "syncretism" has a pejorative image for most Christians. However, all world religions have enriched the image of the divine through syncretistic activities with their own selections and modifications. I use the word without any pejorative implications.

5. Kraemer, *Her Share of Blessings*, 22-29.

6. For Dionysus religion, see Kraemer, *Her Share of Blessings*, 36-48. See also Ross Shepard Kraemer, "Ecstasy and Possession: The Attraction of Women to the Cult of Dionysus," *Harvard Theological Review* 72/1-2 (1979): 55-80; Albert Henrichs, "Changing Dionysiac Identities," in *Jewish and Christian Self-Definition: The Greco-Roman World*, vol. 3, ed. B. F. Meyer and E. P. Sanders (Philadelphia: Fortress Press, 1982), 137-60, 213-36.

7. *Diodorus of Sysily* 1.25, Loeb Classical Library (Cambridge, Mass: Harvard University Press, 1950-67). For Isis religion, see Kraemer, *Her Share of Blessings*, 71-79; Howard Clark Kee, *Medicine, Miracle and Magic in New Testament Times* (Cambridge: Cambridge University Press, 1986), 67-68. Regarding Isis and Roman rulers, see Kee, *Medicine, Miracle and Magic*, 83-84.

8. Regarding Greco-Roman female deities, see Kraemer, *Her Share of Blessings*, 80-81; Elisabeth Schüssler Fiorenza, *In Memory of Her: A Feminist Theological Reconstruction of Christian Origins* (New York: Crossroad, 1983), 224-25. For a bibliographical overview on women in the Greco-Roman religions, see Ross Shepard Kraemer, "Women in the Religions of the Greco-Roman World," *Religious Studies Review* 9/2 (1983): 127-39.

9. Regarding Egyptian queens and kings, see S. Kent Brown, "History of Egypt: Greco-Roman Period," *Anchor Bible Dictionary*, vol. 2 (New York: Doubleday, 1992), 367-74; Hal Taussig, "Wisdom/Sophia, Hellenistic Queens," in *Women and Goddess Traditions in Antiquity and Today*, ed. Karen L. King (Minneapolis, Minn.: Fortress Press, 1997), 264-80; Gail P. Corrington, "Power and the Man of Power in the Context of Hellenistic Popular Belief," *Helios* 13/1 (1986): 75-86; Boring et al., *Hellenistic Commentary to the Christian Testament*, 104-5.

10. Regarding Roman emperors, see, e.g., Elisabeth Schüssler Fiorenza, *Revelation: Vision of a Just World* (Minneapolis, Minn.: Fortress Press, 1991), 80; Mary Rose D'Angelo, "Abba and 'Father': Imperial Theology and the Jesus Traditions," *Journal of Biblical Literature* 111 (1992): 611-30; Jarl Fossum, "Son of God," *Anchor Bible Dictionary*, 6:128-37; Martin Percival Charlesworth, "Some Observations on Ruler-Cult Especially in Rome," *Harvard Theological Review* 38 (1935): 5-44; R. J. Cassidy, *John's Gospel in New Perspective: Christology and the Realities of Roman Power* (Maryknoll, N.Y.: Orbis Books, 1992), 10; Craig R. Koester, "'The Savior of the World' (John 4:42)," *Journal of Biblical Literature* 109 (1990): 665-80; Warren Carter,

"Contested Claims: Roman Imperial Theology and Matthew's Gospel," *Biblical Theology Bulletin* 29/2 (1999): 56-67.

11. See, e.g., E. C. John, "Israel and Inculturation: An Appraisal," *Jeevadhara* 14 (1984): 87-94.

12. Ellen Van Wolde, *A Semiotic Analysis of Genesis 2-3: A Semiotic Theory and Method of Analysis Applied to the Story of the Garden of Eden* (Assen: Van Gorcum, 1989), 203-4 (I am indebted for this information to Kathleen Patricia Rushton); Tikva Frymer-Kensky, *In the Wake of the Goddesses: Women, Culture, and the Biblical Transformation of Pagan Myth* (New York: The Free Press, 1992); Johanna W. H. van Wijk-Bos, *Reimagining God: The Case for Scriptural Diversity* (Louisville, Ky.: Westminster John Knox Press, 1995), 89-98.

13. *Shadhay* (breasts) also appears in the Song of Songs 1:13; 8:10. Regarding female aspects of the god, see Phyllis Trible, *God and the Rhetoric of Sexuality* (Philadelphia: Fortress Press, 1978), 31-71; van Wijk-Bos, *Reimagining God*, 50-88.

14. Van Wijk-Bos, *Reimagining God*, 50-65. Trible, *God and the Rhetoric of Sexuality*, 31-59.

15. Susan Ackerman, "The Queen Mother and the Cult in the Ancient Near East," in *Women and Goddess Traditions in Antiquity and Today*, ed. Karen L. King (Minneapolis, Minn.: Fortress Press, 1997), 179-209. Regarding Yahweh and Asherah as partner deities, see David N. Freedman, "Yahweh of Samaria and His Asherah," *Biblical Archeologist* 50 (1987): 241-49. See also Rachel C. Rasmussen, "Deborah the Woman Warrior," in *Anti-Covenant: Counter-Reading Women's Lives in the Hebrew Bible*, ed. Mieke Bal (Sheffield, England: Sheffield Academic Press, 1989), 79-93.

16. Frymer-Kensky, *In the Wake of the Goddesses*, 153-55.

17. Susan Ackerman, "And the Women Knead Dough: The Worship of the Queen of Heaven in Sixth-Century Judah," in *Gender and Difference in Ancient Israel*, ed. Peggy L. Day (Minneapolis, Minn.: Fortress Press, 1989), 109-24. Peggy L. Day points out that "Ackerman's study underlines the disparity between religion as it was popularly practiced and the theological imperialism that characterizes many of the biblical texts" ("Introduction," in Day, *Gender and Difference in Ancient Israel*, 5-6).

18. Regarding female figurines, see Ackerman, "And the Women Knead Dough," 109-24. Regarding worship and images of female deities among ancient Jewish people, see Raphael Patai, *The Hebrew Goddess* (Detroit, Mich.: Wayne State University Press, 1990); Frymer-Kensky, *In the Wake of the Goddesses*, 153-155; and Freedman, "Yahweh of Samaria and His Asherah," 241-49.

19. John S. Kloppenborg, "Isis and Sophia in the Book of Wisdom," *Harvard Theological Review* 75/1 (1982): 57-84; Raymond Brown, *The Gospel according to John* (New York: Doubleday, 1966); Elisabeth Schüssler Fiorenza, "Wisdom Mythology and the Christological Hymns of the Christian Testament," in *Aspects of Wisdom in Judaism and Early Christianity*, ed. Robert L. Wilken (Notre Dame, Ind.: University of Notre Dame Press, 1975), 17-41; John Ashton, "The Transformation of Wisdom: A Study of the Prologue of John's Gospel," *New Testament Studies* 32/2 (1986): 161-86; Martin Scott, *Sophia and the Johannine Jesus* (Sheffield, England: Sheffield Academic Press, 1992), 80-115; Boring et al., *Hellenistic Commentary to the Christian Testament*, 238; Elaine M. Wainwright, "Jesus Sophia: An Image Obscured in the Johannine Prologue," *The Bible Today* 36/2 (1998): 92-97. Margaret Davies points out the inadequacy of translating *logos* as "word" (*Rhetoric and Reference in the Fourth Gospel* [Sheffield, England: Sheffield Academic Press, 1992], 121).

20. Schüssler Fiorenza, *In Memory of Her*, 130-36; Elisabeth Schüssler Fiorenza, *Jesus: Miriam's Child, Sophia's Prophet: Critical Issues in Feminist Christology* (New York: Continuum, 1994), 131-39.

21. Quotation is from E. P. Sanders, *Judaism: Practice and Belief, 63 BCE—66 CE* (London: SCM Press, 1992), 76; see also Jacob Neusner, "Varieties of Judaism in the Formative Age," in *Jewish Spirituality: From the Bible through the Middle Ages*, ed. Arthur Green (New York: Crossroad, 1986), 171-97.

22. Ross Shepard Kraemer, "Hellenistic Jewish Women: The Epigraphical Evidence," *Society of Biblical Literature Seminar Papers* (1986): 94-105; Shaye J. D. Cohen, "Menstruants and the Sacred in Judaism and Christianity," in *Women's History and Ancient History*, ed. Sarah B. Pomeroy (Chapel Hill, N.C.: University of North Carolina Press, 1991), 273-99; Amy-Jill Levine, "Second Temple Judaism, Jesus, and Women: Yeast of Eden," *Biblical Interpretation* 2/1 (1994): 8-33.

23. Quotation is from Wayne A. Meeks, "Moses as God and King," in *Religions in Antiquity*, ed. Jacob Neusner (Leiden: E. J. Brill, 1968), 354; Erwin R. Goodenough, *Jewish Symbols in the Greco-Roman Period*, vol. 2, ed. Jacob Neusner (Princeton, N.J.: Princeton University Press, 1988), 295.

24. Morton Smith, "Goodenough's Jewish Symbols in Retrospect," *Journal of Biblical Literature* 86 (1967): 53-68. Smith notes that the idea of the subordinate gods is also present in the third-century Christian church father Clement of Alexandria (60-65). Regarding magical spells, see Morton Smith, "The Jewish Elements in the Magical Papyri," *Society of Biblical Literature Seminar Papers* (1986): 455-62; Bernadette J. Brooten, *Love between Women: Early Christian Responses to Female Homoeroticism* (Chicago: University of Chicago Press, 1996), 73-113. Regarding the diversity of Judaisms and its implications for women, see Ross Shepard Kraemer, "Non-Literary Evidence for Jewish Women in Rome and Egypt," *Helios* 13/2 (1987): 85-101; Levine, "Second Temple Judaism"; Valerie Abrahamsen, "Women at Philippi: The Pagan and Christian Evidence," *Journal of Feminist Studies in Religion* 3/2 (1987): 17-30; and Valerie Abrahamsen, "Christianity and the Rock Reliefs at Philippi," *Biblical Archeology Review* (1988): 46-56.

25. Kraemer, *Her Share of Blessings*, 123.

26. Wayne O. McCready, "Johannine Self-Understanding and the Synagogue Episode of John 9," in *Self-Definition and Self-Discovery in Early Christianity: A Study in Changing Horizons*, ed. David J. Hawkin and Tom Robinson (Lewiston, N.Y.: Edwin Mellen, 1990), 147-66.

27. Bernadette J. Brooten, *Women Leaders in the Ancient Synagogue: Inscriptional Evidence and Background Issues* (Chico, Calif.: Scholars Press, 1982). In Greek, women leaders' titles are *archegissa/archegos, presbytera/presbyteresa/presbyterissa, meter synagoges/mater synagogae/pateressa, hiereia/hierissa*. See also Kraemer, "Hellenistic Jewish Women"; idem, "Non-Literary Evidence"; idem, *Her Share of Blessings*, 106-127; see also Shaye J. D. Cohen, "Women in the Synagogues of Antiquity," *Conservative Judaism* 34/2 (1980): 23-29. It is true that we do not know how common women's leadership was in first-century synagogues. It may be that the number of women who held these leadership titles was small. I would argue, however, that women's virtual leadership activities cannot be equated with the number of title holders. It is my experience in today's Japan that in many churches women often participate in leadership activities while formal titles often go to men. If the gender division of work in the first-century world was stronger than in today's Japan, and I assume so, should we not also assume some similar possibilities in the nascent synagogues?

28. Quotation is from Schüssler Fiorenza, *In Memory of Her*, 138. See also Luise Schottroff, *Let the Oppressed Go Free: Feminist Perspectives on the New Testament* (Louisville, Ky.: Westminster John Knox Press, 1993), 104.

29. Regarding the practice of open table fellowship, see Kathleen E. Corley, *Private Women, Public Meals: Social Conflict and Women in the Synoptic Tradition* (Peabody, Mass.: Hendrickson Publications, 1993), 184-86.

30. Schüssler Fiorenza, *In Memory of Her*, 205-41.

31. Regarding house churches, see ibid., 162-68, 175-84.

32. Regarding the community of siblings without a father, see ibid., 147-51; see also Schottroff, *Lydia's Impatient Sisters: A Feminist Social History of Early Christianity* (Louisville, Ky.: Westminster John Knox Press, 1995), 214-16; Scott S. Bartchy, "Undermining Ancient Patriarchy: The Apostle Paul's Vision of a Society of Siblings," *Biblical Theology Bulletin* 29/2 (1999): 68-78.

33. Elisabeth Schüssler Fiorenza, "Word, Spirit and Power: Women in Early Christian Communities," in *Women of Spirit: Female Leadership in the Jewish and Christian Traditions*, ed. Rosemary Ruether and Eleanor McLaughlin (New York: Simon & Schuster, 1979), 30-70; Mary Rose D'Angelo, "Women Partners in the New Testament," *Journal of Feminist Studies in Religion* 6/1 (1990): 65-86; Ivoni R. Reimer, *Women in the Acts of the Apostles: A Feminist Liberation Perspective* (Minneapolis, Minn.: Fortress Press, 1995), 210.

34. Regarding Junia, see Bernadette J. Brooten, "'Junia . . . Outstanding among the Apostles' (Romans 16:7)," in *Women Priests*, ed. Leonard Swidler and Arlene Swidler (New York: Paulist Press, 1977), 141-44. See also Schüssler Fiorenza, *In Memory of Her*, 172. Regarding slave names, see Miriam Therese Winter, *Womanword: A Feminist Lectionary and Psalter: Women of the New Testament* (New York: Crossroad, 1990), 241-42. Regarding female pair missionaries, see D'Angelo, "Women Partners in the New Testament."

35. Schüssler Fiorenza, *In Memory of Her*, 171; "The 'Quilting' of Women's History: Phoebe of Cenchreae," in *Embodied Love: Sensuality and Relationship as Feminist Values*, ed. Paula M. Cooey, Sharon A. Farmer, and Mary Ellen Ross (San Francisco: Harper & Row, 1987), 35-49.

36. Carter, "Contested Claims."

37. Mary Rose D'Angelo points out that "in the first century, the announcement 'God reigns' (or shall soon reign) must have implied for nearly every hearer: 'God reigns—and not the emperor'" (D'Angelo, "Re-Membering Jesus: Women, Prophecy, and Resistance in the Memory of the Early Churches," *Horizons* 19/2 [1992]: 199-218).

38. On the kingly Jesus, see Raymond E. Brown, *The Death of the Messiah: A Commentary on the Passion Narratives in the Four Gospels*, vol. 1 (New York: Doubleday, 1994), 35.

39. R. J. Cassidy maintains that the Johannine gospel includes many reflections of the Johannine communities' struggles and resistance under Roman colonial rule (Cassidy, *John's Gospel in New Perspective*, 3-10, 26-38, 81-87). See more on this topic in chapter 7.

40. Frank Kermode points out that in contrast to the synoptic gospels in John "no centurion proclaims Roman acceptance of Jesus as Son of God, or as innocent" (Frank Kermode, "John," in *The Literary Guide to the Bible*, ed. Robert Alter and Frank Kermode [London: Collins, 1987], 440-466, 464). Similarly, David Rensberger states, "Only in this gospel do the Roman cohort and its commander appear alongside. . . . There is an official Roman interest in the arrest of Jesus from the very beginning in the Johannine gospel" (David Rensberger, *Johannine Faith and Liberating Community* [Philadelphia: Westminster Press, 1988], 90).

41. Luise Schottroff has critically pointed out that the Johannine gospel has been interpreted as a spiritual gospel or the "text of an apolitical conventicle and/or of an otherworldly Christianity" (Luise Schottroff, "Important Aspects of the Gospel for the Future," in *"What Is John?,"* ed. Fernando Segovia [Atlanta, Ga.: Scholars Press, 1996], 208). The Johannine language of a political resistance seems to be one of the most important aspects that is rendered particularly invisible in the dominant scholarship of the Johannine gospel.

#### 4    *Prophecy and "I Am" Revelation*

1. Biblical translations in this chapter are my own. See Introduction n. 17.

2. Migaku Sato, *Q und Prophetie. . . . Studien zur Gattungs—und Traditions-geschichte der Quelle Q* (1988), 411, quoted from M. Eugene Boring, *The Continuing Voices of Jesus: Christian Prophecy and the Gospel Tradition* (Louisville, Ky.: Westminster John Knox Press, 1991), 17. David E. Aune, *Prophecy in Early Christianity and the Ancient Mediterranean World* (Grand Rapids, Mich.: Eerdmans, 1983), 187. See also Mary Rose D'Angelo, "Re-Membering Jesus: Women, Prophecy, and Resistance in the Memory of the Early Churches," *Horizons* 19/2 (1992): 199-218.

3. Josephus, *Jewish War*, 5.14.368.

4. Quotations are from *Antiquities* 20.6.168; *Jewish War*, 2.13.4.259. Richard A. Horsley, "Messianic Movements in Judaism," *Anchor Bible Dictionary*, vol. 4 (New York: Doubleday, 1992), 796.

5. H. Wheeler Robinson, "The Hebrew Conception of Corporate Personality," in *Werden und Wesen Desciples Alten Testaments*, ed. J. Hempel (1936), 49, quoted in Aubrey R. Johnson, *The One and the Many in the Israelite Conception of God* (Cardiff: University of Wales Press, 1961), 8; Susan Thistlethwaite, "Inclusive Language and Linguistic Blindness," *Theology Today* 43/4 (1987): 533-39; Johnson, *The One and the Many*, 6.

6. See Johnson, *The One and the Many*, 35-38. David E. Aune suggests a liturgical setting of antiphonal singing for the free switching of the speaker. This may be a possibility, but it does not negate the aspects of corporate personality (David E. Aune, "The Odes of Solomon and Early Christian Prophecy," *New Testament Studies* 28/4 [1982]: 435-60).

7. Regarding the Sophia imagery behind the following biblical texts, see Elisabeth Schüssler Fiorenza, *In Memory of Her: A Feminist Theological Reconstruction of Christian Origins* (New York: Crossroad, 1983), 130-36.

8. T. E. Pollard, "The Father-Son and God-Believer Relationships according to St. John: A Brief Study of John's Use of Prepositions," in *L'Evangile de Jean: Sources, Redaction, Théologie*, ed. M. de Jonge (Leuven: Leuven University Press, 1977), 363-69; Marinus de Jonge, *Jesus: Stranger from Heaven and Son of God: Jesus Christ and the Christians in Johannine Perspective* (Missoula, Mont.: Scholars Press, 1977), 147-48; Margaret Davies, *Rhetoric and Reference in the Fourth Gospel* (Sheffield: Sheffield Academic Press, 1992), 131-34. Susan Thistlethwaite says that the father metaphor also "conveys a sense of corporate life of God's kin group. . . . When the will of God is done, none is excluded from this extended family" (Thistlethwaite, "Inclusive Language and Linguistic Blindness," 536).

9. Kathleen Patricia Rushton observes that the word "son" actual occurs 27 times while "father" occurs 118, and the explicitly sustained coordination of father-son is found only in 5:19-27 (Kathleen Patricia Rushton, "The Parable of Jn 16:21: A Feminist Socio-Rhetorical Reading of a (Pro)creative Metaphor for the Death-Glory of Jesus" [Ph.D. diss., School of Theology, Griffith University, Australia, 2000], 179-222).

10. Aune, *Prophecy in Early Christianity*, 235-36; Boring, *The Continuing Voices of Jesus*, 39, 43.

11. Boring, *The Continuing Voices of Jesus*, 43, 16. See also D'Angelo, "Re-Membering Jesus: Women, Prophecy, and Resistance."

12. Quotation is from Aune, *Prophecy in Early Christianity*, 70, see also 16-17, 68-70, 320-21. Eduard Norden sees the origin of the "I am" formula in archaic Babylon and Egypt, where it was originally reserved for gods and later adopted by rulers as the earthly representatives of the gods (see D. Bruce Woll, *Johannine Christology in Conflict:*

*Authority, Rank, and Succession in the First Farewell Discourse* [Chico, Calif.: Scholars Press, 1981], 59-60).

13. "Akkadian Oracles and Prophecies," in *The Ancient Near East*, vol. 2, ed. J. B. Pritchard (Princeton, N.J.: Princeton University Press, 1975), 168-69.

14. John J. Collins, "Sibylline Oracles: A New Translation and Introduction," in *The Old Testament Pseudepigrapha*, vol. 1, ed. J. H. Charlesworth (New York: Doubleday, 1983), 317-472; John J. Collins, "Sibylline Oracles," *Anchor Bible Dictionary*, 6:2-6; Aune, *Prophecy in Early Christianity*, 19-83; Amy-Jill Levine, "The Sibylline Oracles," in *Searching the Scriptures*, vol. 2, ed. Elisabeth Schüssler Fiorenza (New York: Crossroad, 1994), 99-108. We should remember, however, that oracles uttered in a woman's name do not necessarily derive from women prophets. A woman's name can be used by men to counter some women prophets. Actually, the extant oracles seem to be those written or edited by men.

15. Ross Shepard Kraemer, ed., *Maenads, Martyrs, Matrons, Monastics: A Sourcebook on Women's Religions in the Greco-Roman World* (Philadelphia: Fortress Press, 1988), 368-70. See also Rose Hofman Arthur, *The Wisdom Goddess: Feminist Motifs in Eight Nag Hammadi Documents* (New York: University Press of America, 1984), 161-62.

16. Jorunn Jacobsen Buckley, "The Thunder, Perfect Mind," *Anchor Bible Dictionary*, 6:545-46; Arthur, *The Wisdom Goddess*, 218-25. See also Kraemer, *Maenads, Martyrs, Matrons, Monastics*, 371-77. Regarding "thunder" as the divine voice, see Eugene Boring, Klaus Berger, and Carsten Colpe, eds., *Hellenistic Commentary to the Christian Testament* (Nashville, Tenn.: Abingdon Press, 1995), 292.

17. Anne McGuire, "Thunder, Perfect Mind," in Schüssler Fiorenza, *Searching the Scriptures*, 2:39-54. George W. MacRae says that the Johannine gospel attempts to present the divine sonship of Jesus as both universal and transcendent (George W. MacRae, "The Fourth Gospel and *Religionsgeschichte*," *Catholic Biblical Quarterly* 32 [1970]: 13-24).

18. Arthur, *The Wisdom Goddess*, 157. In the "Book of Dinanukht" in the *Right Ginza*, the "I am" sayings of a female divine figure have contrasting and antithetical predicates and show striking parallels with those in *Thunder* (see Jorunn J. Buckley, "Two Female Gnostic Revealers," *Harvard Theological Review* 19/3 [1980]: 259-69).

19. James H. Charlesworth, "Jewish Hymns, Odes, and Prayers (ca. 167 B.C.E.—135 C.E.)," in *Early Judaism and Its Modern Interpreters*, ed. Robert A. Kraft and George W. E. Nickelsburg (Philadelphia: Fortress Press, 1986), 411-36; Susan Ashbrook Harvey, "The Odes of Solomon," in Schüssler Fiorenza, *Searching the Scriptures*, 2:86-98.

20. Harvey also points out a change that occurred in Syriac literature at the end of the fourth century. The Holy Spirit that had been referred to in feminine terms was changed to almost exclusively masculine terms. This was at the time Christianity was established as the state religion of the Roman Empire (Harvey, "The Odes of Solomon," 94-96).

21. Elizabeth A. Johnson, *She Who Is: The Mystery of God in Feminist Theological Discourse* (New York: Crossroad, 1992), 91. See also Martin Scott, *Sophia and the Johannine Jesus* (Sheffield, England: Sheffield Academic Press, 1992), 81-115; Elisabeth Schüssler Fiorenza, "Wisdom Mythology and the Christological Hymns of the Christian Testament," in *Aspects of Wisdom in Judaism and Early Christianity*, ed. Robert L. Wilken (Notre Dame, Ind.: University of Notre Dame Press, 1975); Boring et al., *Hellenistic Commentary*, 238; Elaine M. Wainwright, "Jesus Sophia: An Image Obscured in the Johannine Prologue," *The Bible Today* 36/2 (1998): 92-97.

22. Regarding the innovative and liberating aspect of the use of the term *logos* in this prologue, see David Rensberger, "Sectarianism and Theological Interpretation in John,"

in *"What Is John?"* ed. Fernando F. Segovia (Atlanta, Ga.: Scholars Press, 1998), 139-56.

23. They are 4:26; 6:20, 35, 41, 48, 51; 8:12, 18, 23x2, 24, 28, 58; 10:7, 9, 11, 14; 11:25; 13:19; 14:6; 15:1, 5; 18:5, 6, 8. Classification of these differ slightly among scholars.

24. Rudolf Bultmann, *The Gospel of John: A Commentary* (Oxford: Basil Blackwell, 1964/71), 225 n. 3, 327 n. 5. Bultmann rejects the idea of Jesus' ontological identification with God and takes them as expressing Jesus' existential identification with God. On the other hand, David M. Ball strongly argues for the ontological identification (David M. Ball, "'My Lord and My God': The Implication of 'I Am' Sayings for Religious Pluralism," in *One God One Lord in a World of Religious Pluralism*, ed. A. D. Clarke and B. W. Winter [Cambridge: Tyndale House, 1991], 53-71).

25. Charles K. Barrett, *Essays on John* (Philadelphia: Westminster Press, 1982), 1-18. He develops this argument following E. M. Sidebottom, *The Christ of the Fourth Gospel* (London: SPCK, 1961), 194. For similar views, see Robert Kysar, *John the Maverick Gospel* (Louisville, Ky.: Westminster John Knox Press, 1993), 27-28; Charles H. Dodd, *The Interpretation of the Fourth Gospel* (Cambridge: Cambridge University Press, 1953), 93-96; Paul Trudinger, "John's Gospel as Testimony to the Non-Deity of Jesus," *Faith and Freedom* 48/2 (1995): 106-10. The quotation is from page 110. John Robinson also asserts that the center of the gospel is not Christ but God, and that the Johannine Jesus is completely the Father's agent, claiming nothing for himself but everything for God the Father. He interprets that Jesus was misunderstood "precisely for speaking without so much as a 'Thus saith the Lord,'" and that the "I" of the Johannine Jesus is "the 'I' of the mystics, who make the most astonishing claims to be one with God, without of course claiming to *be* God" (John A. T. Robinson, *The Priority of John* [London: SCM Press, 1985], 387).

26. Scott, *Sophia*, 83-173. See also Schüssler Fiorenza, *In Memory of Her*, 133-34; Davies, *Rhetoric*, 87; Wainwright, "Jesus Sophia."

27. Dorothy A. Lee states, "There is an implied restoration of divinity to women in the roles they are given in the narrative. What we see reflected in them is the sending, self-giving, serving, covenanting, mothering God. Nevertheless, the connection is never made explicit in the Fourth Gospel" (Dorothy A. Lee, "Beyond Suspicion? The Fatherhood of God in the Fourth Gospel," *Pacifica* 8 [1995]: 140-54, 153).

28. Quotation is from Solomon D. Goitein, "Women as Creators of Biblical Genres," *Prooftexts* 8 (1988): 1-33, 13.

29. See Levine, "The Sibylline Oracles"; Rebecca Lesses, "The Daughters of Job," in Schüssler Fiorenza, *Searching the Scriptures*, 2:139-47.

30. Thomas Overholt, *Channels of Prophecy: The Social Dynamics of Prophetic Activity* (Minneapolis, Minn.: Fortress Press, 1989), 126-27.

31. In male literature these women prophets were later domesticated (Eusebius, *Ecclesial History* 3.39.7-17, quoted by Schüssler Fiorenza, *In Memory of Her*, 299). See also F. Scott Spencer, "Out of Mind, Out of Voice: Slave-Girls and Prophetic Daughters in Luke-Acts," *Biblical Interpretation* 7/2 (1999): 133-55. (The NRSV translates the above girl's "pythian spirit" as "spirit of divination" [Acts 16:16-18], which is a further degradation of her prophetic gift.)

32. Jerome Murphy-O'Connor, "Corinth," *Anchor Bible Dictionary*, 1:1134-39.

33. Antoinette C. Wire, *The Corinthian Women Prophets: A Reconstruction through Paul's Rhetoric* (Minneapolis, Minn.: Fortress Press, 1990), 138-40. See also Elisabeth Schüssler Fiorenza, "Rhetorical Situation and Historical Reconstruction in 1 Corinthians," *New Testament Studies* 33 (1987): 386-403.

34. Elisabeth Schüssler Fiorenza, *Revelation: Vision of a Just World* (Minneapolis, Minn.: Fortress Press, 1991), 133-35. Regarding the city, see John E. Etambaugh, "Thyatira," *Anchor Bible Dictionary*, 6:546.

35. Schüssler Fiorenza, *Revelation*, 133-35.

## 5 Healing and Sign-Working

1. Regarding the early Christian communities as both prophetic and healing communities, see Elaine M. Wainwright, "'Your Faith Has Made You Well': Jesus, Women and Healing in the Gospel of Matthew," in *Transformative Encounters: Jesus and Women Re-viewed*, ed. Ingrid Rosa Kitzberger (Leiden: E. J. Brill, 2000), 224-44.

2. Regarding miracles and signs, see Elaine M. Wainwright, "The Matthean Jesus and the Healing of Women," in *The Gospel of Matthew in Current Study: Studies in Memory of William Thompson, S.J.*, ed. David E. Aune (Grand Rapids, Mich.: Eerdmans, 2001), 74-95.

3. Morton Smith, *Jesus the Magician* (New York: Harper & Row, 1978), 9; Paul J. Achtemeier, "Jesus and the Disciples as Miracle Workers in the Apocryphal New Testament," in *Aspects of Religious Propaganda in Judaism and Early Christianity*, ed. Elisabeth Schüssler Fiorenza (Notre Dame, Ind.: University of Notre Dame Press, 1976), 149-86; Richard A. Horsley, *Galilee: History, Politics, People* (Valley Forge, Pa.: Trinity Press International, 1995), 122, 199, 220; Luise Schottroff, "The Sayings Source Q," in *Searching the Scriptures*, ed. Elisabeth Schüssler Fiorenza, vol. 2 (New York: Crossroad, 1994), 510-34.

4. Regarding magical spells, see Morton Smith, "The Jewish Elements in the Magical Papyri," *Society of Biblical Literature Seminar Papers* (1986): 455-62; Bernadette J. Brooten, *Love between Women: Early Christian Responses to Female Homoeroticism* (Chicago: University of Chicago Press, 1996), 73-113.

5. For sign/miracle-working as the customary means for religious propaganda, see Pietra J. J. Botha, "The Social Dynamics of the Early Transmission of the Jesus Tradition," *Neotestamentica* 27.2 (1993); Gail P. Corrington, "Power and the Man of Power in the Context of Hellenistic Popular Belief," *Helios* 13/1 (1986): 75-86.

6. *Diodorus of Sysily* 1.25, Loeb Classical Library (Cambridge, Mass.: Harvard University Press, 1950-67). See also Anne McGuire, "Thunder, Perfect Mind," in Schüssler Fiorenza, *Searching the Scriptures*, 2:54 n. 24.

7. Ralph J. Coffman, "Historical Jesus the Healer: Cultural Interpretations of the Healing Cults of the Graeco-Roman World as the Basis for Jesus Movements," *Society of Biblical Literature Seminar Papers* (1993): 412-43; Wainwright, "Your Faith Has Made You Well."

8. Jarl Fossum, "Son of God," *Anchor Bible Dictionary*, vol. 6 (New York: Doubleday, 1992), 128-37; Brendan Byrne, "Sons of God," *Anchor Bible Dictionary*, 6:156-59.

9. Smith, *Jesus the Magician*, 9-19; Eugene Boring, Klaus Berger, and Carsten Colpe, eds., *Hellenistic Commentary to the Christian Testament* (Nashville, Tenn.: Abingdon Press, 1995), 245, 259, 285; Botha, "The Social Dynamics," 205-31; Corrington, "Power and the Man of Power in the Context of Hellenistic Popular Belief."

10. Elisabeth Schüssler Fiorenza, "Miracles, Mission, and Apologetics: An Introduction," in Schüssler Fiorenza, *Aspects of Religious Propaganda in Judaism and Early Christianity;* Achtemeier, "Jesus and the Disciples as Miracle Workers"; Smith, *Jesus the Magician*, 14; Geza Vermes, *Jesus the Jew: A Historian's Reading of the Gospels* (London: Collins, 1973), 67-99.

11. Achtemeier, "Jesus and the Disciples as Miracle Workers," 151-53.

12. Wayne A. Meeks, "Moses as God and King," in *Religions in Antiquity*, ed. Jacob Neusner (Leiden: E. J. Brill, 1968), 354-71.

13. Schüssler Fiorenza, "Miracles, Mission, and Apologetics."

14. John J. Pilch, "Sickness and Healing in Luke-Acts," in *The Social World of Luke-Acts: Models for Interpretation*, ed. Jerome H. Neyrey (Peabody, Mass.: Hendrickson Publications, 1991), 181-209.

15. Regarding these terms and concepts, see Arthur Kleinman, *Patients and Healers in the Context of Culture: An Exploration of the Borderland between Anthropology, Medicine, and Psychiatry* (Berkeley and Los Angeles: University of California Press, 1980), 294-95. The differentiated use of the terms "sickness," "disease," and "illness" is in modern medical anthropology, not in the ancient texts (Pilch, "Sickness and Healing in Luke-Acts").

16. Harold Remus, *Jesus as Healer* (Cambridge: Cambridge University Press, 1997), 118.

17. For this section, see Pilch, "Sickness and Healing in Luke-Acts," and Howard Clark Kee, *Medicine, Miracle and Magic in New Testament Times* (Cambridge: Cambridge University Press, 1986), 9-65.

18. Kee, *Medicine, Miracle and Magic in New Testament Times*, 122.

19. Quotations are respectively from *Fleshes* 19, *Diseases of Women* 1.68, *Gynecology* 3, quoted in Wainwright, "Your Faith Has Made You Well." For this and the following sections I am indebted to the work of Elaine Wainwright.

20. Tal Ilan, *Jewish Women in Greco-Roman Palestine* (Peabody, Mass.: Hendrickson Publications, 1995), 189. Regarding the midwifery in the Greco-Roman period, see Valerie French, "Midwives and Maternity Care in the Roman World" *Helios* 13/2 (1987): 69-84.

21. Wainwright, "Your Faith Has Made You Well."

22. Anne Llewellyn Barstow's study tells about the long history of women as midwives and healers who handed down the knowledge of midwifery, medicinal herbs, and other experiential healing techniques orally. These women delivered babies, cured male impotence and female infertility, provided contraceptives, advised on problems of nursing, and worked as village therapists and healers. Her study also tells us how in medieval Europe these "sought-after" healers were hunted as witches (Anne Llewellyn Barstow, *Witchcraze: A New History of the European Witch Hunts* [London: HarperCollins, 1994], 109-27); also see idem, "On Studying Witchcraft as Women's History: A Historiography of the European Witch Persecutions," *Journal of Feminist Studies in Religion* 4/2 (1988): 7-19.

23. Antoinette Clark Wire, "Ancient Miracle Stories and Women's Social World," *Forum* 2 (1986): 77-84.

24. According to Marianne Sawicki, among first-century prophets "resurrection" meant a "realtime experience" (Marianne Sawicki, *Seeing the Lord: Resurrection and Early Christian Practices* [Minneapolis, Minn.: Fortress Press, 1994], 85). Regarding the cross-cultural human experience of communication with the dead in altered states of consciousness and how Jewish people in the Greco-Roman time might have experienced the resurrection, see John J. Pilch, "Appearances of the Risen Jesus in Cultural Context: Experiences of Alternate Reality," *Biblical Theology Bulletin* 28/2 (1998): 52-60. Regarding the diverse resurrection beliefs of the first century, see Emil Schürer et al, eds., *The History of the Jewish People in the Age of Jesus Christ: 175 BC—AD135*, vol. 2 (Edinburgh: T & T Clark, 1973-87), 539-47; George J. Riley, *Resurrection Reconsidered: Thomas and John in Controversy* (Minneapolis, Minn.: Fortress Press, 1995), 7-68. Regarding a distinction between resurrection and raising of the dead, see

John P. Meier, *A Marginal Jew: Rethinking the Historical Jesus*, vol. 2 (New York: Doubleday, 1994), 775-77.

25. At the same time, we should be cautious not to assume that such non-patriarchal or counter-patriarchal stories existed only among Jews and Christians. Instead, there may have been counter-cultural sign stories of ordinary Greco-Roman women that did not survive in the extant elite male literature. Regarding the counter-cultural sign stories involving women in the Christian Testament, see Joanna Dewey, "Jesus' Healings of Women: Conformity and Non-Conformity to Dominant Cultural Values as Clues for Historical Reconstructions," *Biblical Theology Bulletin* 24 (1994): 122-31.

26. Schüssler Fiorenza, *In Memory of Her*, 49, 51.

27. Virginia Burrus, *Chastity as Autonomy: Women in the Stories of Apocryphal Acts* (Lewiston, N.Y.: Edwin Mellen, 1987).

28. Scholars assume that the Johannine gospel presents seven signs of Jesus (1 through 7 in the following list), corresponding to Moses. See Douglas K. Clark, "Signs in Wisdom and John," *Catholic Biblical Quarterly* 45/2 (1983): 201-9. Signs 8 through 12 are performed in more private settings than signs 1 through 7, but both types of signs are written in the gospel "so that you may come to believe" (20:30), and "have life in his name" (20:31). Thus, I consider all of them as sign stories in this gospel.

29. For the Dionysus story and the Johannine communities' syncretistic activities, see David R. Cartlidge and David L. Dungan, *Documents for the Study of the Gospels* (Philadelphia: Fortress Press, 1980), 165; Helmut Koester, *Ancient Christian Gospels: Their History and Development* (Philadelphia: Trinity Press International, 1990), 205.

30. Regarding Asklepios's sanctuary and the graffitti, see Coffman, "Historical Jesus the Healer," 434.

## 6    Storytelling and Tradition-Making

1. Phyllis A. Bird, "Images of Women in the Old Testament," in *Religion and Sexism: Images of Woman in the Jewish and Christian Traditions*, ed. Rosemary Radford Ruether (New York: Simon & Schuster, 1974), 41-88; Kathleen M. O'Connor, "Jeremiah," in *The Women's Bible Commentary*, ed. Carol A. Newsom and Sharon H. Ringe (London: SPCK, 1992), 169-77; Gale A. Yee, "Hosea," in Newsom and Ringe, *The Women's Bible Commentary*, 195-202; Judith E. Sanderson, "Amos," in Newsom and Ringe, *The Women's Bible Commentary*, 205-09; Tikva Frymer-Kensky, "Deuteronomy," in Newsom and Ringe, *The Women's Bible Commentary*, 52-62.

2. Quotations are from Esther Fuchs, "The Literary Characterization of Mothers and Sexual Politics in the Hebrew Bible," *Semeia* 46 (1989): 165, 162. See also J. Cheryl Exum, "The Mothers of Israel: The Patriarchal Narratives from a Feminist Perspective," *Bible Review* 2/1 (1986): 60-67.

3. Carol Meyers, "'To Her Mother's House': Considering a Counterpart to the Israelite *BBet 'ab*," in *The Bible and the Politics of Exegesis: Essays in Honor of Norman K. Gottwald on His Sixty-Fifth Birthday*, ed. David Jobling, Peggy L. Day, and Gerald T. Sheppard (Cleveland, Ohio: Pilgrim Press, 1991), 39-51. See also Carol Meyers, *Discovering Eve: Ancient Israelite Women in Context* (Oxford: Oxford University Press, 1988).

4. Claudia V. Camp, *Wisdom and the Feminine in the Book of Proverbs* (Sheffield: Almond, 1985), 85-87.

5. In the case of Job (2:9-10), although he first rebukes his wife for her advice, later he actually does exactly what she said: to come to terms with God squarely, rather than remaining just pious and passive. See Ilana Pardes, *Countertraditions in the Bible: A Feminist Approach* (Cambridge: Harvard University Press, 1992), 145-54.

6. Meyers, *Discovering Eve*, 150; S. D. Goitein, "Women as Creators of Biblical Genres," *Prooftexts* 8 (1988): 1-33; Camp, *Wisdom and the Feminine in the Book of Proverbs*, 165-66.

7. "Birth song" (Gen 29:35; 30:13; Ruth 4:14-15; 1 Sam 2:1-5); "naming speech" (Gen 4:1, 25; 29-30; 1 Chr 4:9; Ex 2:10; 1 Sam 4:20-22); "vow" (1 Sam 1:10-11; Prv 7:14; 31:2; Jer 44:19); "prayer" (1 Sam 13a); "wisdom speech" (2 Sam 14, 20; 25:29-31; Prv 1-9; 25:15; 15:1); "warning speech" (Prv 7; 31:1-9); "victory song" (Ex 15:20-21; Judg 5:7; 11:34a; 1 Sam 18:6-7); "mockery song" (2 Sam 1:20; Isa 37:22-25; 2 Kgs 19:21-24; Judg 5:15-30; Jer 38:22); "lament" (2 Chr 35:25; Jer 9:6-21, 17-21; 31:15; Judg 6:28; 11:40; Lam 1:11b-13, 15b-16). See Athalya Brenner and Fokkelien van Dijk-Hemmes, *On Gendering Texts: Female and Male Voices in the Hebrew Bible* (Leiden: E. J. Brill, 1993), 3-25, 25-32. Regarding the naming speech, see also Pardes, *Countertraditions in the Bible*, 39-59; Goitein, "Women as Creators of Biblical Genres."

8. Emanuel Feldman, *Biblical and Post-Biblical Defilement and Mourning: Law as Theology* (New York: Yeshiva University Press, Ktav Publishing House, Inc., 1977), 120-37; Goitein, "Women as Creators of Biblical Genres"; Anna Caraveli, "The Bitter Wounding: The Lament as Social Protest in Rural Greece," in *Gender and Power in Rural Greece*, ed. Jill Dubisch (Princeton, N.J.: Princeton University Press, 1986), 169-94; Gail Holst-Warhaft, *Dangerous Voices: Women's Laments and Greek Literature* (London: Routledge, 1992), 4-12, 111; Rosalind Thomas, *Literacy and Orality in Ancient Greece* (Cambridge: Cambridge University Press, 1992), 105-19. Regarding first-century Jewish literature, see Pseudo Philo's *Biblical Antiquities*, 32.1-33.6; 40.1-9. A look at these texts will follow below.

9. Goitein, "Women as Creators of Biblical Genres"; Leonie J. Archer, *Her Price Is beyond Rubies: The Jewish Woman in Graeco-Roman Palestine* (Sheffield: Sheffield Academic Press, 1990), 281.

10. Robert Garland, "The Well-Ordered Corpse: An Investigation into the Motives behind Greek Funerary Legislation," *Bulletin of the Institute of Classical Studies* 36 (1989): 1-15; Holst-Warhaft, *Dangerous Voices*, 3, 114, 121.

11. Regarding the change of ethos, see Holst-Warhalt, *Dangerous Voices*, 98. Regarding the story of Mohammed, see Goitein, "Women as Creators of Biblical Genres." Itumeleng J. Mosala speaks about the prohibition of lament singing in twentieth-century South Africa under apartheid (Itumeleng J. Mosala, *Biblical Hermeneutics and Black Theology in South Africa* [Grand Rapids, Mich.: Eerdmans, 1989], 151).

12. The earliest extant Jewish mourning tractate, *Mourning*, comes from the eighth century C.E., but internal evidence suggests its literary formulation possibly dates back to the end of the third century C.E. It is remarkable that nowhere in the tractate is any prohibition or inhibition of "exaggerated expressions of grief" or "excessive" wailing mentioned. Rather, it is clearly mentioned that weeping for the dead is mandatory and "a man's sins are forgiven if he sheds tears for the dead" (Dov Zlotnick, trans., *The Tractate "Mourning" (Semahot): Regulations Relating to Death, Burial, and Mourning*, ed. William Scott Green and Calvin Goldscheider, Chicago Studies in the History of Judaism [New Haven, Conn.: Yale University, 1966], 24). To be sure, the tractate is very sexist, and women are no longer assigned significant roles in the mourning rituals. This may reflect general misogynistic trends found especially in second- and third-century Jewish and Christian literature. Regarding funerary restrictions on women, see Kathleen E. Corley, "Women and the Crucifixion and Burial of Jesus: 'He Was Buried: On the Third Day He Was Raised,'" *Forum* New Series 1/1 (1998): 181-225.

13. *Republic* 2.377C; *Geography* 1, 2, 8, C19. Behind the vehement denunciation found in 1 Timothy, scholars assume, were groups of women called "widows" who

were "doers of the word" (Bonnie Bowman Thurston, *The Widows: A Women's Ministry in the Early Church* [Minneapolis, Minn.: Fortress Press, 1989], 113). See also Elisabeth Schüssler Fiorenza, *In Memory of Her: A Feminist Theological Reconstruction of Christian Origins* (New York: Crossroad, 1983), 309-15; Joanna Dewey, "1 Timothy," in Newsom and Ringe, *The Women's Bible Commentary*.

14. Keith R. Bradley, "Wet-nursing at Rome: A Study in Social Relations," in *The Family in Ancient Rome: New Perspectives*, ed. Beryl Rawson (Ithaca, N.Y.: Cornell University Press, 1986), 201-29; Marianne Sawicki, *Seeing the Lord: Resurrection and Early Christian Practices* (Minneapolis, Minn.: Fortress Press, 1994), 267.

15. Daniel J. Harrington, "Palestinian Adaptations of Biblical Narratives and Prophecies: I. The Bible Rewritten (Narratives), and III. Future Research," in *Early Judaism and Its Modern Interpreters*, ed. Robert A. Kraft and George W. E. Nickelsburg (Philadelphia: Fortress Press; Atlanta, Ga.: Scholars Press, 1986), 239-47, 253-55, quotations are from 239-40.

16. Regarding the re-visioning of the entire heritage by a variety of Jewish groups, see Jacob Neusner, *The Way of Torah: An Introduction to Judaism* (Belmont, Calif.: Wadsworth, 1993), 9-10. Some scholars think that the writing of the Johannine gospel itself can be seen as a radical re-visioning of Jewish tradition (see Kysar, "The Gospel of John," *Anchor Bible Dictionary*, vol. 6 [New York: Doubleday, 1992], 912-31).

17. See Cheryl Anne Brown, *No Longer Be Silent: First Century Jewish Portraits of Biblical Women* (Louisville, Ky.: Westminster John Knox Press, 1992), 18-26. For many other stories that help us imagine first-century women's storytelling activities, see Karen L. King, ed., *Images of the Feminine in Gnosticism: Studies in Antiquity and Christianity* (Philadelphia: Fortress Press, 1988); Elisabeth Schüssler Fiorenza, ed., *Searching the Scriptures*, 2 vols. (New York: Crossroad, 1994). Regarding the power of stories we tell, see Joanna Dewey, "From Storytelling to Written Text: The Loss of Early Christian Women's Voices," *Biblical Theology Bulletin* 26 (1996): 1-8.

18. There is also a stark contrast between Jephthah's vow and Hannah's vow. In her prayer Hannah makes a vow to offer her son to God as her sacrifice if God gives her a son. Hannah birthed a son, Samuel, and she offered him as she vowed. The mother's vow brought about a long, prestigious life for her son as a prophet, while the father's vow brought about his daughter's violent, premature death (see Fokkelien van Dijk-Hemmes, "Traces of Women's Texts in the Hebrew Bible," in *On Gendering Texts*, 91-92).

19. *Biblical Antiquities* 40.1-9. The quotation is from Cynthia Backer, "Pseudo-Philo and the Transformation of Jephthah's Daughter," in *Anti-Covenant: Counter-Reading Women's Lives in the Hebrew Bible*, ed. Mieke Bal (Sheffield: Sheffield Academic Press, 1989), 199. See also "Lament for Debora," *Biblical Antiquities* 40.1-9.

20. J. Cheryl Exum, "Murder They Wrote: Ideology and the Manipulation of Female Presence in Biblical Narrative," in *The Pleasure of Her Text: Feminist Readings of Biblical and Historical Texts*, ed. Alice Bach (Philadelphia: Trinity Press International, 1990), 63. Regarding the possible link between this story and Tammus Festival and Ishtal, see Karel Van Der Toorn, *From Her Cradle to Her Grave: The Role of Religion in the Life of the Israelite and Babylonian Woman*, trans. Sara J. Denning-Bolle (Sheffield: Sheffield Academic Press, 1994), 117-20.

21. For a retelling of Moses competing against Greek heroes, see John G. Gager, *Moses in Greco-Roman Paganism* (Nashville, Tenn.: Abingdon Press, 1972), 77.

22. J. Cheryl Exum, "'You Shall Let Every Daughter Live': A Study of Exodus 1.8-2.10," in *A Feminist Companion to Exodus to Deuteronomy*, ed. Athalya Brenner (Sheffield: Sheffield Academic Press, 1994), 37-61; J. Cheryl Exum, "Second Thoughts

about Secondary Characters: Women in Exodus 1.8-2.10," in Brenner, *A Feminist Companion to Exodus to Deuteronomy*, 75-87; Jopie Siebert-Hommes, "But If She Be a Daughter . . . She May Live!: 'Daughters' and 'Sons' in Exodus 1-2," in Brenner, *A Feminist Companion to Exodus to Deuteronomy*, 62-74.

23. Phyllis Trible, "Bringing Miriam Out of the Shadows," *Bible Review* 5/1 (1989): 34; Pardes, *Countertraditions in the Bible*, 3-11; Eileen Schuller, "Women of the Exodus in Biblical Retelling of the Second Temple Period," in *Gender and Difference in Ancient Israel*, ed. Peggy L. Day (Minneapolis, Minn.: Fortress Press, 1989), 178-94. For a reading of Miriam as a priest, see Rita J. Burns, *Has the Lord Indeed Spoken Only Through Moses?: A Study of the Biblical Portrait of Miriam* (Atlanta, Ga.: Scholars Press, 1987).

24. Regarding the Therapeutrides, see "Religious Celibates" in chapter 2 in this volume.

25. Linda Bennett Elder, "Judith," in Schüssler Fiorenza, *Searching the Scriptures*, 2:455-69.

26. Regarding Judith's story as a new Exodus, see Schroer, "Book of Sophia," in Schüssler Fiorenza, *Searching the Scriptures*, vol. 2. The quotation is from Schüssler Fiorenza, *In Memory of Her*, 18. Archeological evidence identifies Bethany *(Beth Ananiah)*, "the village of Mary and her sister Martha" (Jn 11:1), as the ancient Ananiah (the merciful god), one of the cities Nebuchadnezzar leveled (L. J. Perkins, "Bethany," *Anchor Bible Dictionary*, 1:702-3). Women in Bethany might have especially loved the retelling of Judith's story.

27. *Testament of Job*, 46-53. Rebecca Lesses, "The Daughters of Job," in Schüssler Fiorenza, *Searching the Scriptures*, 2:139-47.

28. Job even gives his daughters "fragrant" names, such as "Day" (or Dove), "Cassia" (cinnamon or a type of perfume), and "Amaltheia's Horn" (a type of eye-shadow, or a Greek legendary she-goat horn that nursed Zeus), that have nothing to do with piety. See Pardes, *Countertraditions in the Bible*, 146-54; Lesses, "The Daughters of Job."

29. Regarding Greco-Roman education, see John T. Townsend, "Education (Israel): Greco-Roman Period," *Anchor Bible Dictionary*, 2:312-17.

30. Quotations are all from Mary Ann Tolbert, *Sowing the Gospel: Mark's World in Literary-Historical Perspective* (Minneapolis, Minn.: Fortress Press, 1989), 70. Regarding literacy in the ancient oral culture, see Joanna Dewey, "Textuality in an Oral Culture: A Survey of the Pauline Traditions," *Semeia* 65 (1995): 37-65; Lucretia B. Yaghjian, "Ancient Reading," in *The Social Sciences and New Testament Interpretation*, ed. Richard L. Rohrbaugh (Peabody, Mass.: Hendrickson, 1996), 206-30; Susan Guettel Cole, "Could Greek Women Read and Write?" in *Reflections of Women in Antiquity*, ed. Helene P. Foley (New York: Gordon and Breach Science, 1981), 219-45. Regarding "popular literature," see Richard I. Pervo, *Profit with Delight: The Literary Genre of the Acts of the Apostles* (Philadelphia: Fortress Press, 1987), 82; Lawrence M. Wills, *The Jewish Novel in the Ancient World* (Ithaca, N.Y.: Cornell University Press, 1995), 28. It was only recently that ancient popular literature was "discovered" by scholars. Since a tiny minority group of privileged people were the preservers of all the literature and they were educated to take seriously only the classics and to despise popular literature, most of the Greco-Roman popular literature was lost from historical memory. However, there are many extant texts of five novels from 200 B.C.E. to 100 C.E. in different geographical areas among different ethnic groups, attesting to the broad stream of popular literature, "too disparate to be attributed to a single readership group" (Pervo, *Profit with Delight*, 82). See also Fred E. H. Schroeder, ed., *Five Thousand Years of Popular Culture: Popular Culture before Printing* (Bowling Green: Bowling Green University Popular Press, 1980).

31. Wills, *The Jewish Novel in the Ancient World*, 15-29, 213-44; Mary Ann Tolbert, "The Gospel in Greco-Roman Culture," in *The Book and the Text: The Bible and Literary Theory*, ed. Regina M. Schwartz (Cambridge: Basil Blackwell, 1990), 258-75; Tolbert, *Sowing the Gospel*, 73; Bryan P. Reardon, *Collected Ancient Greek Novels* (Berkeley and Los Angeles: University of California Press, 1989), 1-16.

32. Dieter Georgi, *The Opponents of Paul in Second Corinthians* (Philadelphia: Fortress Press, 1986), 99-102.

33. Tolbert, *Sowing the Gospel*, 71, 73. It is also interesting to observe differences in length between the Greek classics and the Christian gospels. While the length of Greek writings varies from fifteen thousand to eighteen thousand words, the gospels are shorter but similar in length: Mk: eleven thousand; Jn: fifteen thousand; Mt: eighteen thousand; Lk: nineteen thousand words (Robert Morgenthaler, *Statistik Des Neutestamentlichen Wortschitzes* [Zurich: Gotthelf, 1958], 166). These lengths are fitting for theatrical storytelling performances.

34. Lord Raglan, *The Hero: A Study in Tradition, Myth, and Drama* (New York: Vintage, 1956), 150; Alan Dundes, "The Hero Pattern and the Life of Jesus," *In Quest of the Hero*, ed. Robert A. Segal (Princeton, N.J.: Princeton University Press, 1990), 179-223. Quotations are from pages 193-94.

35. Regarding meaning-making, Elaine M. Wainwright says: "The accounts of the death and resurrection of Jesus have a long history of traditioning. . . . They are the result of long-term Christian *poiesis*, shaped by the traditioning and meaning-making of women and men who struggled to make sense of the death of their companion and friend, Jesus" (Elaine M. Wainwright, *Shall We Look for Another?: A Feminist Rereading of the Matthean Jesus* [Maryknoll, N.Y.: Orbis Books, 1998], 101). Kathleen P. Rushton has convincingly argued that the transformative metaphor of a woman in childbirth (Jn 16:21) originated from Johannine women's meaning-making of Jesus' violent death (Kathleen Patricia Rushton, "The Parable of Jn 16:21: A Feminist Socio-Rhetorical Reading of a (Pro)creative Metaphor for the Death-Glory of Jesus" [Ph.D. diss., School of Theology, Faculty of Arts, Griffith University, Australia, 2000]).

36. Regarding the plausibility that the passion tradition originated in women's lament singing, see Corley, "Women and the Crucifixion and Burial of Jesus" and "Lamentation and Gospel: Women's Voices in Passion Tradition" (paper for the annual meeting of the Society of Biblical Literature, 2000). Corley sees elements of the "noble death" of heroes in classic literature also present in the gospels' passion narrative. See also Sawicki, *Seeing the Lord*, 267-75.

37. Regarding Jesus' death as a result of state violence under Roman imperial rule, see Schüssler Fiorenza, *In Memory of Her*, 105, and Mary Rose D'Angelo, "The Concrete Foundation of Christianity: Re-Membering Jesus," *Proceedings of the Catholic Theological Society of America* 49 (1994): 135-46. Paula Fredricksen's study illustrates how the message of divine vindication of Jesus' ministry "regardless of" his violent death by crucifixion gradually became "because of" the cross (Paula Fredricksen, *From Jesus to Christ: The Origins of the New Testament Images of Jesus* [New Haven, Conn.: Yale University Press, 1988]).

38. Virginia Burrus, "Chastity as Autonomy: Women in the Stories of the Apocryphal Acts," *Semeia* 38 (1986): 101-17.

39. Quotation is from Virginia Burrus, *Chastity as Autonomy: Women in the Stories of Apocryphal Acts* (Lewiston, N.Y.: Edwin Mellen, 1987), 104.

40. Burrus, *Chastity as Autonomy*, 73-84, 116-18. Regarding novels and fairy tales (and some folklore), which serve the patriarchal status quo, see Karen E. Rowe, "Feminism and Fairy Tales," *Women's Studies* 6 (1979): 237-57; Rosan A. Jordan and F. A. de Caro, "Women and the Study of Folklore," *Signs* (1986): 500-518. See also Dennis

Ronald MacDonald, *The Legend and the Apostle: The Battle for Paul in Story and Canon* (Philadelphia: Westminster Press, 1983), 17, 53.

41. James C. Scott, *Domination and the Arts of Resistance: Hidden Transcripts* (New Haven, Conn.: Yale University Press, 1990), ix-xiii; idem, "Protest and Profanation: Agrarian Revolt and the Little Tradition," *Theory and Society* 4 (1977): 1-39, 211-46.

42. Joanna Dewey, "From Storytelling to Written Text," 3. In oral transmission stories are modified by storytellers, who adjust the stories to the audience and occasion. People in the Greco-Roman world seem to have felt quite free to modify the stories in their own ways. Even the "quotations" from classical literature and proverbial sayings were freely modified in order to make them more appropriate to the intended context, and this custom was regarded as a legitimate and acceptable activity (Paul J. Achtemeier, "*Omne Verbum Sonat:* The New Testament and the Oral Environment of Late Western Antiquity," *Journal of Biblical Literature* 109/1 [1990]: 3-27). David Barr states, "A fundamental aspect of early Christian preaching was telling stories, and this story was part of the earliest Christian proclamation of the gospel" (David L. Barr, *New Testament Story: An Introduction* [Belmont, Calif.: Wadsworth, 1995], 30).

43. Dewey, "From Storytelling to Written Text."

44. Dennis Ronald MacDonald, "From Audita to Legenda: Oral and Written Miracle Stories," *Forum* 2/4 (1986): 15-26.

45. Ibid., 24.

46. Regarding the change of church location and the diminishing of women's voices, see Pauline Allsop, "'There Were Also Women': The Gospel according to Anna" (D.Min. diss., Episcopal Divinity School, Cambridge, Massachusetts, 1996), 41-43, 48-50.

47. Ibid., 51-52.

### 7   Persecution and Patriarchalization

1. Martin Percival Charlesworth, "Some Observations on Ruler-Cult Especially in Rome," *Harvard Theological Review* 38 (1935): 5-44; Fergus Millar, "The Imperial Cult and the Persecutions," in *Le Culte des Souverains dans L'empire Romain*, ed. Willen den Boer (Geneva: Fondation Hardt, 1972), 143-75.

2. Josephus, *Jewish War,* 2.10, 184-203.

3. Christoper D. Stanley, "Ethnic Conflict between 'Jews' and 'Greeks' in the Greco-Roman Era" (paper presented at the annual meeting of the Society of Biblical Literature, 1995).

4. Bryan W. Jones, "Claudius," *Anchor Bible Dictionary*, vol. 1 (New York: Doubleday, 1992), 1054-55. Miriam T. Griffin, "Nero," *Anchor Bible Dictionary*, 4:1076-81.

5. Elisabeth Schüssler Fiorenza, *The Book of Revelation: Justice and Judgment* (Philadelphia: Fortress Press, 1985), 193. Regarding expulsion from synagogues, see M. Eugene Boring, Klaus Berger, and Carsten Colpe, eds., *Hellenistic Commentary to the New Testament* (Nashville, Tenn.: Abingdon Press, 1995), 302.

6. For criticism on this interpretation, see Steven T. Katz, "Issues in the Separation of Judaism and Christianity after 70 c.e.: A Reconsideration," *Journal of Biblical Literature* 103/1 (1984): 43-76.

7. Ibid., 64-69; Reuven Kimelman, "*Birkat Ha-Minim* and the Lack of Evidence for an Anti-Christian Jewish Prayer in Late Antiquity," in *Jewish and Christian Self-Definition*, ed. E. P. Sanders, A. I. Baumgarten, and Alan Mendelson (Philadelphia: Fortress Press, 1981), 226-44; Claudia J. Setzer, *Jewish Responses to Early Christians: History and Polemics, 30-150 c.e.* (Minneapolis, Minn.: Fortress Press, 1994), 74.

8. It has been interpreted that the "Sanhedrin" in Jerusalem was the Jewish supreme judicial court (Jn 11:47; Mk 14:64; Mt 26:66; Lk 22:30). However, the word "sanhedrin" *(synedrion)*, literally a "sitting down with," is one of many general terms for meetings and assemblies. In the Greco-Roman period regional Jewish community leaders who met in an assembly *(syndrion* or *boule)* were held responsible by the Roman governance for keeping order in their society. There was a central council in Jerusalem, but it was only in the second to third centuries that the council obtained relatively fixed membership, structure, and powers (Anthony J. Saldarini, "Sanhedrin," in *Anchor Bible Dictionary*, 5:975-80). Jacob Neusner states that "there never has been a single encompassing Judaism," "There have been only diverse Judaisms," and "In the long history of the Jews, groups of people who regarded themselves as 'Israel'—that is, groups of Jewish people—have framed many Judaisms" (Jacob Neusner, *The Way of Torah: An Introduction to Judaism* [Belmont, Calif.: Wadsworth, 1993], 6-7). See also Ross Shepard Kraemer, "On the Meaning of the Term 'Jew' in Greco-Roman Inscriptions," *Harvard Theological Review* 82/1 (1989): 35-53; Shaye J. D. Cohen, "Crossing the Boundary and Becoming a Jew," *Harvard Theological Review* 82/1 (1989): 13-33; Wayne O. McCready, "Johannine Self-Understanding and the Synagogue Episode of John 9," in *Self-Definition and Self-Discovery in Early Christianity: A Study in Changing Horizons*, ed. David J. Hawkin and Tom Robinson (Lewiston, N.Y.: Edwin Mellen Press, 1990), 147-66.

9. Elisabeth Schüssler Fiorenza, *In Memory of Her: A Feminist Theological Reconstruction of Christian Origins* (New York: Crossroad, 1983), 109-10.

10. Setzer, *Jewish Responses to Early Christians*, 167-68, 176.

11. Setzer, *Jewish Responses to Early Christians*, 170. Regarding educational flogging, see John T. Townsend, "Education (Israel): Greco-Roman Period," *Anchor Bible Dictionary*, 2:314.

12. Setzer notes that perhaps this handing over of fellow Jewish people (Jewish Christians) to the Roman authorities was the "last resort" for some Jewish communities in tragic circumstances (Setzer, *Jewish Responses to Early Christians*, 176, 172). See also David Rensberger, *Johannine Faith and Liberating Community* (Philadelphia: Westminster Press, 1988), 27.

13. Charlesworth, "Some Observations on Ruler-Cult Especially in Rome," 5-44; Millar, "The Imperial Cult and the Persecutions."

14. Norman Perrin and Dennis C. Duling, *The New Testament: An Introduction* (San Diego, Calif.: Harcourt Brace Jovanovich, 1982), 113-15; Francine Cardman, "Acts of the Women Martyrs," *Anglical Theological Review* 70/2 (1988): 144-50.

15. See Schüssler Fiorenza, *In Memory of Her*, 173-75; Sheila E. McGinn, "The Acts of Thecla," in *Searching the Scriptures*, vol. 2, ed. Elisabeth Schüssler Fiorenza (New York: Crossroad, 1994), 800-828.

16. Quotations are from Herbert Musurillo, *Acts of the Christian Martyrs* (Oxford: Clarendon, 1972), 72, 77-81. I owe this information to Pauline Alsop.

17. Rosemary Rader, "Perpetua," in *A Lost Tradition: Women Writers of the Early Church*, ed. Wilson-Kastner et al. (Washington, D.C.: University Press of America, 1981), 1-32.

18. Luise Schottroff, *Lydia's Impatient Sisters: A Feminist Social History of Early Christianity* (Louisville, Ky.: Westminster John Knox Press, 1995), 104-5. See also Cardman, "Acts of the Women Martyrs."

19. On the general liberating ethos of the early Greco-Roman world, see Kathleen E. Corley, "Were the Women around Jesus Really Prostitutes? Women in the Context of Greco-Roman Meals," *Society of Biblical Literature Seminar Papers* (1989): 487-521.

20. Regarding Jesus' comment on women's blessings in the Lukan texts, Craig and Kristjansson offer an excellent critical feminist reading showing how this text reinforces, rather than undermines, the patriarchal dichotomy of male/word/speech versus female/body/silence. While I appreciate their reading, I also think that the text had an emancipating aspect when heard in a context of more blatant patriarchalism that attempted to constrain women's activities primarily to childbearing and domestic tasks (see Kerry M. Craig and Margret A. Kristjansson, "Women Reading as Men/ Women Reading as Women: A Structural Analysis for the Historical Project," *Semeia* 51 [1990]: 119-36).

21. Schüssler Fiorenza, *In Memory of Her*, 306; Edgar Hennecke and Wilhelm Schneemelcher, eds., *New Testament Apocrypha*, vol. 1, (Philadelphia: Westminster Press, 1963/64), 340-44.

22. "The Didache, or Teaching of the Twelve Apostles," in *Apostolic Fathers*, vol. 1, Loeb Classical Library (Cambridge, Mass.: Harvard University Press, 1950), 308-33; Charles Taylor, "Translation of the *Teaching of the Twelve Apostles*," in *Didache: The Unknown Teaching of the Twelve Apostles*, ed. Brent S. Walters (San Jose, Calif.: Ante-Nicene Archive, 1991). Quotations are from nos. 195, 196, and 198.

23. For *Didascalia Apostolorum*, see R. Hugh Connolly, *Didascalia Apostolorum: The Syriac Version Translated and Accompanied by the Verona Latin Fragments* (Oxford: Clarendon, 1929). The following quotations are from chapters 3 and 15.

24. Regarding the pastoral epistles, see Linda M. Maloney, "The Pastoral Epistles," in Schüssler Fiorenza, *Searching the Scriptures*, 2:361-80.

25. My examination of the use of shame vocabulary in the entire Christian Testament shows that terms related to shame are used without gender differentiation. The only two exceptions are 1 Timothy 2:9 (dress modestly) and 1 Corinthians 14:35 (women should not speak in church). Susan Treggiari's study tells us that such a concept of gender-specific shame as female shame is not found in non-Christian literature in the Greco-Roman world (Susan Treggiari, "Honor and Shame in the Roman World" [lecture, Harvard Divinity School, Cambridge, Massachusetts, 1992]). These observations question the validity of the anthropological theory of polarized gender-specific shame as well as other gender-related social codes (Satoko Yamaguchi, "'Female Shame' and the New Testament" (paper presented at Catholic Biblical Association/Society of Biblical Literature regional conference, Worcester, Massachusetts, 1994).

26. Schüssler Fiorenza, *In Memory of Her*, 243-314. See also Schüssler Fiorenza, *Searching the Scriptures*; Karen L. King, ed., *Images of the Feminine in Gnosticism: Studies in Antiquity and Christianity* (Philadelphia: Fortress Press, 1997). A eucharistic fresco from the end of the first century C.E. shows a woman presiding at a eucharist (not a full meal of *agape*) in a catacomb where a vigil was being held (Dorothy Irvin, "The Ministry of Women in the Early Church: The Archaeological Evidence," *Duke Divinity School Review* 45/2 [1980]: 76-86).

27. Jerome, *Jerome to Ctesiphon*, quoted in Ross Shepard Kraemer, *Her Share of the Blessings: Women's Religions among Pagans, Jews, and Christians in the Greco-Roman World* (Oxford: Oxford University Press, 1992), 157.

28. Susanna Elm, "Montanist Oracles," in Schüssler Fiorenza, *Searching the Scriptures*, 2:31-38; Elaine C. Huber, *Women and the Authority of Inspiration: A Reexamination of Two Prophetic Movements from a Contemporary Feminist Perspective* (Lanham, Md.: University Press of America, 1985), 20. The naming process of this movement makes me wonder whether or not similar things happened to other movements, including the reign-of-God movement that has been called the "Jesus movement." I wonder whether the movement, in its earliest stage, was not practicing a more egalitarian co-leadership among male and female prophets, true to the equality of spirit, rather

than a hierarchical relationship between the single male leader and his disciples. Mary Rose D'Angelo also questions the traditional hierarchical understanding of the reign-of-God movement (Mary Rose D'Angelo, "Re-Membering Jesus: Women, Prophecy, and Resistance in the Memory of the Early Churches," *Horizons* 19/2 [1992]: 199-218).

29. Tertullian, *On the Soul,* 9, quoted in Ross Shepard Kraemer, ed., *Maenads, Martyrs, Matrons, Monastics: A Sourcebook on Women's Religions in the Greco-Roman World* (Philadelphia: Fortress Press, 1988), 224.

30. Hippolytus, *Refutation of Heresies,* 8.12, quoted in Kraemer, *Maenads, Martyrs, Matrons, Monastics,* 225. See also Karen Jo Torjesen, *When Women Were Priests: Women's Leadership in the Early Church and the Scandal of Their Subordination in the Rise of Christianity* (San Francisco: Harper San Francisco, 1993), 299.

31. Origen, fragments on 1 Corinthians, quoted in Huber, *Women and the Authority of Inspiration,* 28. Regarding the writing of books, see Schüssler Fiorenza, *In Memory of Her,* 309; Kraemer, *Her Share of the Blessings,* 165; Eusebius, *History of the Church,* 5.18.13, quoted in Torjesen, *When Women Were Priests,* 299. See also Epiphanius, *Medicine Box,* 49.2, quoted in Kraemer, *Maenads, Martyrs, Matrons, Monastics,* 163. Epiphanius uses the term "founder" for Quintilla, about whom we do not yet know much.

32. Kraemer, *Her Share of the Blessings,* 165.

33. Procopius, *Anecdota,* quoted in Huber, *Women and the Authority of Inspiration,* 63. Guy Edmund Smith, "Montanism and Related Movements" (thesis, Bonebrake Theological Seminary, Dayton, Ohio, 1953), 34, quoted in Huber, *Women and the Authority of Inspiration,* 62.

### PART TWO

#### 8 The Story and Its Characters

1. Biblical translations in this chapter are my own. See Introduction n. 17.

2. For a critical feminist reading of this story, see Sandra M. Schneiders, "Women in the Fourth Gospel and the Role of Women in the Contemporary Church," *Biblical Theology Bulletin* 12 (1982): 35-45; Elisabeth Schüssler Fiorenza, "A Feminist Critical Interpretation for Liberation: Martha and Mary: Lk. 10:38-42," *Religion and Intellectual Life* 41/2 (1986): 21-36; Adele Reinhartz, "From Narrative to History: The Resurrection of Mary and Martha," in *"Women Like This": New Perspectives on Jewish Women in the Greco-Roman World,* ed. Amy-Jill Levine (Atlanta, Ga.: Scholars Press, 1991), 174-76; and a few others.

3. It should be noted that a *raising* of the dead in sign stories in the Christian Testament is not really a resurrection but a resuscitation of a person who was thought to have died. The person will physically die again. As we take into consideration the tendency toward enhancement of the miraculous in storytelling performances, it is likely that a raising story was originally a healing story of a person near to death or suffering a death-like disease. Regarding the components of a miracle story, see Gerd Theissen, *The Miracle Stories of the Early Christian Tradition,* trans. Francis McDonagh (Philadelphia: Fortress Press, 1983), 72-80; Antoinette Clark Wire, "The Structure of the Gospel Miracle Stories and Their Tellers," *Semeia* 11 (1978): 83-113. For some reconstructions of traditions and redactions, see Rudulf Bultmann, *The Gospel of John: A Commentary* (Oxford: Basil Blackwell, 1971), 414; W. Nicol, *The Semeia in the Fourth Gospel: Tradition and Redaction* (Leiden: E. J. Brill, 1972), 21, 37-39, 60;

Robert Tomson Fortna, *The Fourth Gospel and Its Predecessor: From Narrative Source to Present Gospel* (Philadelphia: Fortress Press, 1988), 94-109, 128-46; Urban C. von Wahlde, *The Earliest Version of John's Gospel: Recovering the Gospel of Signs* (Wilmington, Del.: Michael Glazier, 1989), 116-28.

4. Dorothy A. Lee, *The Symbolic Narratives of the Fourth Gospel: The Interplay of Form and Meaning* (Sheffield: Sheffield Academic Press, 1994), 188. For the common use of a chiastic form and the "interwoven tapestry," see Joanna Dewey, "Mark as Interwoven Tapestry: Forecasts and Echoes for a Listening Audience," *Catholic Biblical Quarterly* 53 (1991): 221-36.

5. On the historical level many scholars agree that the temple episode was the last public action Jesus took before his arrest, and that this triggered the final plot of some Judean authority figures to kill Jesus. However, the Johannine gospel places the raising miracle, Jesus' life-giving ministry, as the final occasion that triggered the Judean authority figures' plot to kill Jesus (see Sandra M. Schneiders, "Death in the Community of Eternal Life: History, Theology, and Spiritaulity in John 11," *Interpretation* 41/1 [1987]: 56).

6. Regarding the characters as representatives of certain groups of people, see Raymond F. Collins, "The Representative Figures of the Fourth Gospel—I," *The Downside Review* 94 (1976): 26-46, 118-32; Mary Ann Tolbert, *Sowing the Gospel: Mark's World in Literary-Historical Perspective* (Minneapolis, Minn.: Fortress Press, 1989), 78.

7. Regarding *parresia*, see M. Eugene Boring, *The Continuing Voices of Jesus: Christian Prophecy and the Gospel Tradition* (Louisville, Ky.: Westminster John Knox Press, 1991), 131.

8. Mark W. G. Stibbe, "The Elusive Christ: A New Reading of the Fourth Gospel," *Journal of Studies in the New Testament* 44 (1991): 19-38.

9. R. Arlan Culpepper, *Anatomy of the Fourth Gospel: A Study in Literary Design* (Philadelphia: Fortress Press, 1983). Many scholars point out that the gospel invites misunderstandings by ambiguous statements, metaphors, and double-entendres in Jesus' conversation (ibid., 160), and by the "surplus of meaning" (ibid., 199) that is not fully exhausted in words and scenes.

10. Tolbert, *Sowing the Gospel*, 41; Frank Thielman, "The Style of the Fourth Gospel and Ancient Literary Critical Concepts of Religious Discourse," in *Persuasive Artistry: Studies in New Testament Rhetoric in Honor of George A. Kennedy*, ed. Duane F. Watson, *Journal for the Study of the New Testament Supplement Series* 50 (1991): 169-83.

11. Regarding the Greco-Roman miracle techniques, see Robert Tomson Fortna, *The Fourth Gospel and Its Predecessor: From Narrative Source to Present Gospel* (Philadelphia: Fortress Press, 1988), 107-8. Some scholars interpret this verse as referring to Jesus' anger toward the despair or faithlessness of Mary and the Jews, or to the death of Lazarus, or to anticipation of his passion (Rudolf Bultmann, *The Gospel of John: A Commentary* [Oxford: Basil Blackwell, 1964/1971], 406); Cullen I. K. Story, "The Mental Attitude of Jesus at Bethany: John 11:33, 38," *New Testament Studies* 37 (1991): 51-66; Barnabas Lindars, "Rebuking the Spirit: A New Analysis of the Lazarus Story of John 11," *New Testament Studies* 38 (1992): 89-104. However, Jesus' heightened emotion cannot be anger against the weeping of Mary and the sympathetic Jewish neighbors around her. The same word "troubled" *(tarasso)* is used again to describe Jesus at the end of his public ministry: "Now is my soul troubled" (12:27). Besides, Jesus shares tears with Mary and Jewish neighbors on his way to the tomb.

12. Schneiders, "Death in the Community of Eternal Life," 54. See also Elizabeth E. Platt, "The Ministry of Mary of Bethany," *Theology Today* 34 (1977): 35.

13. Some scholars interpret that the gospel presents Jesus here with extraordinary divine potency or divinity equal to God (e.g., Jerome H. Neyrey, "'My Lord and My God': The Divinity of Jesus in John's Gospel," *Society of Biblical Literature Seminar Papers* [1986]: 152-71). However, the character Jesus does not make any claim for his own divine power to raise the dead. In the gospel the character Jesus has been making his derivative status and power very clear (e.g., 5:24, 31; 8:24). In accordance with this presentation, here Jesus ascribes saving power to God. For opinions that the use of the father-son metaphor in the gospel does not ascribe divinity to Jesus, see, for example, T. E. Pollard, "The Father-Son and God-Believer Relationships according to St. John: A Brief Study of John's Use of Prepositions," in *L'Evangile de Jean: Sources, Redaction, Théologie,* ed. M. de Jonge (Leuven: Leuven University Press, 1977), 262-69.

14. Charles Kingsley Barrett, *Essays on John* (Philadelphia: Westminster Press, 1982), 13. See also John A. T. Robinson, *The Priority of John* (London: SCM Press, 1985), 349.

15. Literally, what Jesus says is, "Lazarus, *deuro, exo*" (11:43). The Greek word *deuro* is an adjectival adverb, used like a verb imperative, meaning "(out): here (come on!)." *Exo* is also an adjectival adverb, meaning "out" or "outside." So Jesus' calling voice may be translated in a vivid colloquial way, "Lazarus, out here, out!" While the colloquial wording might have come from an earlier tradition, the double use of adjectival adverbs symbolically emphasizes Jesus' call to Lazarus to come *out.* Ironically, the Greek word used for Jesus' "shouting" *(kragazo)* for life for Lazarus echoes the Jews' shouting *(kragazo)* for Jesus' death (18:40; 19:6, 12, 15). See Raymond E. Brown, *The Gospel and Epistles of John: A Concise Commentary* (Collegeville, Minn.: Liturgical Press, 1988), 65; Lindars, "Rebuking the Spirit," 100. See Martin Scott, *Sophia and the Johannine Jesus* (Sheffield: Sheffield Academic Press, 1992), 169, regarding the "descent-go away" combination in this gospel. Robert Kysar says that the gospel sets "the Christ event within the framework of the Exodus-Passover theme" ("The Gospel of John," *Anchor Bible Dictionary*, vol. 3 [New York: Doubleday, 1992], 926). For the exodus theme in the gospel, see also Helmut Koester, "The Story of the Johannine Tradition," *Sewanee Theological Review* 36 (1992): 17-32.

16. Douglas K. Clark argues that the telling of the seven signs of Jesus in his lifetime in the gospel is the retelling of the same in Exodus (Clark, "Signs in Wisdom and John," *Catholic Biblical Quarterly* 45/2 [1983]: 205). Moses was identified and called "my beloved" of God, "son of God," and even "God" (see Wayne A. Meeks, "Moses as God and King," in *Religions in Antiquity,* ed. Jacob Neusner [Leiden: E. J. Brill, 1968], 357). Therefore, it is quite understandable that Jesus, the leader of the new exodus, who is to be better and mightier than the old hero, has to be presented with all these titles and identifications and more. Sarah J. Tanzer states, "The distancing from the 'Jews' and from Jewish festivals and the negative portrayal of the Jews would have a great hortatory effect on secret Christian Jews . . . not to be afraid to distance themselves from their Jewish customs. . . . After all, their primary identity was as Jews" (Sarah J. Tanzer, "Secret Christian Jews in John," in *The Future of Early Christianity,* ed. Birger A. Pearson, A. Thomas Kraabel, George W. E. Nickelsburg, and Norman R. Peterson [Minneapolis, Minn.: Fortress Press, 1991], 290-300).

17. Oona Ajzenstat, "Jesus as the New Odysseus: An Analysis of a Literary Source of John 9 and 10" (paper presented at the annual meeting of the Academy of American Religion/Society of Biblical Literature, 1995). Viewing Odysseus's exodus as a subtext offers some clues for understanding problems in these chapters, such as why Jesus is identified not only as the good shepherd but also as the door in 10:7. (In the *Odyssey,* a stone door symbolizes a transition from the cave of darkness/death to light/

life, and Odysseus makes the stone door open for their escape. For his men, he is the door to life.) And, why does the setting suddenly change in 10:22? (It corresponds with the *Odyssey*'s setting change in 471.) And in John 10:40? (It also corresponds to 541.)

At the same time, the metaphors in John 9—10 seem to have subtexts other than the *Odyssey*. These other subtexts may include both Jewish traditional and Greco-Roman literature. For example, metaphors derived from shepherding echo Ezekiel 34, Jeremiah 23:1-4, Ezra 5, and many other parts of the Hebrew Bible. In Jewish traditions the leadership role of the prophets was compared to that of the shepherd. On the other hand, since Plato's *Republic* (fourth century B.C.E.), the metaphor of shepherding was also frequently used for ruling and governing in Greek and Greco-Roman literature (Charles H. Talbert, *Reading John: A Literary and Theological Commentary on the Four Gospels and the Johannine Epistles* [New York: Crossroad, 1992], 167; M. Eugene Boring, Klaus Berger, and Carsten Colpe, eds., *Hellenistic Commentary to the New Testament* [Nashville, Tenn.: Abingdon Press, 1995], 286). Another Greek subtext may be the allegory of the cave in Plato's *Republic* (7.1-11), in which human beings are bound in a cave where they can see only reflections of reality and by escaping from or going out of the cave, some are able to see true reality (Boring et al., *Hellenistic Commentary*, 280-81).

The Johannine gospel seems to have enriched the imagery and the meaning of its narrative by making many allusions both to conventional Jewish traditions as well as to various popularly known Greco-Roman literature. Craig Koester points to "Johannine symbolism [which] would have been accessible to and entertaining to a spectrum of readers" and assumes the communities' missionary engagement (Craig Koester, *Symbolism in the Fourth Gospel: Meaning, Mystery, Community* [Minneapolis, Minn.: Fortress Press, 1995], xi).

18. Regarding their being disciples, see Elisabeth Schüssler Fiorenza, *In Memory of Her: A Feminist Theological Reconstruction of Christian Origins* (New York: Crossroad, 1983), 329; idem, "A Feminist Critical Interpretation for Liberation," 31; Jeffrey Lloyd Staley, *Reading with a Passion: Rhetoric, Autobiography, and the American West in the Gospel of John* (New York: Continuum, 1995), 65. In the entire gospel only Martha, Mary, and Lazarus are identified by name as Jesus' friends (11:5). In the Greco-Roman world the term "friend" refers both to loving relationships and to the hierarchical but supposedly mutually beneficial patron-client relationship (Alan C. Mitchell, "The Social Function of Friendship in Acts 2:44-47 and 4:32-37," *Journal of Biblical Literature* 111/2 [1992]: 255-72). The identification of being someone's "friend" had a political connotation (e.g., "Caesar's friend" in Jn 19:12; see also Richard J. Cassidy, *John's Gospel in New Perspective: Christology and the Realities of Roman Power* [Maryknoll, N.Y.: Orbis Books, 1992], 81-87; Sharon H. Ringe, *Wisdom's Friends: Community and Christology in the Fourth Gospel* [Louisville, Ky.: Westminster John Knox Press, 1999], 65). Regarding the word "lord" (*kyrios*), while it was applied for the Hebrew word *YHWH* in *LXX*, the same word was also generally used for a master and lord, and as a reverent address, "Sir."

19. Regarding Martha's statement as the beginning part of a lament, see Ardy Bass, "Martha and Jesus," *The Bible Today* 32 (1994): 90-94.

20. This confession uses a traditional Jewish expression; the phrase "one who is to come into the world" was specifically connected to the Jewish people's long-held expectation for the coming of a prophet like Moses, Elijah, or Elisha (Raymond E. Brown, *The Gospel according to John*, vol. 1 [New York: Doubleday, 1966], 234-35). For the Jewishness of this notion, see also Marinus de Jonge, *Jesus: Stranger from Heaven and Son of God: Jesus Christ and the Christians in Johannine Perspective* (Missoula, Mont.:

Scholars Press, 1977), 84; Margaret Davies, *Rhetoric and Reference in the Fourth Gospel* (Sheffield: Sheffield Academic Press, 1992), 52. See also Gail R. O'Day, *The Word Disclosed: John's Story and Narrative Preaching* (St. Louis: CBP Press, 1987), 88; Dorothy A. Lee, *The Symbolic Narratives of the Fourth Gospel: The Interplay of Form and Meaning* (Sheffield: Sheffield Academic Press, 1994), 206.

21. Lee, *The Symbolic Narratives;* Mark W. G. Stibbe, *John: A Readings Commentary* (Sheffield: JSOT, 1992), 125; For the recognition that Martha, rather than Peter in 6:69, is the spokesperson of the faith of the community, see Sandra M. Schneiders, "Women in the Fourth Gospel and the Role of Women in the Contemporary Church," *Biblical Theology Bulletin* 12 (1982): 41; Schüssler Fiorenza, *In Memory of Her*, 329, among many others.

22. Many scholars think that Martha's objection here makes it seem as if she does not believe in Jesus' power to raise Lazarus, and many scholars have reassessed her faith and are divided in their conclusions. See George W. MacRae, *Invitation to John: A Commentary on the Gospel of John with Complete Text from the Jerusalem Bible* (New York: Doubleday, 1978), 141; Stephen E. Dollar, *The Significance of Women in the Fourth Gospel* (Ann Arbor, Mich.: University Microfilms International, 1983), 123; Schneiders, "Women in the Fourth Gospel," 41; Lee, *The Symbolic Narratives of the Fourth Gospel*, 202.

23. Elsewhere in the Johannine gospel different Greek words are used for "servants." For example, *doulos* (15:15), and *hup'retai* (18:36).

24. Elisabeth Moltmann-Wendel talks about injustice done to Martha in the way she has been remembered in Christian traditions (Moltmann-Wendel, *The Women around Jesus: Reflection on Authentic Personhood* [New York: Crossroad, 1982], 22). It seems likely that more and more such injustices will be discovered as feminist studies proceed. Adele Reinhartz thinks that the story of dinner in Bethany, in which women are hosting and are present in Jesus' inner circle, provides a counterbalance to the calling narrative in which no females are mentioned (Adele Reinhartz, "The Gospel of John," in *Searching the Scriptures*, vol. 2, ed. Elisabeth Schüssler Fiorenza [New York: Crossroad, 1994], 583).

25. Regarding the non-conflictual relationship between the sisters, see Schüssler Fiorenza, "A Feminist Critical Interpretation for Liberation," 32; Turid Karlsen Seim, "Roles of Women in the Gospel of John," *Aspects on the Johannine Literature: Papers Presented at a Conference of Scandinavian New Testament Exegetes at Uppsala, June 16-19, 1986*, ed. Lars Hartman and Birger Olsson (Uppsala: Almovist and Wiksell, 1987), 73.

26. Observing the lack of hostile Judeans or Jewish people in the stories related to women, many scholars assume that it is the result of the use of traditional material; that is, the earlier traditions reflect the communal situation in which they could be optimistic, but later they have undergone severe conflict with local synagogue members and experienced dislocation—with their Jewish roots being torn up–which has led to a dualistic exclusivist view (e.g., Raymond E. Brown, *The Community of the Beloved Disciple: The Life, Loves, and Hates of an Individual Church in New Testament Times* [New York: Paulist Press, 1979], 166-67; Robert Kysar, *John, the Maverick Gospel* [Louisville, Ky.: Westminster John Knox Press, 1993], 70, 75-76). While I do not deny such a tendency, I think that there were still diverse opinions within Johannine communities at the time of the gospel's composition. The gospel's manipulative presentation of characters implies the existence of various groups and opinions (Brown, *The Community of the Beloved Disciple*, 88-108). Furthermore, Martha's assent for the character Jesus' last enactment of the new exodus (11:39) seems to be important and something the author/s wanted to obtain. This would imply that many women did

not share in the author/s' idea of dissociation from "the Judeans" or the exodus from "the Judeans."

27. Schüssler Fiorenza, "A Feminist Critical Interpretation for Liberation," 31.

28. Mark Stibbe sees the authorial identification of Lazarus as the Beloved Disciple (Stibbe, *John*, 126).

29. In John, 11:2; 12:3; 13:5; in Luke, only in the anointing story, 7:38, 44. Nowhere else in the Christian Testament does the word appear.

30. John Christopher Thomas, *Footwashing in John 13 and the Johannine Community* (Sheffield: Sheffield Academic Press, 1991), 42, 187.

31. Elisabeth Schüssler Fiorenza says that the Johannine gospel's rhetorical use of this story counteracts the picture of the all-male Last Supper (*In Memory of Her*, xiv).

32. Schüssler Fiorenza, *In Memory of Her*, xiii-xiv; Fortna, *The Fourth Gospel and Its Predecessor*, 140-42; Elaine M. Wainwright, *Toward a Feminist Critical Reading of the Gospel according to Matthew* (Berlin: Walter de Gruyter, 1991), 126-28; Dollar, *The Significance of Women in the Fourth Gospel* , 131-34.

33. J. F. Coakley, "The Anointing at Bethany and the Priority of John," *Journal of Biblical Literature* 107/2 (1988): 241-56. See also Athenaeus, *Deipnosophists* 12.553: "There was a custom at Athens, among persons who lived in luxury, of anointing [*enaleiphein*] even the feet with perfumes" (Loeb Classical Library, trans. Charles B. Gulick [Cambridge, Mass.: Harvard University, 1941], 5.513; Thomas, *Footwashing in John 13 and the Johannine Community*, 42, 187).

34. Regarding funeral preparations, see S. Safrai, M. Stern, with D. Flusser and W. C. van Unik, eds., *The Jewish People in the First Century* (Assen: Van Gorcum, 1976), 773-87. See also an excellent summary of Jewish, Greek, and Roman funeral customs in Kathleen E. Corley, "Women and the Crucifixion and Burial of Jesus: 'He Was Buried: On the Third Day He Was Raised,'" *Forum* New Series 1/1 (1998): 181-225.

35. Marianne Sawicki, *Seeing the Lord: Resurrection and Early Christian Practices* (Minneapolis, Minn.: Fortress Press, 1994), 162-63.

36. Sawicki reconstructs the anointing story as a woman's poiesis (meaning-making) of Jesus' death. I admit her reconstruction is persuasive, but I think a historical woman behind this story is plausible, especially since the story is told in all the canonical gospels. Kathleen E. Corley argues for a historical core of the woman's anointing story ("The Anointing of Jesus in the Synoptic Tradition," paper presented at the Jesus Seminar, 1994). Winsome Munro states that it is plausible that the anointing woman was a prophet, a historical figure, in the earliest Christian movements ("A Woman's Anointing of Jesus: A Response to Papers by Corley and Winter," paper presented at the Jesus Seminar, 1994).

37. In *Secret Mark*, a text of which only two fragments were found, there is a raising story of a young man on the fourth day in Bethany. There, the raised young man asks Jesus to stay with him, and Jesus does so. This indicates that there may have been different versions of this story in which Lazarus's role is not passive and silent. Regarding *Secret Mark*, see Raymond E. Brown, "The Relation of 'The Secret Gospel of Mark' to the Fourth Gospel," *Catholic Biblical Quarterly* 36 (1974): 466-85; Moody D. Smith, "John," *Harper's Bible Commentary*, ed. James L. Mays et al. (San Francisco: Harper & Row, 1988), 1044-76; Helmut Koester, *Ancient Christian Gospels: Their History and Development* (Philadelphia: Trinity Press International, 1999), 280, 296; Robin M. Jensen, "The Raising of Lazarus," *Bible Review* (1995): 20-28, 45.

38. See Schneiders, "Death in the Community of Eternal Life," 44-56.

39. See George J. Riley, *Resurrection Reconsidered: Thomas and John in Controversy* (Minneapolis, Minn.: Fortress Press, 1995), 122-24. Regarding the parallel or variant

passages between the Johannine gospel and the Gospel of Thomas, see Helmut Koester, "The Story of the Johannine Tradition," 20-22.

40. Scholars detect several groups of people with whom the author/s of the Johannine gospel might have engaged in theological debates. See, for example, Brown, *The Community of the Beloved Disciple*, 62-91, 168-69; Jouette M. Bassler, "The Galileans: A Neglected Factor in Johannine Community Research," *Catholic Biblical Quarterly* 43 (1981): 243-57; Culpepper, *Anatomy of the Fourth Gospel*, 221-25. Elaine M. Wainwright talks about different voices within Matthean communities, among which certain voices gradually became dominant by suppressing others ("Go Quickly and Tell— Alternative Voices Remembering Jesus and Shaping Ministry," paper presented at the Australian Catholic Biblical Association Meeting in Sydney, 1995). Hisako Kinukawa's study has restored some of the silenced and marginalized voices of women within Markan communities (*Women and Jesus in Mark: A Japanese Feminist Perspective* [Maryknoll, N.Y.: Orbis Books, 1994], 4). The same seems to apply to the Johannine communities.

41. See R. S. Sugirtharajah, "For You Always Have the Poor with You: An Example of Hermeneutics of Suspicion," *Asian Journal of Theology* 4.1 (1990): 102-7.

42. Adele Reinhartz says that the gospel "provides meager support" for a view that contrasts "Jewish authorities" and "ordinary Judeans" (Adele Reinhartz, "The Johannine Community and Its Jewish Neighbors," in *What Is John?*, ed. Fernando F. Segovia [Atlanta, Ga.: Scholars Press, 1998], 111-38). True, the crowd or "ordinary Judeans" are not courageous fighters, but in my view they are still presented as contrasting with authority figures.

43. David Rensberger, "Sectarianism and Theological Interpretation in John," in Segovia, *What Is John?*, 90-92. See also Louis H. Feldman, "New Testament Antisemitic?," *Moment* (1990): 50.

44. Jesus' work of gathering the scattered children of God evokes the divine Sophia imagery (Mt 23:37; Lk 13:34). Regarding the gathering, see Talbert, *Reading John*, 177; Johannes Beutler, "Two Ways of Gathering: The Plot to Kill Jesus in John 11.47-53," *New Testament Studies* 40 (1994): 399-406. Lawrence M. Wills's study shows that the portrayal of the crowd in the Lukan gospel as "a chaotic and explosive force" parallels "the 'imperial sociology' of Roman historians" ("The Depiction of the Jews in Acts," *Journal of Biblical Literature* 110/4 [1991]: 631-54, quotations at 634, 650). The portrayal of the crowd in the Johannine gospel contrasts with such a view.

45. Regarding the gospels' double meanings, see Davies, *Rhetoric and Reference in the Fourth Gospel*, 347; E. Richard, "Expressions of Double Meaning and Their Function in the Gospel of John," *New Testament Studies* 31 (1985): 96-112.

## 9   Ethnicity, Class, and Gender of the Story World

1. Biblical translations in this chapter are my own. See Introduction n. 17.

2. Regarding women's names, see Tal Ilan, "Notes on the Distribution of Jewish Women's Names in Palestine in the Second Temple and Mishnaic Periods," *Journal of Jewish Studies* 40/2 (1989): 186-200. Regarding the name Lazarus, see Raymond F. Collins, "Lazarus," *Anchor Bible Dictionary*, vol. 4 (New York: Doubleday, 1992), 265-66. Regarding the name Martha, see Raymond F. Collins, "Martha," *Anchor Bible Dictionary*, 4:573-74.

3. Regarding the word "for" *(hyper)*, as in "for the benefit of," see Marianne Meye Thompson, *The Incarnate Word: Perspectives on Jesus in the Fourth Gospel* (Peabody, Mass.: Hendrickson Publishing, 1988), 92. "One for all" was the Greco-Roman common ideal around the time (Eugene M. Boring, Klaus Berger, Carsten Colpe, eds., *Hellenistic Commentary to the New Testament* [Nashville, Tenn.: Abingdon Press, 1995],

288, 290). Regarding the political connotation of the "for," see Gerard S. Sloyan, *John: Interpretation: A Bible Commentary for Teaching and Preaching* (Atlanta, Ga.: John Knox, 1988), 146.

4. On the use of *laos* and *ethnos*, see Severino Pancaro, "'People of God' in St. John's Gospel," *New Testament Studies* 16 (1967-8): 114-29. Regarding "Greeks," see Johannes Beutler, "Greeks Come to See Jesus," *Biblica* 71/3 (1990): 333-47.

5. In the synoptic gospels different groups of "the Jews" are referred to by different terms. Among Jewish leaders are high priests (Mt—25 times, Mk—22 times, Lk—15 times), Sadducees (Mt—7, Mk—1, Lk—1), scribes (Mt—23, Mk—21, Lk—14), elders (Mt—30, Mk—12, Lk—5), and Pharisees (Mt—30, Mk—12, Lk—27). "The Judeans" *(hoi Ioudaioi)*, appears only a few times (Mt—5, Mk—6, Lk— ). In the Johannine gospel "high priest" is used 21 times, and Pharisees 19 times; there is no mention of Sadducees, scribes, or elders, but "the Judeans" appear 71 times (the word's occurrence in the story of "the woman taken in adultery" is not included, because the story is an interpolation). The very generalized and frequent use of "the Judeans" in this gospel creates a negative image of "the Judeans" as a whole, and this peculiar usage seems intentional. It does not necessarily mean, however, that the Johannine gospel is anti-Jewish or anti-Semitic. See R. Arlan Culpepper, "The Gospel of John and the Jews," *Review and Expositor* 84/2 (1987): 273-88; Daniel J. Harrington, "'The Jews' in John's Gospel," *The Bible Today* 27/4 (1989): 203-09; Wilfried Harrington, "The Johannine Jesus," *Scripture in Church* 24/94 (1994): 233-40.

6. See, for example, Turid Karlsen Seim, "The Gospel of Luke," in *Searching the Scriptures*, ed. Elisabeth Schüssler Fiorenza (New York: Crossroad, 1994), 2:745; Charles H. Talbert, *Reading John: A Literary and Theological Commentary on the Fourth Gospel and the Johannine Epistles* (New York: Crossorad, 1992), 173; Frank Thielman, "The Style of the Fourth Gospel and Ancient Literary Critical Concepts of Religious Discourse," in *Persuasive Artistry: Studies in New Testament Rhetoric in Honor of George A. Kennedy*, ed. Duane F. Watson, *Journal for the Study of the New Testament Supplement Series* 50 (1991): 169-83.

7. Leonie J. Archer, *Her Price Is beyond Rubies: The Jewish Woman in Graeco-Roman Palestine* (Sheffield: Sheffield Academic Press, 1990), 281; Kathleen E. Corley, "Were the Women around Jesus Really Prostitutes? Woman in the Context of Greco-Roman Meals," *Society of Biblical Literature Seminar Papers* (1989): 487-521.

8. Archer, *Her Price Is beyond Rubies*, 254-55; Ze'ev Safrai and M. Stern, *The Jewish People in the First Century* (Assen: Van Gorcum, 1976), 775.

9. Craig Koester says, "there is no indication that Mary belonged to one of the wealthiest classes. . . . The ointment was apparently a major expenditure" (Craig Koester, *Symbolism in the Fourth Gospel: Meaning, Mystery, Community* [Minneapolis, Minn.: Fortress Press, 1995], 113).

10. Robert Tomson Fortna, *The Fourth Gospel and Its Predecessor: From Narrative Source to Present Gospel* (Philadelphia: Fortress Press, 1988), 6.

11. Henry George Liddell and Robert Scott, *Greek-English Lexicon: A New Edition*, rev. ed. (Oxford: Clarendon, 1966), 383, 486-87, 578, 935, 1200, 1600. In ancient literature *keiriais* were used for bed-making or for bandages, but there is no example of their use as burial cloths other than in this passage. The fact that this use of *keiriais* does not appear in the extant literature does not necessarily mean they were not used as burial cloths, but it does suggest that their use as burial cloths was not the preferred choice for decent burials.

12. See Gerda Lerner, *The Creation of Patriarchy* (New York: Oxford University Press, 1986), 139. In contrast to the story of Mary and Martha in the Lukan version

(Lk 10:38-42), there is no conflict between the sisters in the Johannine version. See Elisabeth Schüssler Fiorenza, "A Feminist Critical Interpretation for Liberation: Martha and Mary: Lk. 10:38-42," *Religion and Intellectual Life* 41/2 (1986): 21-36.

13. Mary Ann Tolbert, *Sowing the Gospel: Mark's World in Literary-Historical Perspective* (Minneapolis, Minn.: Fortress Press, 1989), 221-22.

14. Regarding the text's disregard for social codes without polemical tones, see Turid Karlsen Seim, "Roles of Women in the Gospel of John," in *Aspects of the Johannine Literature: Papers Presented at a Conference on Scandinavian New Testament Exegetes at Uppsala, June 16-19, 1986*, ed. Lars Hartman and Birger Olsson (Uppsala: Almovist and Wiksell, 1987), 70. Actually, not only in this story but in the entire Johannine gospel, no woman is presented as staying inside the house. Even if the gospel is intent on persuading the audience to follow Jesus as leader of the new exodus, the exterior or "public" presence of all the women characters is a subversive gender construction.

15. In his article on the text Jeffrey Lloyd Staley focuses on the two sisters, while most male scholars have focused on the two males, Jesus and Lazarus. He argues that Jesus' delay in attending to the sisters' need results in their brother's death and gives them a chance to act on their own. That is, each of them is empowered to "ever bolder speech and action" (Jeffrey Lloyd Staley, *Reading with a Passion: Rhetoric, Autobiography, and the American West in the Gospel of John* [New York: Continuum, 1995], 76-77). This is an interesting interpretation. In patriarchal societies, in general, the absence or loss of males often functions as the only chance for women to take on bold speech and action.

16. Mary Rose D'Angelo suggests that it is possible that Martha and Mary were a missionary pair as "sisters" or as "a minister and her sister" (Mary Rose D'Angelo, "Women Partners in the New Testament," *Journal of Feminist Studies in Religion* 6/1 [1990]: 65-86).

17. See, for example, Sandra M. Schneiders, "Women in the Fourth Gospel and the Role of Women in the Contemporary Church," *Biblical Theology Bulletin* 12 (1982): 35-45; John Rena, "Women in the Gospel of John," *Eglise et Théologie* 17 (1986): 131-47; Seim, "Roles of Women in the Gospel of John," 56-73; Jeffrey Lloyd Staley, *The Print's First Kiss: A Rhetorical Investigation of the Implied Reader in the Fourth Gospel* (Atlanta, Ga.: Scholars Press, 1988), 69-70.

18. For a similar observation, see Ingrid Rosa Kitzberger, "Mary of Bethany and Mary of Magdala—Two Female Characters in the Johannine Passion Narrative: A Feminist, Narrative-Critical Reader-Response," *New Testament Studies* 41 (1995): 564-86.

19. In her study Kathleen P. Rushton has observed an ironic contrast between the symbolic world of women (less visible, but understanding and accomplishing the work of God) and that of men (visible, but in betrayal and misunderstanding). Rushton questions "whether the traditions comprising the stories of women, the birth traditions and aspects of the presentation of the death of Jesus, were shaped by women who may even have been members of the Johannine influential school" (Kathleen P. Rushton, "The Parable of John 16:21: A Feminist Socio-Rhetorical Reading of a (Pro)creative Metaphor for the Death-Glory of Jesus" [Ph.D. diss., School of Theology, Griffith University, Australia, 2000], 185).

### 10 *Martha, Mary, and Christian Women (and Men) Today*

1. Sheila Greeve Davaney says that "new possibilities" emerge "out of creative reconstruals of our plural inheritances" (Sheila Greeve Davaney, "Continuing the Story, but Departing the Text: A Historicist Interpretation of Feminist Norms," in *Horizons*

*in Feminist Theology: Identity, Tradition, and Norms,* ed. Rebecca S. Chopp and Sheila Greeve Davaney [Minneapolis, Minn.: Fortress Press, 1997], 215-31).

2. Chung Hyun Kyung, "Welcome the Spirit; Hear Her Cries: The Holy Spirit, Creation, and the Culture of Life," *Christianity and Crisis* 51/10-11 (1991): 220-23. If Japanese Christians had been present, they would likely have been most astonished by Chung's "syncretistic" performance. Japanese churches have been extremely careful to maintain an "authentic" Christian faith, avoiding any sign of the "syncretistic," and are still captive to the Western-colonized spirituality that identifies only the Western form as purely Christian. See also Kwok Pui-lan, "The Image of the 'White Lady': Gender and Race in Christian Mission," *Concilium* 6 (1991): 19-27; idem, *Discovering the Bible in the Non-Biblical World* (Maryknoll, N.Y.: Orbis Books, 1995).

3. Regarding the political danger of uncritical syncretism, see Satoko Yamaguchi, "The Invention of Traditions: The Case of Shintoism," *In God's Image* 18/4 (1999): 40-46.

# Bibliography

Abrahamsen, Valerie. "Christianity and the Rock Reliefs at Philippi." *Biblical Archaeologist* (1988): 46-56.
———. "Women at Philippi: The Pagan and Christian Evidence." *Journal of Feminist Studies in Religion* 3/2 (1987): 17-30.
Achtemeier, Paul J. "Jesus and the Disciples as Miracle Workers in the Apocryphal New Testament." In *Aspects of Religious Propaganda in Judaism and Early Christianity*, edited by Elisabeth Schüssler Fiorenza. Notre Dame, Ind.: University of Notre Dame Press, 1976, 149-86.
———. "*Omne Verbum Sonat:* The New Testament and the Oral Environment of Late Western Antiquity." *Journal of Biblical Literature* 109/1 (1990): 3-27.
Ackerman, Susan. "And the Women Knead Dough: The Worship of the Queen of Heaven in Sixth Century Judah." In *Gender and Difference in Ancient Israel*, edited by Peggy L. Day. Minneapolis, Minn.: Fortress Press, 1989, 109-24.
———. "The Queen Mother and the Cult in the Ancient Near East." In *Women and Goddess Traditions in Antiquity and Today*, edited by Karen L. King. Minneapolis, Minn.: Fortress Press, 1997, 179-209.
Ajzenstat, Oona, "Jesus as the New Odysseus: An Analysis of a Literary Source of John 9 and 10." Paper presented at AAR/SBL, 1995.
Alexander, Philip S., "Rabbinic Judaism and the New Testament." *Zeitschrift für das neutestamentliche Wissenschaft* 74 (1983): 237-46.
Allsop, Pauline, "'There Were Also Women': The Gospel according to Anna." Doctor of Ministry diss., Episcopal Divinity School, Cambridge, Mass., 1996.
Anderson, Janice Capel, and S. D. Moore. *Mark and Method: New Approaches in Biblical Studies*. Minneapolis, Minn.: Fortress Press, 1992.
Anderson, Robert T. "Samaritans." *Anchor Bible Dictionary*. Vol. 5. New York: Doubleday, 1992, 940-47.
Archer, Leonie J. *Her Price Is beyond Rubies: The Jewish Woman in Graeco-Roman Palestine*. Sheffield: Sheffield Academic Press, 1990.
Arlandson, James Malcolm. *Women, Class, and Society in Early Christianity: Models from Luke-Acts*. Peabody, Mass.: Hendrickson Publications, 1997.
Arthur, Rose Hofman. *The Wisdom Goddess: Feminist Motifs in Eight Nag Hammadi Documents*. New York: University Press of America, 1984.
Ashton, John. "The Transformation of Wisdom: A Study of the Prologue of John's Gospel." *New Testament Studies* 32/2 (1986): 161-86.
Aune, David E. "The Odes of Solomon and Early Christian Prophecy." *New Testament Studies* 28/4 (1982): 435-60.
———. *Prophecy in Early Christianity and the Ancient Mediterranean World*. Grand Rapids, Mich.: Eerdmans, 1983.
Bach, Alice, ed. *The Pleasure of Her Text: Feminist Readings of Biblical and Historical Texts*. Philadelphia: Trinity Press International, 1990.

Backer, Cynthia. "Pseudo-Philo and the Transformation of Jephthah's Daughter." In *Anti-Covenant: Counter-Reading Women's Lives in the Hebrew Bible,* edited by Mieke Bal. Sheffield: Sheffield Academic Press, 1989, 195-209.

Bailey, Kenneth E. "Informal Controlled Oral Tradition and the Synoptic Gospels." *Asian Journal of Theology* 5/1 (1991): 34-54.

Bal, Mieke, ed. *Anti-Covenant: Counter-Reading Women's Lives in the Hebrew Bible.* Sheffield: Sheffield Academic Press, 1989.

Ball, David M. "'My Lord and My God': The Implication of 'I Am' Sayings for Religious Pluralism." In *One God One Lord in a World of Religious Pluralism,* edited by A. D. Clarke and B. W. Winter. Cambridge: Tyndale House, 1991, 53-71.

Barr, David L. *New Testament Story: An Introduction.* Belmont, Calif.: Wadsworth, 1995.

Barrett, Charles Kingsley. *Essays on John.* Philadelphia: Westminster Press, 1982.

Barstow, Anne Llewellyn. "On Studying Witchcraft as Women's History: A Historiography of the European Witch Persecutions." *Journal of Feminist Studies in Religion* 4/2 (1988): 7-19.

———. *Witchcraze: A New History of the European Witch Hunts.* London: Harper-Collins, 1994.

Bartchy, S. Scott. "Undermining Ancient Patriarchy: The Apostle Paul's Vision of a Society of Siblings." *Biblical Theology Bulletin* 29/2 (1999): 68-78.

Bass, Ardy. "Martha and Jesus." *The Bible Today* 32 (1994): 90-94.

Bassler, Jouette M. "The Galileans: A Neglected Factor in Johannine Community Research." *Catholic Biblical Quarterly* 43 (1981): 243-57.

Beutler, Johannes. "Greeks Come to See Jesus." *Biblica* 71/3 (1990): 333-47.

———. "Two Ways of Gathering: The Plot to Kill Jesus in John 11.47-53." *New Testament Studies* 40 (1994): 399-406.

Bird, Phyllis A. "Images of Women in the Old Testament." In *Religion and Sexism: Images of Woman in the Jewish and Christian Traditions,* edited by Rosemary Radford Ruether. New York: Simon and Schuster, 1974, 41-88.

Boring, M. Eugene. *The Continuing Voices of Jesus: Christian Prophecy and the Gospel Tradition.* Louisville, Ky.: Westminster John Knox, 1991.

Boring, M. Eugene, Klaus Berger, and Carsten Colpe, eds. *Hellenistic Commentary to the New Testament.* Nashville, Tenn.: Abingdon Press, 1995.

Botha, Pieter J. J. "Letter Writing and Oral Communication in Antiquity." *Scriptura* 42 (1992): 17-34.

———. "The Social Dynamics of the Early Transmission of the Jesus Tradition." *Neotestamentica* 27/2 (1993): 205-31.

Bradley, Keith R. "Wet-nursing at Rome: A Study in Social Relations." In *The Family in Ancient Rome: New Perspectives,* edited by Beryl Rawson. Ithaca, N.Y.: Cornell University Press, 1986, 201-29.

Brenner, Athalya, and Fokkelien van Dijk-Hemmes. *On Gendering Texts: Female and Male Voices in the Hebrew Bible.* Leiden: E. J. Brill, 1993.

Brodie, T. L. *The Quest for the Origin of John's Gospel: A Source-Oriented Approach.* New York: Oxford University Press, 1993.

Brooten, Bernadette J. "Early Christian Women and Their Cultural Contexts." *Feminist Perspectives on Biblical Scholarship,* edited by A. Yarbro Collins. Atlanta, Ga.: Scholars Press, 1985, 65-92.

———. "Jewish Women's History in the Roman Period: A Task for Christian Theology." *Harvard Theological Review* 79 (1986) 22-30.

———. "'Junia . . . Outstanding among the Apostles' (Romans 16:7)." In *Women Priests*, edited by Leonard Swidler and Arlene Swidler. New York: Paulist Press, 1977, 141-44.

———. *Love between Women: Early Christian Responses to Female Homoeroticism*. Chicago: The University of Chicago Press, 1996.

———. *Women Leaders in the Ancient Synagogue: Inscriptional Evidence and Background Issues*. Chico, Calif.: Scholars Press, 1982.

Brown, Cheryl Anne. *No Longer Be Silent: First Century Jewish Portraits of Biblical Women*. Louisville, Ky.: Westminster John Knox, 1992.

Brown, Raymond E. *The Community of the Beloved Disciple: The Life, Loves, and Hates of an Individual Church in New Testament Times*. New York: Paulist Press, 1979.

———. *The Death of the Messiah: A Commentary on the Passion Narratives in the Four Gospels*. 2 vols. New York: Doubleday, 1994.

———. *The Gospel according to John*. 2 vols. Garden City, N.Y.: Doubleday, 1966/1970.

———. *The Gospel and Epistles of John: A Concise Commentary*. Collegeville, Minn.: Liturgical Press, 1988.

———. "The Relation of 'The Secret Gospel of Mark' to the Fourth Gospel." *Catholic Biblical Quarterly* 36 (1974): 466-85.

Brown, S. Kent, "History of Egypt: Greco-Roman Period." *Anchor Bible Dictionary*. Vol. 2. New York: Doubleday, 1992, 367-74.

Buckley, Jorunn Jacobsen. "Two Female Gnostic Revealers." *Harvard Theological Review* 19/3 (1980): 259-69.

———. "The Thunder, Perfect Mind." *Anchor Bible Dictionary*. Vol. 6. New York: Doubleday, 1992, 545-46.

Bultmann, Rudolf. *The Gospel of John: A Commentary*. Oxford: Basil Blackwell, 1964/71.

Burns, Rita J. *Has the Lord Indeed Spoken Only through Moses?: A Study of the Biblical Portrait of Miriam*. Atlanta, Ga.: Scholars Press, 1987.

Burrus, Virginia. "Chastity as Autonomy: Women in the Stories of the Apocryphal Acts." *Semeia* 38 (1986): 101-17.

———. *Chastity as Autonomy: Women in the Stories of Apocryphal Acts*. Lewiston, N.Y.: Edwin Mellen Press, 1987.

Byrne, Brendan. *Lazarus: A Contemporary Reading of John 11:1-46*. Collegeville, Minn.: Liturgical Press, 1990.

———. "Sons of God." *Anchor Bible Dictionary*. Vol. 6. New York: Doubleday, 1992, 156-59.

Camp, Claudia V. *Wisdom and the Feminine in the Book of Proverbs*. Sheffield: Almond Press, 1985.

Caraveli, Anna. "The Bitter Wounding: The Lament as Social Protest in Rural Greece." In *Gender and Power in Rural Greece*, edited by Jill Dubisch. Princeton, N.J.: Princeton University Press, 1986, 169-94.

Cardman, Francine. "Acts of the Women Martyrs." *Anglican Theological Review* 70/2 (1988): 144-50.

Carter, Warren. "Contested Claims: Roman Imperial Theology and Matthew's Gospel." *The Bible Today* 29/2 (1999): 56-67.

Cartlidge, David R., and David L. Dungan. *Documents for the Study of the Gospels*. Philadelphia: Fortress Press, 1980.

Cassidy, R. J. *John's Gospel in New Perspective: Christology and the Realities of Roman Power*. Maryknoll, N.Y.: Orbis Books, 1992.

Ceresko, Anthony R. *Introduction to the Old Testament: A Liberation Perspective*. Rev. and exp. ed. Maryknoll, N.Y.: Orbis Books, 2001.

Charlesworth, James H. "Jewish Hymns, Odes, and Prayers (ca. 167 BCE—135 CE)." In *Early Judaism and Its Modern Interpreters*, edited by Robert A. Kraft and George W. E. Nickelsburg. Philadelphia: Fortress Press, 1986, 411-36.

———. "Reinterpreting John: How the Dead Sea Scrolls Have Revolutionized Our Understanding of the Gospel of John." *Bible Review* 9 (1993): 18-25, 54.

Charlesworth, Martin Percival. "Some Observations on Ruler-Cult Especially in Rome." *Harvard Theological Review* 38 (1935): 5-44.

Chung, Hyun Kyung. "Welcome the Spirit; Hear Her Cries: The Holy Spirit, Creation, and the Culture of Life." *Christianity and Crisis* 51/10-11 (1991): 220-23.

Clark, Douglas K. "Signs in Wisdom and John." *Catholic Biblical Quarterly* 45/2 (1983): 201-9.

Clark, Gillian. *Women in the Ancient World: Greece and Rome*. Oxford: Oxford University Press, 1989.

Coakley, J. F. "The Anointing at Bethany and the Priority of John." *Journal of Biblical Literature* 107/2 (1988): 241-56.

Coffman, Ralph J. "Historical Jesus the Healer: Cultural Interpretations of the Healing Cults of the Graeco-Roman World as the Basis for Jesus Movements." *Society of Biblical Literature Seminar Papers* (1993): 412-43.

Cohen, Shaye J. D. "Crossing the Boundary and Becoming a Jew." *Harvard Theological Review* 82/1 (1989): 13-33.

———. "Menstruants and the Sacred in Judaism and Christianity." *Women's History and Ancient History*, edited by Sarah B. Pomeroy. Chapel Hill, N.C.: The University of North Carolina Press, 1991, 273-99.

———. "Women in the Synagogues of Antiquity." *Conservative Judaism* 34/2 (1980): 23-29.

Cole, Susan Guettel. "Could Greek Women Read and Write?" in *Reflections of Women in Antiquity*, edited by Helene P. Foley. New York: Gordon and Breach Science, 1981, 219-45.

Collins, John J. "Sibylline Oracles." *Anchor Bible Dictionary*. Vol. 6. New York: Doubleday, 1992, 2-6.

———. "Sibylline Oracles: A New Translation and Introduction." In *The Old Testament Pseudepigrapha*, edited by J. H. Charlesworth. New York: Doubleday, 1983, 1:317-472.

Collins, Raymond F. "The Representative Figures of the Fourth Gospel—I." *The Downside Review* 94 (1976): 26-46, 118-32.

Connolly, R. Hugh. *Didascalia Apostolorum: The Syriac Version Translated and Accompanied by the Verona Latin Fragments*. Oxford: Clarendon, 1929.

Corley, Kathleen E. "The Anointing of Jesus in the Synoptic Tradition." Presented at the Jesus Seminar in Santa Rosa, March 2-6, 1994.

———. "Lamentation and Gospel: Women's Voices in Passion Tradition." Unpublished manuscript, used with permission.

———. *Private Women, Public Meals: Social Conflict and Women in the Synoptic Tradition*. Peabody, Mass.: Hendrickson Publications, 1993.

———. "Were the Women around Jesus Really Prostitutes? Women in the Context of Greco-Roman Meals." *Society of Biblical Literature Seminar Papers* (1989): 487-521.

———. "Women and the Crucifixion and Burial of Jesus: 'He Was Buried: On the Third Day He Was Raised.'" *Forum* New Series 1/1 (1998): 181-225.

Corrington, Gail Paterson. "Power and the Man of Power in the Context of Hellenistic Popular Belief." *Helios* 13/1 (1986): 75-86.

Craig, Kerry M., and Margret A. Kristjansson. "Women Reading as Men, Women Reading as Women: A Structural Analysis for the Historical Project." *Semeia* 51 (1990): 119-36.

Culpepper, R. Arlan. *Anatomy of the Fourth Gospel: A Study in Literary Design.* Philadelphia: Fortress Press, 1983.

———. "The Gospel of John and the Jews." *Review and Expositor* 84/2 (1987): 273-88.

———. *John, the Son of Zebedee: The Life of a Legend.* Columbia, S.C.: University of South Carolina Press, 1993.

D'Angelo, Mary Rose. "Women Partners in the New Testament." *Journal of Feminist Studies in Religion* 6/1 (1990): 65-86.

———. "*Abba* and 'Father': Imperial Theology and the Jesus Traditions." *Journal of Biblical Literature* 111 (1992): 611-30.

———. "Re-Membering Jesus: Women, Prophecy, and Resistance in the Memory of the Early Churches." *Horizons* 19/2 (1992): 199-218.

———. "The Concrete Foundation of Christianity: Re-Membering Jesus." *Proceedings of the Catholic Theological Society of America* 49 (1994): 135-46.

Davaney, Sheila Greeve. "Continuing the Story, but Departing the Text: A Historicist Interpretation of Feminist Norms." In *Horizons in Feminist Theology: Identity, Tradition, and Norms,* edited by Rebecca S. Chopp and Sheila Greeve Davaney. Minneapolis, Minn.: Fortress Press, 1997, 215-31.

Davies, Margaret. *Rhetoric and Reference in the Fourth Gospel,* Sheffield: Sheffield Academic Press, 1992.

Day, Peggy L. "Why Is Anat a Warrior and Hunter?" In *The Bible and the Politics of Exegesis: Essays in Honor of Norman K. Gottwald on His Sixty-Fifth Birthday,* edited by David Jobling, Peggy L. Day, and Gerald T. Sheppard. Cleveland, Ohio: Pilgrim Press, 1991, 141-46.

Day, Peggy L., ed. *Gender and Difference in Ancient Israel.* Minneapolis, Minn.: Fortress Press, 1989.

de Jonge, Marinus. *Jesus: Stranger from Heaven and Son of God: Jesus Christ and the Christians in Johannine Perspective.* Missoula, Mont.: Scholars Press, 1977.

Destro, Adriana, and Mauro Pesce, "Kinship, Discipleship, and Movement: An Anthropological Study of John's Gospel." *Biblical Interpretation* 3/3 (1995): 266-84.

Dewey, Joanna. "1 Timothy." In *The Women's Bible Commentary,* edited by Carol A. Newsom and Sharon H. Ringe. London: SPCK, 1992, 353-58.

———. "From Storytelling to Written Text: The Loss of Early Christian Women's Voices." *Biblical Theology Bulletin* 26 (1996): 1-8.

———. "Jesus' Healings of Women: Conformity and Non-Conformity to Dominant Cultural Values as Clues for Historical Reconstructions." *Biblical Theology Bulletin* 24 (1994): 122-31.

———. "Mark as Aural Narrative: Structures as Clues to Understanding." *Sewanee Theological Review* 36/1 (1992): 45-56.

———. "Mark as Interwoven Tapestry: Forecasts and Echoes for a Listening Audience." *Catholic Biblical Quarterly* 53 (1991): 221-36.

———. "Textuality in an Oral Culture: A Survey of the Pauline Traditions." *Semeia* 65 (1995): 37-65.

Dodd, Charles Harold. *The Interpretation of the Fourth Gospel.* Cambridge: The University Press, 1953.

Dollar, Stephen E. *The Significance of Women in the Fourth Gospel.* Ann Arbor, Mich.: University Microfilms International, 1983.

Donahue, John R. "Tax Collector." *Anchor Bible Dictionary.* Vol. 6. New York: Doubleday, 1992, 337-38.

Dundes, Alan. "The Hero Pattern and the Life of Jesus." In *In Quest of the Hero,* edited by Robert A. Segal. Princeton, N.J.: Princeton University Press, 1990, 179-223.

Dunn, James D. G. "Let John Be John: A Gospel for Its Time." In *Das Evangelium und die Evangelien: Vortrage vom Tubinger Symposium 1982,* edited by Peter Stuhlmacher. Tubingen: J. C. B. Mohr (Paul Siebeck), 1983, 309-39.

Edwards, Douglas R. "Dress and Ornamentation." *Anchor Bible Dictionary.* Vol. 2. New York: Doubleday, 1992, 232-38.

Elder, Linda Bennett. "Judith." In *Searching the Scriptures,* edited by Elisabeth Schüssler Fiorenza. New York: Crossroad, 1994, 2:455-69.

Elliott, John H. "Patronage and Clientism in Early Christian Society: A Short Reading Guide." *Forum* 3/4 (1987): 39-48.

Elm, Susanna. "Montanist Oracles." *Searching the Scriptures,* edited by Elisabeth Schüssler Fiorenza. New York: Crossroad, 1994, 2:131-38.

Etambaugh, John E. "Thyatira." *Anchor Bible Dictionary.* Vol. 6. New York: Doubleday, 1992, 546.

Evans, Craig A. *Word and Glory: On the Exegetical and Theological Background of John's Prologue.* Sheffield: Sheffield Academic Press, 1993.

Exum, J. Cheryl. "The Mothers of Israel: The Patriarchal Narratives from a Feminist Perspective." *Bible Review* 2/1 (1986): 60-67.

———. "Murder They Wrote: Ideology and the Manipulation of Female Presence in Biblical Narrative." In *The Pleasure of Her Text: Feminist Readings of Biblical and Historical Texts,* edited by Alice Bach. Philadelphia: Trinity Press International, 1990, 45-67.

———. "Second Thoughts about Secondary Characters: Women in Exodus 1.8— 2.10." In *A Feminist Companion to Exodus to Deuteronomy,* edited by Athalya Brenner. Sheffield: Sheffield Academic Press, 1994, 75-87.

———. "'You Shall Let Every Daughter Live': A Study of Exodus 1.8—2.10." In *A Feminist Companion to Exodus to Deuteronomy,* edited by Athalya Brenner. Sheffield: Sheffield Academic Press, 1994, 37-61.

Fabella, Virginia. "A Common Methodology for Diverse Christologies?" In *With Passion and Compassion: Third World Women Doing Theology,* edited by Virginia Fabella and Mercy Amba Oduyoye. Maryknoll, N.Y.: Orbis Books, 1988, 108-17.

Farley, Edward. "Re-thinking the God-terms—Tradition: The God-term of Social Remembering." *Toronto Journal of Theology* 9/1 (1993): 67-77.

Feldman, Emanuel. *Biblical and Post-Biblical Defilement and Mourning: Law as Theology.* New York: Yeshiva University Press, Ktav Publishing House, 1977.

Feldman, Louis H. "New Testament Antisemitic?" *Moment* (1990): 32-35, 50-52.

———. *Jew and Gentile in the Ancient World: Attitudes and Interactions from Alexander to Justinian.* Princeton, N.J.: Princeton University Press, 1993.

Fortna, Robert Tomson. *The Fourth Gospel and Its Predecessor: From Narrative Source to Present Gospel.* Philadelphia: Fortress Press, 1988.

Fossum, Jarl. "Son of God." *Anchor Bible Dictionary.* Vol. 6. New York: Doubleday, 1992, 128-37.

Fredriksen, Paula. *From Jesus to Christ: The Origins of the New Testament Images of Jesus.* New Haven, Conn.: Yale University Press, 1988.

Freedman, David Noel. "Yahweh of Samaria and His Asherah." *Biblical Archaeologist* 50 (1987), 241-49.

French, Valerie. "Midwives and Maternity Care in the Roman World." *Helios* 13/2 (1987): 69-84.

Frymer-Kensky, Tikva, *In the Wake of the Goddesses: Women, Culture, and the Biblical Transformation of Pagan Myth.* New York: The Free Press, 1992.

———. "Deuteronomy." *The Women's Bible Commentary,* edited by Carol A. Newsom and Sharon H. Ringe. London: SPCK, 1992, 52-62.

Fuchs, Esther. "The Literary Characterization of Mothers and Sexual Politics in the Hebrew Bible." *Semeia* 46 (1989): 151-66.

Gager, John G. *Moses in Greco-Roman Paganism.* Nashville, Tenn.: Abingdon Press, 1972.

Gardner, Jane F. *Women in Roman Law and Society.* Bloomington, Ind.: Indiana University Press, 1986.

Gardner, Jane F., and Thomas Wiedemann. *The Roman Household: A Sourcebook.* New York: Routledge, 1991.

Garland, Robert. "The Well-Ordered Corpse: An Investigation into the Motives behind Greek Funerary Legislation." *Bulletin of the Institute of Classical Studies* 36 (1989): 1-15.

Georgi, Dieter. *The Opponents of Paul in Second Corinthians.* Philadelphia: Fortress Press, 1986.

Goitein, S. D. "Women as Creators of Biblical Genres." *Prooftexts* 8 (1988): 1-33.

Goodenough, Erwin R. *Jewish Symbols in the Greco-Roman Period.* Abridged ed., edited by Jacob Neusner. Princeton, N.J.: Princeton University Press. 1988.

Gottwald, Norman K. *The Hebrew Bible: A Socio-Literary Introduction.* Philadelphia: Fortress Press, 1985.

Griffin, Miriam T. "Nero." *Anchor Bible Dictionary.* Vol. 4. New York: Doubleday, 1992, 1076-81.

Haines-Eitzen, Kim. "'Girls Trained in Beautiful Writing': Female Scribes in Roman Antiquity and Early Christianity." *Journal of Early Christian Studies* 6/4 (1998): 629-46.

Hanson, K. C. "The Galilean Fishing Economy and the Jesus Tradition." *The Bible Today* 27/3 (1997): 99-111.

Hanson, K. C., and Douglas E. Oakman. *Palestine in the Time of Jesus: Social Structures and Social Conflicts.* Minneapolis, Minn.: Fortress Press, 1998.

Harrington, Daniel J. "'The Jews' in John's Gospel." *The Bible Today* 27/4 (1989): 203-9.

———. "Palestinian Adaptations of Biblical Narratives and Prophecies: I. The Bible Rewritten (Narratives)" and "III. Future Research." In *Early Judaism and Its Modern Interpreters,* edited by Robert A. Kraft and George W. E. Nickelsburg. Philadelphia: Fortress Press; Atlanta, Ga.: Scholars Press, 1986, 239-47, 253-55.

Harrington, Wilfried. "The Johannine Jesus." *Scripture in Church* 24.94 (1994): 233-40.

Harris, William V. *Ancient Literacy.* Cambridge, Mass.: Harvard University Press, 1989.

Harvey, Susan Ashbrook. "The Odes of Solomon." In *Searching the Scriptures,* edited by Elisabeth Schüssler Fiorenza. New York: Crossroad, 1994, 2:86-98.

Hennecke, Edgar, and Wilhelm Schneemelcher, eds. *New Testament Apocrypha.* 2 vols. Philadelphia: Westminster Press, 1963/1964.

Henrichs, Albert. "Changing Dionysiac Identities." In *Jewish and Christian Self-Definition: The Greco-Roman World,* edited by B. F. Meyer and E. P. Sanders. Philadelphia: Fortress Press, 1982, 3:137-60, 213-36.

Holst-Warhaft, Gail. *Dangerous Voices: Women's Laments and Greek Literature.* London: Routledge, 1992.

Horsley, Richard A. *Galilee: History, Politics, People.* Valley Forge, Pa.: Trinity Press International, 1995.

——. "Messianic Movements in Judaism." *Anchor Bible Dictionary.* Vol. 4. New York: Doubleday, 1992, 791-97.

——. "Popular Messianic Movements around the Time of Jesus." *Catholic Biblical Quarterly* 46 (1984): 471-95.

Huber, Elaine C. *Women and the Authority of Inspiration: A Reexamination of Two Prophetic Movements from a Contemporary Feminist Perspective.* Lanham, Md.: University Press of America, 1985.

Ilan, Tal. "How Women Differed." *Biblical Archaeology Review* 24/2 (1998): 38-39, 68.

——. *Jewish Women in Greco-Roman Palestine.* Peabody, Mass.: Hendrickson Publications, 1995.

——. "Notes on the Distribution of Jewish Women's Names in Palestine in the Second Temple and Mishnaic Periods." *Journal of Jewish Studies* 40/2 (1989): 186-200.

Irvin, Dorothy. "The Ministry of Women in the Early Church: The Archaeological Evidence." *Duke Divinity School Review* 45/2 (1980): 76-86.

Jensen, Robin M. "The Raising of Lazarus." *Bible Review* (1995): 20-28, 45.

Jewett, Robert. "Tenement Churches and Pauline Love Feasts." *Quarterly Review* 14/1 (1994): 43-58.

John, E. C. "Israel and Inculturation: An Appraisal." *Jeevadhara* 14 (1984): 87-94.

Johnson, Aubrey R. *The One and the Many in the Israelite Conception of God.* Cardiff: University of Wales Press, 1961.

Johnson, Elizabeth A. *She Who Is: The Mystery of God in Feminist Theological Discourse.* New York: Crossroad, 1993.

Jones, Bryan W. "Claudius." *Anchor Bible Dictionary.* Vol. 1. New York: Doubleday, 1992, 1054-55.

Jones, Donald L., "Roman Imperial Cult." *Anchor Bible Dictionary.* Vol. 5. New York: Doubleday, 1992, 806-9.

Jordan, Rosan A., and F. A. de Caro, "Women and the Study of Folklore." *Signs* (1986): 500-518.

Katz, Steven T. "Issues in the Separation of Judaism and Christianity after 70 CE: A Reconsideration." *Journal of Biblical Literature* 103/1 (1984): 43-76.

Kee, Howard Clark. *Medicine, Miracle, and Magic in New Testament Times.* Cambridge: Cambridge University Press, 1986.

——. "Myth and Miracle: Isis, Wisdom, and the Logos of John." In *Myth, Symbol, and Reality,* edited by Alan M. Olson. Notre Dame, Ind.: University of Notre Dame Press, 1980, 145-64.

Kermode, Frank. "John." In *The Literary Guide to the Bible,* edited by Robert Alter and Frank Kermode. London: Collins, 1987, 440-66.

Kimelman, Reuven. "*Birkat Ha-Minim* and the Lack of Evidence for an Anti-Christian Jewish Prayer in Late Antiquity." In *Jewish and Christian Self-Definition,* edited by E. P. Sanders, A. I. Baumgarten, and Alan Mendelson. Philadelphia: Fortress Press, 1981, 226-44.

King, Karen L., ed. *Images of the Feminine in Gnosticism: Studies in Antiquity and Christianity.* Philadelphia: Fortress Press, 1988.

Kinukawa, Hisako. *Women and Jesus in Mark: A Japanese Feminist Perspective.* Maryknoll, N.Y.: Orbis Books, 1994.

Kitzberger, Ingrid Rosa. "Love and Footwashing: John 13:1-20 and Luke 7:36-50 Read Intertextually." *Biblical Interpretation* 2/2 (1994): 190-206.

―――. "Mary of Bethany and Mary of Magdala—Two Female Characters in the Johannine Passion Narrative: A Feminist, Narrative-Critical Reader-Response." *New Testament Studies* 41 (1995): 564-86.

Kleinman, Arthur. *Patients and Healers in the Context of Culture: An Exploration of the Borderland between Anthropology, Medicine, and Psychiatry.* Berkeley and Los Angeles: University of California Press, 1980.

Kloppenborg, John S. "Isis and Sophia in the Book of Wisdom." *Harvard Theological Review* 75/1 (1982): 57-84.

Koester, Craig R. "'The Savior of the World' (John 4:42)." *Journal of Biblical Literature* 109 (1990): 665-80.

―――. *Symbolism in the Fourth Gospel: Meaning, Mystery, Community.* Minneapolis, Minn.: Fortress Press, 1995

Koester, Helmut. *Ancient Christian Gospels: Their History and Development.* Philadelphia: Trinity Press International, 1990.

―――. "The Story of the Johannine Tradition." *Sewanee Theological Review* 36 (1992): 17-32.

Kraemer, Ross Shepard. "Ecstasy and Possession: The Attraction of Women to the Cult of Dionysus." *Harvard Theological Review* 72/1-2 (1979): 55-80.

―――. "Hellenistic Jewish Women: The Epigraphical Evidence." *Society of Biblical Literature Seminar Papers* (1986): 183-200.

―――. *Her Share of the Blessings: Women's Religions among Pagans, Jews, and Christians in the Greco-Roman World.* Oxford: Oxford University Press, 1992.

―――. "On the Meaning of the Term 'Jew' in Greco-Roman Inscriptions." *Harvard Theological Review* 82/1 (1989): 35-53.

―――. "Monastic Jewish Women in Greco-Roman Egypt: Philo Judaeus on the Therapeutrides." *Signs* 14/2 (1989): 342-70.

―――. "Non-Literary Evidence for Jewish Women in Rome and Egypt." *Helios* 13/2 (1987): 85-101.

―――. "Women in the Religions of the Greco-Roman World." *Religious Studies Review* 9/2 (1983): 127-39.

Kraemer, Ross Shepard, ed. *Maenads, Martyrs, Matrons, Monastics: A Sourcebook on Women's Religions in the Greco-Roman World.* Philadelphia: Fortress Press, 1988.

Kwok Pui-lan. *Discovering the Bible in the Non-Biblical World.* Maryknoll, N.Y.: Orbis Books, 1995.

―――. "The Future of Feminist Theology: An Asian Perspective." In *Feminist Theology from the Third World: A Reader*, edited by Ursula King. Maryknoll, N.Y.: Orbis Books, 1994, 63-76.

―――. "The Image of the 'White Lady': Gender and Race in Christian Mission." *Concilium* 6 (1991): 19-27.

Kysar, Robert. "Coming Hermeneutical Earthquake in Johannine Interpretation." In *What Is John? Literary and Social Readings of the Fourth Gospel*, vol. 1, edited by Fernando Segovia. Atlanta, Ga.: Scholars Press, 1996, 185-89.

―――. *The Fourth Evangelist and His Gospel: An Examination of Contemporary Scholarship.* Minneapolis, Minn.: Augsburg Fortress Press, 1975.

―――. "The Gospel of John." *Anchor Bible Dictionary.* Vol. 3. New York: Doubleday, 1992, 912-31.

―――. *John, the Maverick Gospel.* Rev. ed. Louisville, Ky.: Westminster John Knox, 1993.

Lee, Dorothy A. "Beyond Suspicion? The Fatherhood of God in the Fourth Gospel." *Pacifica* 8 (1995): 140-54.

———. *The Symbolic Narratives of the Fourth Gospel: The Interplay of Form and Meaning*. Sheffield: Sheffield Academic Press, 1994.

Lefkowitz, Mary R., and Maureen B. Fant. *Women in Greece and Rome*. Toronto: Samuel-Stevens, 1977.

Lerner, Gerda. *The Creation of Patriarchy*. New York: Oxford University Press, 1986.

Lesses, Rebecca. "The Daughters of Job." In *Searching the Scriptures*, edited by Elisabeth Schüssler Fiorenza. New York: Crossroad, 1994, 2:139-47.

Levine, Amy-Jill. "Second Temple Judaism, Jesus, and Women: Yeast of Eden." *Biblical Interpretation* 2/1 (1994): 8-33.

———. "The Sibylline Oracles." In *Searching the Scriptures*, edited by Elisabeth Schüssler Fiorenza. New York: Crossroad, 1994, 2:99-108.

Liddell, Henry George and Robert Scott, *Greek-English Lexicon: A New Edition*. Rev. ed. Oxford: Clarendon, 1966.

Lindars, Barnabas. "Rebuking the Spirit: A New Analysis of the Lazarus Story of John 11." *New Testament Studies* 38 (1992): 89-104.

Love, Stuart L. "The Household: A Major Social Component for Gender Analysis in the Gospel of Matthew." *Biblical Theology Bulletin* 23/1 (1993): 21-31.

MacDonald, Dennis Ronald. "From *Audita* to *Legenda*: Oral and Written Miracle Stories." *Forum* 2/4 (1986): 15-26.

———. *The Legend and the Apostle: The Battle for Paul in Story and Canon*. Philadelphia: Westminster Press, 1983.

MacRae, George W. "The Fourth Gospel and *Religionsgeschichte*." *Catholic Biblical Quarterly* 32 (1970): 13-24.

Malina, Bruce J. *The Gospel of John in Sociolinguistic Perspective*. Berkeley, Calif.: Graduate Theological Union and University of California-Berkeley, 1985.

Maloney, Linda M. "The Pastoral Epistles." In *Searching the Scriptures*, edited by Elisabeth Schüssler Fiorenza. New York: Crossroad, 1994, 2:361-80.

McCready, Wayne O. "Johannine Self-Understanding and the Synagogue Episode of John 9." In *Self-Definition and Self-Discovery in Early Christianity: A Study in Changing Horizons*, edited by David J. Hawkin and Tom Robinson. Lewiston, N.Y.: Edwin Mellen Press, 1990, 147-66.

McGinn, Sheila E. "The Acts of Thecla." In *Searching the Scriptures*, edited by Elisabeth Schüssler Fiorenza. New York: Crossroad, 1994, 2:800-828.

McGuire, Anne. "Thunder, Perfect Mind." In *Searching the Scriptures*, edited by Elisabeth Schüssler Fiorenza. New York: Crossroad, 1994, 2:39-54.

Meeks, Wayne A. "Moses as God and King." In *Religions in Antiquity*, edited by Jacob Neusner. Leiden: E. J. Brill, 1968, 354-71.

Meier, John P. *A Marginal Jew: Rethinking the Historical Jesus*. 2 vols. New York: Doubleday, 1991/1994.

Meyers, Carol. *Discovering Eve: Ancient Israelite Women in Context*. Oxford: Oxford University Press, 1988.

———. "'To Her Mother's House': Considering a Counterpart to the Israelite *BBet 'ab*." In *The Bible and the Politics of Exegesis: Essays in Honor of Norman K. Gottwald on His Sixty-Fifth Birthday*, edited by David Jobling, Peggy L. Day, and Gerald T. Sheppard. Cleveland, Ohio: Pilgrim Press, 1991, 39-51.

Millar, Fergus. "The Imperial Cult and the Persecutions." In *Le Culte des Souverains dans L'empire Romain*, edited by Willen den Boer. Geneva: Fondation Hardt, 1972, 143-75.

Mitchell, Alan C. "The Social Function of Friendship in Acts 2:44-47 and 4:32-37." *Journal of Biblical Literature* 111/2 (1992): 255-72.

Moltmann-Wendel, Elisabeth. *The Women around Jesus: Reflection on Authentic Personhood.* New York: Crossroad, 1982.

Morgenthaler, Robert. *Statistik Des Neutestamentlichen Wortschitzes.* Zurich/Frankfurt am Main: Gotthelf, 1958.

Mosala, Itumeleng J. *Biblical Hermeneutics and Black Theology in South Africa.* Grand Rapids, Mich.: Eerdmans, 1989.

Mueller, Steve. "Thoughts on the 'Thirtysomething' Jesus." *The Bible Today* 37/2 (1999): 91-95.

Munro, Winsome. "A Woman's Anointing of Jesus: A Response to Papers by Corley and Winter." Paper presented at the Jesus Seminar, 1994.

Murphy-O'Connor, Jerome. "Corinth." *Anchor Bible Dictionary.* Vol. 1. New York: Doubleday, 1992, 1134-39.

———. "Fishers of Fish, Fishers of Men." *Bible Review* 15/3 (1999): 22-27, 48-49.

———. "On the Road and on the Sea with St. Paul: Traveling Conditions in the First Century." *Bible Review* 1/2 (1985): 38-47.

———. "Prisca and Aquila." *Bible Review* 8/6 (1992): 40-62.

Musurillo, Herbert. *Acts of the Christian Martyrs.* Oxford: Clarendon, 1972.

Neusner, Jacob. "Varieties of Judaism in the Formative Age." In *Jewish Spirituality: From the Bible through the Middle Ages,* edited by Arthur Green. New York: Crossroad, 1986, 171-97.

———. *The Way of Torah: An Introduction to Judaism.* Belmont, Calif.: Wadsworth, 1993.

Neyrey, Jerome H. "'My Lord and My God': The Divinity of Jesus in John's Gospel." *Society of Biblical Literature Seminar Papers* (1986): 152-71.

Nicol, W. *The Semeia in the Fourth Gospel: Tradition and Redaction.* Leiden: E. J. Brill, 1972.

Oakman, Douglass E. "The Archaeology of First-Century Galilee and the Social Interpretation of the Historical Jesus." *Society of Biblical Literature Seminar Papers* (1994): 220-5l.

———. *Jesus and the Economic Questions of His Day.* Lewiston, N.Y.: Edwin Mellen Press, 1986.

———. "Was Jesus a Peasant?: Implications for Reading the Samaritan Story (Luke 10:30-35)." *Biblical Theology Bulletin* 22/3 (1992): 117-25.

O'Collins, Gerald G. "Crucifixion." *Anchor Bible Dictionary.* Vol. 2. New York: Doubleday, 1992, 207-9.

O'Connor, Kathleen M. "Jeremiah." In *The Women's Bible Commentary,* edited by Carol A. Newsom and Sharon H. Ringe. Louisville, Ky.: Westminster John Knox; London: SPCK, 1992, 169-77.

O'Day, Gail R. *The Word Disclosed: John's Story and Narrative Preaching.* St. Louis: CBP Press, 1987.

Osiek, Carolyn. "The Family in Early Christianity: 'Family Values' Revisited." *Catholic Biblical Quarterly* 58/1 (1996): 1-24.

———. "Forum: Gospel and Enculturation: The Long Road." *Religion and Theology* 6/1 (1999): 83-92.

———. "Slavery in the Second Testament World." *The Bible Today* 22/2 (1992): 174-79.

Overholt, Thomas W. *Channels of Prophecy: The Social Dynamics of Prophetic Activity.* Minneapolis, Minn.: Fortress Press, 1989.

Packer, James E. "Housing and Population in Imperial Ostia and Rome." *Journal of Roman Studies* 57 (1967): 80-95.

Pancaro, Severino, "'People of God' in St. John's Gospel." *New Testament Studies* 16 (1967-68): 114-29.

Pardes, Ilana. *Countertraditions in the Bible: A Feminist Approach.* Cambridge: Harvard University Press, 1992.

Patai, Raphael. *The Hebrew Goddess.* Detroit, Mich.: Wayne State University Press, 1990.

Perkins, L. J. "Bethany." *Anchor Bible Dictionary.* Vol. 1. New York: Doubleday, 1992, 702-3.

Perrin, Norman and Dennis C. Duling. *The New Testament: An Introduction.* San Diego, Calif.: Harcourt Brace Jovanovich, 1982.

Pervo, Richard I. *Profit with Delight: The Literary Genre of the Acts of the Apostles.* Philadelphia: Fortress Press, 1987.

Pilch, John J. "Appearances of the Risen Jesus in Cultural Context: Experiences of Alternate Reality." *Biblical Theology Bulletin* 28/2 (1998): 52-60.

————. *The Cultural Dictionary of the Bible.* Collegeville, Minn.: Liturgical Press, 1999.

————. "Sickness and Healing in Luke-Acts." In *The Social World of Luke-Acts: Models for Interpretation,* edited by Jerome H. Neyrey. Peabody, Mass.: Hendrickson Publications, 1991, 181-209.

Platt, Elizabeth E. "The Ministry of Mary of Bethany." *Theology Today* 34 (1977): 29-39.

Pollard, T. E. "The Father-Son and God-Believer Relationships according to St. John: A Brief Study of John's Use of Prepositions." In *L'Evangile de Jean: Sources, Redaction, Theologie,* edited by M. de Jonge. Leuven: Leuven University Press, 1977, 363-69.

Pomeroy, Sarah B. *Goddesses, Whores, Wives, and Slaves: Women in Classical Antiquity.* New York: Schocken Books, 1975.

Pritchard, J. B., ed. *The Ancient Near East.* 2 vols. Princeton, N.J.: Princeton University Press, 1975.

Rader, Rosemary. "Perpetua." In *A Lost Tradition: Women Writers of the Early Church,* edited by Patricia Wilson-Kastner, G. Ronald Kastner, Ann Millin, Rosemary Rader, and Jeremiah Reedy. Washington, D.C.: University Press of America, 1981, 1-32.

Raglan, Lord. *The Hero: A Study in Tradition, Myth, and Drama.* New York: Vintage Books, 1956.

Rasmussen, Rachel C. "Deborah the Woman Warrior." In *Anti-Covenant: Counter-Reading Women's Lives in the Hebrew Bible,* edited by Mieke Bal. Sheffield: Sheffield Academic Press, 1989, 79-93.

Reimer, Ivoni R. *Women in the Acts of the Apostles: A Feminist Liberation Perspective.* Minneapolis, Minn.: Fortress Press, 1995.

Reinhartz, Adele. "From Narrative to History: The Resurrection of Mary and Martha." In *"Women Like This": New Perspectives on Jewish Women in the Greco-Roman World,* edited by Amy-Jill Levine. Atlanta, Ga.: Scholars Press, 1991, 174-76.

————. "The Gospel of John." In *Searching the Scriptures,* edited by Elisabeth Schüssler Fiorenza. New York: Crossroad, 1994, 2:561-600.

————. "The Johannine Community and Its Jewish Neighbors: A Reappraisal." In *"What Is John?,"* edited by Fernando F. Segovia. Atlanta, Ga.: Scholars Press, 1998, 2:111-38.

Remus, Harold E. *Jesus as Healer.* Cambridge: Cambridge University Press, 1997.

Rena, John. "Women in the Gospel of John." *Eglise et Theologie* 17 (1986): 131-47.

Rensberger, David. *Johannine Faith and Liberating Community*. Philadelphia: Westminster Press, 1988.

———. "Sectarianism and Theological Interpretation in John." In *"What Is John?": Literary and Social Readings of the Fourth Gospel*, vol. 2, edited by Fernando F. Segovia. Atlanta, Ga.: Scholars Press, 1998, 139-56.

Richard, E. "Expressions of Double Meaning and Their Function in the Gospel of John." *New Testament Studies* 31 (1985): 96-112.

Riley, George J. *Resurrection Reconsidered: Thomas and John in Controversy*. Minneapolis, Minn.: Fortress Press, 1995.

Ringe, Sharon H. *Wisdom's Friends: Community and Christology in the Fourth Gospel*. Louisville, Ky.: Westminster John Knox, 1999.

Robinson, John A. T. *The Priority of John*. London: SCM Press, 1985.

Rohrbaugh, Richard L., ed. *The Social Sciences and New Testament Interpretation*. Peabody, Mass.: Hendrickson Publications, 1996.

Rowe, Karen E. "Feminism and Fairy Tales." *Women's Studies* 6 (1979): 237-57.

Ruether, Rosemary Radford. "The Female Nature of God: A Problem in Contemporary Religious Life." In *God As Father?*, edited by Johannes-Baptist Metz and Edward Schillebeeckx. Edinburgh: T & T Clark, 1981, 61-66.

———. "How Not to Reinvent the Wheel: Feminist Theology in the Academy." *Christianity and Crisis* (1985): 57-62.

Rushton, Kathleen Patricia. "The Parable of John 16:21: A Feminist Socio-Rhetorical Reading of a (Pro)creative Metaphor for the Death-Glory of Jesus." Ph.D. diss., School of Theology, Faculty of Arts, Griffith University, Australia, 2000.

Sacks, Karen Brodkin. "Toward a Unified Theory of Class, Race, and Gender." *American Ethnologist* 16 (1989): 534-50.

Safrai, S., and M. Stern, with D. Flusser and W. C. van Unik, eds. *The Jewish People in the First Century*. Assen: Van Gorcum, 1976.

Safrai, Ze-ev. *The Economy of Roman Palestine*. London: Routledge, 1994.

Saldarini, Anthony J. "Babatha's Story." *Biblical Archaeology Review* 24/2 (1998): 28-37, 72-74.

———. "Sanhedrin." *Anchor Bible Dictionary*. Vol. 5. New York: Doubleday, 1992, 975-80.

Sanders, E. P., *Judaism: Practice and Belief, 63 BCE—66 CE*. London: SCM Press, 1992.

Sanderson, Judith E. "Amos." In *The Women's Bible Commentary*, edited by Carol A. Newsom and Sharon H. Ringe. London: SPCK, 1992, 205-9.

Sawicki, Marianne. *Seeing the Lord: Resurrection and Early Christian Practices*. Minneapolis, Minn.: Fortress Press, 1994.

Schaberg, Jane. "Luke." In *The Women's Bible Commentary*, edited by Carol A. Newsom and Sharon H. Ringe. London: SPCK, 1992, 275-92.

Schneiders, Sandra M. "'Because of the Woman's Testimony . . . ': Reexamining the Issue of Authorship in the Fourth Gospel." *New Testament Studies* 44/4 (1998): 513-35.

———. "Death in the Community of Eternal Life: History, Theology, and Spirituality in John 11." *Interpretation* 41/1 (1987): 44-56.

———. *The Revelatory Text: Interpreting the New Testament as Sacred Scripture*. San Francisco: HarperSan Francisco, 1991.

———. "Women in the Fourth Gospel and the Role of Women in the Contemporary Church." *Biblical Theology Bulletin* 12 (1982): 35-45.

Schottroff, Luise. "Discussion of a Feminist Introduction Using the AFECT Project as a Starting Point." Paper presented at the Annual Meeting of the Society of Biblical Literature, 1993.

———. "Important Aspects of the Gospel for the Future." In *"What Is John?": Literary and Social Readings of the Fourth Gospel*, vol. 1, edited by Fernando Segovia. Atlanta, Ga.: Scholars Press, 1996, 1:205-10.

———. *Let the Oppressed Go Free: Feminist Perspectives on the New Testament*. Louisville, Ky.: Westminster John Knox, 1993.

———. *Lydia's Impatient Sisters: A Feminist Social History of Early Christianity*. Louisville, Ky.: Westminster John Knox, 1995.

———. "Die Samaritanerin am Brunnen (John 4)." In *Auf Israel hören. Sozialgeschichtliche Bibelauslegung*, edited by Renate Jost, Rainer Kessler, and Christoph M. Raisig. Lucerne: 1992, 115-32.

———. "The Sayings Source Q." In *Searching the Scriptures*, edited by Elisabeth Schüssler Fiorenza. New York: Crossroad, 1994, 2:510-34.

Schroeder, Fred E. H., ed. *Five Thousand Years of Popular Culture: Popular Culture before Printing*. Bowling Green, Ky.: Bowling Green University Popular Press, 1980.

Schroer, Silvia. "The Book of Sophia." In *Searching the Scriptures*, edited by Elisabeth Schüssler Fiorenza. New York: Crossroad, 1994, 2:17-38.

Schuller, Eileen. "Women of the Exodus in Biblical Retelling of the Second Temple Period." In *Gender and Difference in Ancient Israel*, edited by Peggy L. Day. Minneapolis, Minn.: Fortress Press, 1989, 178-94.

Schürer, Emil, et al. *The History of the Jewish People in the Age of Jesus Christ 175 BC—AD135)*. 3 vols. Edinburgh: T & T Clark, 1973.

Schüssler Fiorenza, Elisabeth. *The Book of Revelation: Justice and Judgment*. Philadelphia: Fortress Press, 1985.

———. *But She Said: Feminist Practices of Biblical Interpretation*. Boston: Beacon Press, 1992.

———. "A Feminist Critical Interpretation for Liberation: Martha and Mary: Lk. 10:38-42." *Religion and Intellectual Life* 41/2 (1986): 21-36.

———. "Feminist Hermeneutics." *Anchor Bible Dictionary*. Vol. 2. New York: Doubleday, 1992, 783-91.

———. *In Memory of Her: A Feminist Theological Reconstruction of Christian Origins*. New York: Crossroad, 1983.

———. *Jesus: Miriam's Child, Sophia's Prophet: Critical Issues in Feminist Christology*. New York: Continuum, 1994.

———. "Miracles, Mission, and Apologetics: An Introduction." In *Aspects of Religious Propaganda in Judaism and Early Christianity*, edited by Elisabeth Schüssler Fiorenza. Notre Dame, Ind.: University of Notre Dame Press, 1976, 1-25.

———. "The 'Quilting' of Women's History: Phoebe of Cenchreae." In *Embodied Love: Sensuality and Relationship as Feminist Values*, edited by Paula M. Cooey, Sharon A. Farmer, and Mary Ellen Ross (San Francisco: Harper & Row, 1987), 35-49.

———. *Revelation: Vision of a Just World*. Minneapolis, Minn.: Fortress Press, 1991.

———. *Rhetoric and Ethic: The Politics of Biblical Studies*. Minneapolis, Minn.: Fortress Press, 1999.

———. "Rhetorical Situation and Historical Reconstruction in 1 Corinthians." *New Testament Studies* 33 (1987): 386-403.

———. "Text and Reality—Reality as Text: The Problem of a Feminist Historical and Social Reconstruction Based on Texts." *Studia Theologica* 43 (1989): 19-34.

———. "Wisdom Mythology and the Christological Hymns of the New Testament."
In *Aspects of Wisdom in Judaism and Early Christianity*, edited by Robert L.
Wilken. Notre Dame, Ind.: University of Notre Dame Press, 1975, 17-41.

———. "Word, Spirit and Power: Women in Early Christian Communities." In *Women
of Spirit: Female Leadership in the Jewish and Christian Traditions*, edited by
Rosemary Ruether and Eleanor McLaughlin. New York: Simon and Schuster,
1979, 30-70.

Schüssler Fiorenza, Elisabeth, ed. *Searching the Scriptures.* 2 vols. New York: Crossroad, 1993/1994.

Scott, James C. *Domination and the Arts of Resistance: Hidden Transcripts.* New Haven, Conn.: Yale University Press, 1990.

———. "Protest and Profanation: Agrarian Revolt and the Little Tradition." *Theory
and Society* 4 (1977): 1-39, 211-46.

Scott, Martin. *Sophia and the Johannine Jesus.* Sheffield: Sheffield Academic Press,
1992.

Seim, Turid Karlsen. "The Gospel of Luke." In *Searching the Scriptures*, edited by
Elisabeth Schüssler Fiorenza. New York: Crossroad, 1994, 2:728-62.

———. "Roles of Women in the Gospel of John." In *Aspects on the Johannine Literature: Papers Presented at a Conference of Scandinavian New Testament Exegetes at Uppsala, June 16-19, 1986*, edited by Lars Hartman and Birger Olsson.
Uppsala: Almovist and Wiksell, 1987.

Setzer, Claudia J. *Jewish Responses to Early Christians: History and Polemics, 30-150
C.E.* Minneapolis, Minn.: Fortress Press, 1994.

Sidebottom, E. M. *The Christ of the Fourth Gospel.* London: SPCK, 1961.

Siebert-Hommes, Jopie. "But If She Be a Daughter . . . She May Live!: 'Daughters'
and 'Sons' in Exodus 1-2." In *A Feminist Companion to Exodus to
Deuteronomy*, edited by Athalya Brenner. Sheffield: Sheffield Academic Press,
1994, 62-74.

Sloyan, Gerard S. *John: Interpretation: A Bible Commentary for Teaching and Preaching.* Atlanta, Ga.: John Knox Press, 1988.

Smith, Morton. "Goodenough's Jewish Symbols in Retrospect." *Journal of Biblical
Literature* 86 (1967): 53-68.

———. *Jesus the Magician.* New York: Harper & Row, 1978.

———. "The Jewish Elements in the Magical Papyri." *Society of Biblical Literature
Seminar Papers* (1986): 455-62.

Staley, Jeffrey Lloyd. *The Print's First Kiss: A Rhetorical Investigation of the Implied
Reader in the Fourth Gospel.* Atlanta, Ga.: Scholars Press, 1988.

———. *Reading with a Passion: Rhetoric, Autobiography, and the American West in the
Gospel of John.* New York: Continuum, 1995.

Stanley, Christopher D. "Ethnic Conflict between 'Jews' and 'Greeks' in the Greco-
Roman Era." Paper presented at the annual meeting of the Society of Biblical Literature, 1995.

Stibbe, Mark W. G. "The Elusive Christ: A New Reading of the Fourth Gospel."
*Journal for the Study of the New Testament* 44 (1991): 19-38.

———. *John: A Readings Commentary.* Sheffield: JSOT, 1992.

Story, Cullen I. K. "The Mental Attitude of Jesus at Bethany: John 11:33, 38." *New
Testament Studies* 37 (1991): 51-66.

Sugirtharajah, R. S. "'For You Always Have the Poor with You': An Example of Hermeneutics of Suspicion." *Asian Journal of Theology* 4/1 (1990): 102-7.

Talbert, Charles H. *Reading John: A Literary and Theological Commentary on the Four
Gospels and the Johannine Epistles.* New York: Crossroad, 1992.

Tanzer, Sarah J. "Secret Christian Jews in John." In *The Future of Early Christianity: Essays in Honor of Helmut Koester*, edited by Birger A. Pearson, A. Thomas Kraabel, George W. E. Nickelsburg, and Norman R. Petersen. Minneapolis, Minn.: Fortress Press, 1991, 290-300.

Taussig, Hal, "Wisdom, Sophia, Hellenistic Queens." In *Women and Goddess Traditions in Antiquity and Today*, edited by Karen L. King. Minneapolis, Minn.: Fortress Press, 1997, 264-80.

Taylor, Charles. "Translation of the *Teaching of the Twelve Apostles*." In *Didache: The Unknown Teaching of the Twelve Apostles*, edited by Brent S. Walters. San Jose, Calif.: Ante-Nicene Archive, 1991.

Theissen, Gerd. *The Miracle Stories of the Early Christian Tradition*. Francis McDonagh, trans. Philadelphia: Fortress Press, 1983.

Thielman, Frank. "The Style of the Fourth Gospel and Ancient Literary Critical Concepts of Religious Discourse." In *Persuasive Artistry: Studies in New Testament Rhetoric in Honor of George A. Kennedy*, edited by Duane F. Watson. *Journal for the New Testament Supplement Series* 50 (1991), 169-83.

Thistlethwaite, Susan. "Inclusive Language and Linguistic Blindness." *Theology Today* 43/4 (1987): 533-39.

Thomas, John Christopher. *Footwashing in John 13 and the Johannine Community*. Sheffield: Sheffield Academic Press, 1991.

Thomas, Rosalind. *Literacy and Orality in Ancient Greece*. Cambridge: Cambridge University Press, 1992.

Thompson, Marianne Meye. *The Incarnate Word: Perspectives on Jesus in the Fourth Gospel*. Peabody, Mass.: Hendrickson Publications, 1988.

Thurston, Bonnie Bowman. *The Widows: A Women's Ministry in the Early Church*. Minneapolis, Minn.: Fortress Press, 1989.

Tolbert, Mary Ann. "The Gospel in Greco-Roman Culture." In *The Book and the Text: The Bible and Literary Theory*, edited by Regina M. Schwartz. Cambridge: Basil Blackwell, 1990, 258-75.

———. *Sowing the Gospel: Mark's World in Literary-Historical Perspective*. Minneapolis, Minn.: Fortress Press, 1989.

Toorn, Karel Van Der. *From Her Cradle to Her Grave: The Role of Religion in the Life of the Israelite and Babylonian Woman*, translated by Sara J. Denning-Bolle. Sheffield: Sheffield Academic Press, 1994.

Torjesen, Karen Jo. *When Women Were Priests: Women's Leadership in the Early Church and the Scandal of Their Subordination in the Rise of Christianity*. San Francisco: Harper San Francisco, 1993.

Townsend, John T. "Education (Israel): Greco-Roman Period." *Anchor Bible Dictionary*. Vol. 2. New York: Doubleday, 1992, 312-17.

Treggiari, Susan. "Honor and Shame in the Roman World." Lecture delivered at Harvard Divinity School, Cambridge, Massachusetts, 1992.

Trible, Phyllis. "Bringing Miriam Out of the Shadows." *Bible Review* 5/1 (1989): 14-25, 34.

———. *God and the Rhetoric of Sexuality*. Philadelphia: Fortress Press, 1978.

Trimble, Jennifer. "Bathwomen and Other Undervalued Phenomena: A Study of PSI 28, a Love Spell between Women." Presentation at Prof. Bernadette Brooten's seminar 1875, Harvard Divinity School, Cambridge, Massachusetts, 1992.

Trudinger, Paul. "John's Gospel as Testimony to the Non-Deity of Jesus." *Faith and Freedom* 48/2 (1995): 106-10.

Van Dijk-Hemmes, Fokkelien. "Traces of Women's Texts in the Hebrew Bible." In *On Gendering Texts: Female and Male Voices in the Hebrew Bible*, edited by

Athalya Brenner and Fokkelien van Dijk-Hemmes. Leiden: E. J. Brill, 1993, 17-109.

Van Wijk-Bos, Johanna W. H. *Reimagining God: The Case for Scriptural Diversity.* Louisville, Ky.: Westminster John Knox, 1995.

Van Wolde, Ellen. *A Semiotic Analysis of Genesis 2—3: A Semiotic Theory and Method of Analysis Applied to the Story of the Garden of Eden.* Assen: Van Gorcum, 1989.

Vermes, Geza. *Jesus the Jew: A Historian's Reading of the Gospels.* London: Collins, 1973.

Von Wahlde, Urban C. *The Earliest Version of John's Gospel: Recovering the Gospel of Signs.* Wilmington, Del.: Michael Glazier, 1989.

Wainwright, Elaine M. "Go Quickly and Tell—Alternative Voices Remembering Jesus and Shaping Ministry." Paper presented at the Australian Catholic Biblical Association Meeting in Sydney, 1995.

———. "Jesus Sophia: An Image Obscured in the Johannine Prologue." *The Bible Today* 36/2 (1998): 92-97.

———. "The Matthean Jesus and the Healing of Women." In *The Gospel of Matthew in Current Study: Studies in Memory of William Thompson, S.J.*, ed. David E. Aune (Grand Rapids, Mich.: Eerdmans, 2001), 74-95.

———. *Shall We Look for Another?: A Feminist Rereading of the Matthean Jesus.* Maryknoll, N.Y.: Orbis Books, 1998.

———. *Toward a Feminist Critical Reading of the Gospel according to Matthew.* Berlin: Walter de Gruyter, 1991.

———. "Weaving a New Web of Creative Remembering." In *Teaching the Bible: The Discourses and Politics of Biblical Pedagogy*, edited by Fernando Segovia and Mary Ann Tolbert. Maryknoll, N.Y.: Orbis Books, 1998, 338-51.

———. "'Your Faith Has Made You Well': Jesus, Women and Healing in the Gospel of Matthew." In *Transformative Encounters: Jesus and Women Re-viewed*, edited by Ingrid Rosa Kitzberger. Leiden: E. J. Brill, 2000, 224-44.

Whibley, Charles. *Apuleius: The Golden Ass.* New York: Boni and Liveright, 1927.

Wikan, Unni. "Shame and Honour: A Contestable Pair." *Man* 19 (1983): 635-52.

Wills, Lawrence M. "The Depiction of the Jews in Acts." *Journal of Biblical Literature* 110/4 (1991): 631-54.

———. *The Jewish Novel in the Ancient World.* Ithaca, N.Y.: Cornell University Press, 1995.

Winter, Miriam Therese. *Womanword: A Feminist Lectionary and Psalter: Women of the New Testament.* New York: Crossroad, 1990.

Wire, Antoinette Clark. "Ancient Miracle Stories and Women's Social World." *Forum* 2 (1986): 77-84.

———. *The Corinthian Women Prophets: A Reconstruction through Paul's Rhetoric.* Minneapolis, Minn.: Fortress Press, 1990.

Witherinton, Ben. "Lydia." *Anchor Bible Dictionary.* Vol. 4. New York: Doubleday, 1992, 422-23.

Woll, D. Bruce. *Johannine Christianity in Conflict: Authority, Rank, and Succession in the First Farewell Discourse.* Chico, Calif.: Scholars Press, 1981.

Wordelman, Amy L. "Everyday Life: Women in the Period of the New Testament." In *The Women's Bible Commentary*, edited by Carol A. Newsom and Sharon H. Ringe. London: SPCK, 1992, 390-96.

Yaghjian, Lukrretia. "Ancient Reading." In *The Social Sciences and New Testament Interpretation*, edited by Richard L. Rohrbaugh. Peabody, Mass.: Hendrickson Publications, 1996, 206-30.

Yamaguchi, Satoko. "'*Female Shame*' and the New Testament." Paper presented at Catholic Biblical Association, Society of Biblical Literature regional conference, Worcester, Massachusetts, 1994.

——. "The Impact of National Histories on the Politics of Identity: The Second Story." *Journal of Asian and Asian American Theology* 2/1 (1997): 95-107.

——. "The Invention of Traditions: The Case of Shintoism." In *In God's Image* 18/4 (1999): 40-46.

——. "Original Christian Messages and Our Christian Identities." In *God's Image* 16/4 (1997): 24-31.

Yee, Gail A. "Hosea." In *The Women's Bible Commentary*, edited by Carol A. Newsom and Sharon H. Ringe. London: SPCK, 1992, 195-202.

Yee, Gale A., ed. *Judges and Method: New Approaches in Biblical Studies.* Minneapolis, Minn.: Fortress Press, 1995.

Zias, Joseph. "Death and Disease in Ancient Israel." *Biblical Archaeology Review* 54/3 (1991): 147-59.

Zlotnick, Dov, trans. *The Tractate "Mourning" (Semahot): Regulations Relating to Death, Burial, and Mourning*, edited by William Scott Green and Calvin Goldscheider. New Haven, Conn.: Yale University Press, 1966.

# Index